SOUL OF A TIGER

A Miraculous True Story of a Family
That Survived the Cambodian Genocide

SreyReath Kuy
SreyRam Kuy

Published by Motivational Press, Inc.
7777 N Wickham Rd, # 12-247
Melbourne, FL 32940
www.MotivationalPress.com

Manufactured in the United States of America.

ISBN: 978-1-62865-040-2

Dedication

This book is dedicated to our mother, whose unfailing love and support helped us to become the people we are today. You pushed, pulled, prodded, and did whatever it took to move us forward. You never gave up on us, even when we fell flat on our backs. Words cannot express the tremendous gratitude we have for your unwavering persistence, loyalty, and unconditional love.

Acknowledgements

- To Sandra W. Potter, PhD, you were the best pre-med advisor. Thank you for never giving up on me.

- Thanks also to Robert P. Doss, PhD, who has been a truly wonderful boss. I appreciate the job and the bonuses to start medical school.

- Randal M. Lepow, DPM—the best residency director and mentor that I could have asked for. I am so grateful for your great advice and support.

- To both James R. Koski, MD and the family of Tom and Faith Norris, PhDs, we wish to thank you for your generous financial support that put both of us through college. Without your help, we would never have had the life-changing opportunity for an education.

- Another person who has made a tremendous difference is Joyce Carver, whose remarkable patience taught this stubborn child her English skills. Yet, you never gave up, even when it looked hopeless.

Disclaimer:

Although this book and the events that transpired are based upon a true story, the names of the individuals characterized have been changed to protect their privacy.

Contents

Chapter One

"Death Bed"

Adying elderly man awoke in his hospital bed, hoping to see his family waiting by his bedside. The stark white room was as white as the loneliness he felt, as he looked around, realizing nobody was there. His wife and two daughters had not shown up. His brother was absent. Having to face the inevitable, he knew it was his own fault that nobody was there to support him or console him through his last few days on earth.

Although he was not afraid, he was disappointed. The situation was disgraceful and he was ashamed for his actions. As he studied his wrinkled hands, the old man couldn't help but feel remorseful for the things he had done. Why had he let his brother talk him into turning against his own family? How could he have been so foolish? Now here he was, sick and weak and all alone. He had betrayed those who loved him the most.

His wife, Rachana, had always been there to care for him, right from the very beginning. When he was first diagnosed with cancer, nearly eight months prior, it seemed like the end of the world. He was nearing the end of his life.

The diagnosis came in June of 1995. Rachana had been working in the hospital where he was admitted. She came to see him every day; first thing in the morning, during lunch breaks, and then again after work. She often stayed until the last visiting hours of 9:00 p.m. There was no question how much she loved him.

For twenty-one days, he stayed there, reflecting upon his life and his present illness. Rachana often brought their two daughters, Sophea, who was twenty-one years old, and Neary, seventeen years old. The treatments were very difficult and painful; however, the girls all took very good care of him. He wanted his wife there all the time but she couldn't spend the nights. It wasn't that he was mistreated by the staff at the hospital; it was just that he wanted her there. She comforted him, with her calm bedside demeanor and soothing voice.

Working every day and caring for her sick husband took its toll on Rachana. She was sleep deprived. She also took care of her two daughters, who were both busy with college and their extra-curricular activities. This left most of the work to the mother of the family, who by the grace of God was needed by everyone. She often overlooked her own needs in exchange for theirs. Besides, she knew her husband was getting excellent care from all the doctors and the nurses.

While sitting beside him one evening, Rachana reached for her husband's hand. She looked into his eyes and said, "Narin, dear, why do you need me in the room at night?"

"I can't close my eyes," he admitted. "Every time I close my eyes, I see ghosts all around me."

"Did you pray last night?" she whispered.

"No," he replied.

So Rachana told him, "Then tonight, before you close your eyes, pray."

He confessed, "I don't know how to pray."

She sat down and patiently taught him how to pray the Lord's Prayer.

The very next morning, Rachana got up, cooked breakfast and lunch, packed for everybody and went to the hospital early enough to check in on her husband. She could hardly wait to find out how he was doing and if he was feeling any better.

When she opened the door of his room, Narin was awake. "Hi, sweetie," she greeted him. "Did you pray last night, like I taught you?"

He answered, "Yes, I did."

She asked, "How was your night then?"

Narin smiled as he said, "I did not see any ghosts. I dreamed that I was standing under a big umbrella. I slept well last night. You see how powerful God is!" He motioned his hands toward the sky. "From now on, I will pray every night."

And he did. After that night, Narin got over his fear of being in a hospital room alone. He looked much better than the day he had first been hospitalized. His skin looked peppier and his eyes sparkled a bit more. He looked well and happy enough to be discharged by his doctors.

On the twenty-first day after the death sentence of terminal cancer, Narin was sent home to be with his family. He planned on "serving out his time" for the next six to nine months by spending as much time with them as he could. However, Sophea and Neary were busy with work and academics. Despite their father's incurability, the girls could not miss school. Their educations were at stake and many thousands of dollars had been spent on their tuitions. They wanted to become doctors and their mother had sacrificed many things to ensure the very best for her daughters. It was for this very reason that Rachana brought her daughters to America from Cambodia, with the hope of a better life.

Over the next few months, as Narin lay at home dying from cancer, he had plenty of time to think. Hopelessness crept into his soul, as much as the very disease that had come upon him. He felt sorry for himself. To fill the lonely hole, Narin began talking more on the phone with his estranged brother. While his wife was working and his daughters were at school trying to become successful in life, Narin carried out a stunning betrayal.

It was uncharacteristic of him, considering all their family had been through in the Killing Fields of Cambodia. They had survived a horrific genocide together, with everybody still in one piece. Even after their entire family moved to the U.S. in September of 1981, things were peaceful and content for them. Rachana and Narin worked very hard and did the best they could to provide for their two daughters.

Although he never handled their money, Rachana always paid their bills on time and was responsible when it came to the family finances. Narin always handed over his paycheck to his wife every week, just as faithfully as there were seven days. Sometimes he would ask how much money they had, but he never questioned it as long as they had the funds to get essentials and to live. That was before his own brother brainwashed Narin, causing poor judgment to precede his family's best interests.

Rachana was a strong bookkeeper and a good handler of the family's assets. From the time of their arrival in the States in September of 1981, until thirteen months thereafter, she had saved enough money for them to buy a brand new car with cash. By October of 1984, she had saved up for a down payment on their first house. It was a cute ranch-style home in Corvallis, Oregon.

Narin's brother and sister-in-law lived about an hour away in Beaverton, near Portland. They began visiting more frequently after Narin and Rachana bought the house. There was a mood of sibling rivalry stirring between the two brothers. Vibol was a couple of years younger than Narin, but he had always known Rachana and her family very well. They were all from the same community of Siem Reap in Cambodia.

Instead of being happy for his brother's success in life, Vibol was jealous. He carried a thwarted sense of values and believed it would be best if the men of the household quit their jobs and stayed at home, forcing their wives to be the breadwinners. He believed that in America, women were too free-spirited and independent to need their husbands and that all marriages would end in divorce. In Vibol's mind, it was only a matter of time before the divorce papers were placed before him—and then what? Should he let a woman decide his fate? He thought not. Within Vibol's household, he had established a position of authority and dominance.

Not long after the purchase of their new home in Corvallis, Narin's brother and family began coming to visit every weekend. This ritual began even before the cancer diagnosis. They tricked Narin into believing in their falsehoods. It was not the first time Vibol had come between their marriage. He and his siblings had also caused a separation between Narin and Rachana just after the war was over in Cambodia. Because of their meddling, the couple was split apart for a full year until they reunited in the refugee camps before their flight to the United States. Unfortunately, Narin was weak and lacked resilience. His incomprehension of God, nor in the truth, had been woven into his head.

When they came to visit on the weekends, Vibol and his wife teamed up against Narin, despite his protests that Rachana was doing a fine job of managing their bills. They had ulterior motives.

"Trust me, it may seem like she is sweet and kind and that she is paying your bills," said Vibol, wickedly. "But she's plotting against you. Guaranteed she has a stash somewhere, like a secret savings account. Women do that, if you let 'em. But you're not going to let her, are you Narin?"

Vibol's father-in-law also believed in these falsehoods. "You're gonna be dead if you work so hard. Your wife will take everything if you get divorced. It happens all the time in the U.S. It's like the divorce capital of the world!" he exclaimed.

In contrast, Vibol's wife had been compliant and obedient to her husband's orders. He managed the money but she was also the income earner of the household, working two or three jobs to support them. Vibol controlled their money and her. His wife lacked the self-esteem to stand up to him.

Narin was also led to believe that all women in the United States have affairs and are unfaithful to their husbands. Narin slowly shifted to the side of the enemy because he was gullible and naïve. The devil did his best to come between his relationship with his wife. Under the influence of weakness and vulnerability, Narin sided with his sibling. He took his brother's advice, quit his job to stay home while Rachana worked multiple jobs to meet the monthly obligations.

Meanwhile, Rachana could not explain the changes in her husband. She stayed busy and worked by herself for four long years, always managing to pay the mortgage and buy the family groceries. It was difficult, but her strong faith kept her going. Her will to love outweighed her husband's new resolve to hate.

Vibol taught his older brother many ways to steal from the family. Narin became secretive and mysterious. While Rachana worked tirelessly at two or three jobs just to support the family, Narin wrote checks to himself. Whenever there were side jobs, he cleared cash under the table. He opened a savings account in his brother's name, as Vibol had requested. This pleased Vibol very much, as well as his in-laws, who were also in on the brainwashing.

As they continued to fill Narin's mind with lies, he grew even more fearful that Rachana would divorce him and take everything. He became so wrought with anxiety that he hid things from her and kept secrets. Narin failed to realize that his brother's quest to break apart their family was working. Vibol and his father-in-law instructed Narin that, as the man of the household, he should take over management of the finances. According to them, he was to control his wife and family.

However, Rachana was a clever woman and very independent-minded. Even though she loved her husband and family, she always stood her ground in matters of sticking to what she believed in.

Unexpectedly, Narin came home from a landscaping job one day that he had performed under the table. "From now on, I think it's best if I handle our money," he stated.

Rachana simply asked, "Why?"

"Well, because my brother handles the money and takes care of his wife at their house," he replied.

"That doesn't explain to me why you want control of our money," she said. "Since you married me, have you ever had any debt that you had to pay for?"

"No," he admitted.

"Have I ever gambled it away?" she asked.

"No," he answered.

"Gone drinking?" she asked.

"No," again.

"Squandered, horded, hidden, coveted or forsaken you for anything in which you contributed money to?" she asked.

Again, "No."

Finally, she said, "Have I ever put you through anything that you had to work hard at?"

This time, he shook his head side to side.

"So how come you don't trust me all of a sudden and want control of our finances?" Rachana simply didn't understand why her husband had turned into such a conniving man, although she suspected Vibol was behind it.

Narin didn't say anymore. Indeed, it was his brother's influence.

After more prodding, Rachana finally agreed later on to divide their money. From that point on, she kept her paycheck and he kept his. Narin had not worked at a steady job for four years, so she had nothing to lose by accepting this clause. Subsequently, Narin finally got a job at Goodwill after much encouragement from his wife. She was sick of working her tail off while he stayed home and moped. She pushed him to do something worthwhile to help them. Narin kept most of his paycheck and gave her five hundred dollars each month to contribute towards their household bills. Nevertheless, it was more than he had done in quite some time, so Rachana didn't complain. Meanwhile, she paid for everything else.

One day, another discussion transpired from a sudden outburst. Out of the blue, Narin asked his wife, "Can we put the house in my brother's and his wife's name?"

Startled, she replied, "What for?"

"So that you can move out of state and collect welfare," he said.

Dumbfounded, she hastily responded, "Now that's just about the dumbest thing I've ever heard. If I did that, I would sell the house first. I'm not that stupid! I have an education, too. Remember? You're not dealing with a dummy here."

Narin's request was once again denied. Even though Rachana had proven to be a loyal and faithful wife and stayed by his side for those three weeks in the hospital, Narin still did not see what he had to lose. His brother's influence was like the devil on his shoulder, instructing him what to do.

Making matters worse in their marriage, Vibol used Narin's cancer as a pressing time limit. Knowing that his brother only had six to nine months left to live, Vibol initiated urgency and action. He knew he had to light a fire under Narin now, if he was to inherit his brother's home and take over their family's assets. The paperwork had to be signed prior to his death.

On the day Narin was sent home from the hospital, there were home health nurses who were assigned to help the Long family cope and manage some of the care responsibilities of a dying elderly man. Hospice workers were also sent to help. But as soon as Rachana and her daughters left for school and work, Narin sent the hospice workers and caretakers away. He nastily explained that he could take care of himself and that their services were unwelcomed.

Based on Vibol's guidance, Narin devised a plan to deceive his family. Because Rachana would not agree to put their house in Vibol's and his wife's name, the only choice left was to send them all to prison. If his wife and daughters went to jail, any heirs in his will would automatically assume their house. So, Narin faked his own care on their behalf.

As soon as he heard the last car door slam and roll out of their driveway, Narin took all of the blankets off his bed, turned down the thermostat in their house, and hid all of the food. When his friends and neighbors came over to check on him, it seemed as if his family was torturing him. It appeared as if they left him in bed with no blankets, no heat, and no food. Feeling sorry for himself, Narin fabricated stories of how they mistreated him. He barely ate. In conjunction with the chemo treatments for cancer, Narin became very frail and thin. This contributed to the illusion of abuse.

One time, he called the City of Corvallis Water Department and had the water disconnected. He disconnected the electricity too. This was in the middle of December. With no heat or water at freezing temperatures, Rachana and her two daughters had to drive across town to shower at a stranger's house. Life was hard and Narin was bent on making it difficult for everyone.

Even though he had some cash in a secret bank account, Narin also stopped contributing any money to support the family. Nobody knew how much it was or where it came from. Instead, he left his money in his will to his nieces, Vibol's daughters. That was done so they would have scholarships. Instead of helping his own daughters, he helped his brother's children. In his mind, Narin didn't need to help his daughters because they had already received scholarships and financial aid. So, he didn't help with the finances for any of their education. He didn't even offer.

These and other plots were all done in the name of betrayal. Narin's friend, who was a retired professor, told Rachana and her daughters that if Narin died in the house, they would press charges and they would all be tried in court and sent to prison. As expected, his wife and children were very angry about his behavior, yet scared for their own well-being at the same time. It was a horrible thing for a husband and father to do, but Narin was led away from his family by his greedy brother and his brother's father-in-law to be led against his family. They would have been entirely pleased to see Rachana and her girls thrown in prison for torturing Narin, even though it was far from the truth.

The truth was Rachana had stuck by his side, despite everything that he was putting them through. She believed in God and that the truth would prevail. She took care of him every day and stayed too busy to think about what would happen if Narin's plan worked. All she knew was that her strength and faith were being tested and that she had been called upon to serve.

As luck would have it, Narin had a burning urge to go to France and visit his other brother before he died. It was his last chance to travel. His doctors cautioned him; however, Narin was very stubborn and determined to go there so that he could visit his other sibling one last time. Sophea bought her father the plane ticket to France as her last gift to him, even though she felt disgusted by all that had transpired. It made her feel good knowing she could fulfill her dying father's last wish, despite her dislike for the way he had treated their family.

Narin did make it to France and stayed with Heng, the eldest of the Long boys. They had stayed in touch but had not seen each other in nearly a decade, since Heng and his wife had last visited the States. However, while in France, Narin's condition took a turn for the worst. Doctors had warned him of the dangers in flying–as his immune system and white blood cell count were very low–but Narin failed to heed their warnings. He became very sick and had to change his return flight to leave France sooner than planned.

On the way home, the plane ride overseas was brutally arduous. Narin's already failing health added nausea, airsickness, and lethargy. His breathing was labored and his head spun like a pinwheel. Black spots filled his eyes like ink splatters. It was the last leg of the flight. If he could just make it home, he could die there in peace. He struggled. He just wanted to die at home. Not on the plane . . . not now. But Narin could not hold on any longer. After the black spots filled entirely and his eyes went completely dark, he collapsed in the aisle of the giant aircraft. It was right as the flight attendant went on the intercom to announce their final descent to the San Francisco International Airport.

Although he didn't remember the incident, Narin vaguely recalled opening his eyes for a moment or two on the ambulance ride to UCSF Medical Center, where cancer specialists had been called to prepare for his arrival.

A paramedic said to someone, "He's awake."

Then the EMT said, "Don't worry, Mr. Long, we're on our way to the hospital right now. Hang in there. We will call your wife to let her know where you are."

"She won't come," Narin whispered. "She won't come . . ."

The paramedic tried to reassure him. "Just get some rest. We're taking great care of you."

Narin closed his eyes. He felt like a big redwood tree had fallen on top of him, with all of its weight and the lifetime of difficulty it had delivered with it. He felt death nearing upon him. He had almost made it home. Almost.

Outside the window, the faint outline of the Golden Gate Bridge hovered above the fog. It was so beautiful. He imagined the bridge looked much like the pearly gates of heaven. Would the angels let him pass, or send him to hell for what he had done? He prayed they would not. He prayed for the chance to make things right again.

Suddenly, he remembered the words Rachana had spoken to him when he was scared in the hospital during those first three weeks of chemotherapy, many months ago. She had stayed by his side the whole time, except at night. She had taught him how to make the ghosts disappear with the power of prayer.

All you have to do is ask with faith, her words of wisdom echoed, ringing in his ears.

Now staring at the drip of the IV that was anchored to the vein in his wrist, he questioned whose side he was on. Drip, drip, drip, drip . . . the IV was methodically melancholy. Mesmerizing. Tranquil. With each silent drip, the clock ticked down to his final breath. But he wasn't quite ready to go, not just yet.

Chapter Two

"The Transition of Dowry"

The teapot whistled as Rachana stepped out of the shower, interrupting the quiet morning. It was the first weekend she'd had off in a few weeks. Her daughters were at the library, studying. Narin was still in France, visiting his brother Heng. She wondered how he was doing. When Narin had left, he was in a lot of pain, but he was determined to go see Heng one last time before the final days of cancer finally took him away. She understood this strong desire since she too had missed loved ones who lived far away overseas.

Rachana quickly dried off and wrapped herself in a towel, dashing quickly to the screaming teapot. It was so loud that it may have stirred the Saturday sleepers who lived nearby.

After pouring her cup, Rachana brought the tea back to her room while she finished getting ready. She had scheduled a social day to help her church since she had been too busy lately to participate in any of their functions. Admittedly, Rachana relished the empty household. There was no complaining husband to care for or daughters busily preparing for school. She had the whole house to herself and loved it!

Just as she snapped her earrings in her earlobes and took the last sip of her tea, Rachana heard the phone ring. Since she was in a hurry, Rachana almost ignored it. However, she thought better against it, just in case it was one of the church ladies calling to change their plans. It wasn't.

"Hello?" Rachana answered breathlessly, after running to catch the phone on the fifth ring.

"Yes, hello. Is this Mrs. Long?" asked a woman on the other end. The voice was unfamiliar.

Rachana said, "Yes, this is she."

"This is Dr. Nancy Bradley from the UCSF Medical Center in San

Francisco. Your husband collapsed on a return flight home from France. He didn't make the last leg of the trip. He had to be admitted right away," explained the doctor.

Rachana looked surprised. He wasn't supposed to have been coming home for another nine days. Something must have happened.

"Is he okay?" she asked, knowing the answer.

"No, I'm afraid not," the doctor said. "Frankly, I don't know if he can even hang on long enough for you to make it here. Unless you fly, you're looking at a nine to ten hour drive."

Rachana thought about it. She thought about not going at all, since Narin had made his own bed. *Why should I bother? He doesn't like us anyway,* she thought, but didn't say out loud. Instead, she told the doctor she would see what she could do to get there as fast as possible. She thanked her for calling.

Even though Narin had put her through a lot of grief the last few years, Rachana knew that she would go. It was in her nature to care. After all, they had been through incredible horrors together. She had to say goodbye. It was time for him to go and be in peace. It was time for Rachana to have peace too. She just had to decide whether to drive or fly.

She called her eldest daughter, Sophea. She told her about Narin's early return from France and about collapsing on the airplane. Sophea was sympathetic, but she too was angry with her father for turning against their family. She had no desire to see him. Nevertheless, he was her father. Sophea told her mother that she would help with the arrangements for her to fly into the San Francisco airport that day.

After they spoke, Rachana set to packing. Her mind was racing, thinking about Narin and wondering if she would make it to the hospital before he died. She felt helpless, so she busied herself with preparation. She packed a simple green overnight bag with enough clothes to last three days. If she had to be there longer, she would just wear what she had or pick up something new.

Sophea called back a little over an hour later. "Mom, I booked you a flight. There will be a shuttle there within forty-five minutes to pick you up and take you to the airport in Portland."

"Okay, I will be ready," Rachana solemnly sighed.

"Be strong mother," reassured Sophea. "You are brave."

"Thank you, dear. I love you, Sophea," she replied.

"Me too," she answered.

After Rachana set the phone back into the receiver, she gathered the rest of her belongings. She collected a few of Narin's too, even though she knew he had his bags from France with him. Some clothing, a few pairs of clean socks, a picture of the two of them, and a Bible were all she placed quietly in a bag. She passed time by waiting for the shuttle to come and pick her up. Rachana also called the church ladies and told them she would be unable to help with the volunteering. They were very understanding and compassionate. They offered to pray for Rachana and her family during this difficult time.

Exactly thirty-five minutes had passed when a large, silver minivan pulled into Rachana's driveway, beeping its horn twice to announce its arrival. She picked up her satchel and opened the door to wave at the driver. He came out of the driver's side to give her a hand with her bag. Then, he gave her a hand stepping up into the back. Rachana was his only passenger.

"Do we have others to pick up?" she asked.

"Not if you want to get to the airport on time," he teased her.

She sat in silence for a few minutes but couldn't resist the urge to speak. Rachana loved to talk to people and was quite outgoing. The driver was a young guy in his mid-thirties. He looked rather polished in his uniformed navy blue shirt and khakis, yet his face was approachably personable.

Rachana asked, "What should I call you?"

"Name's Edgar. Some call me Eddie. Some call me Grrr . . ." he joked.

She smiled. "I'm Rachana. Some call me Cha-Cha. How far to the airport?"

He said, "Sit tight because we have about an hour and a half ride."

She was silent again for a few minutes, but the anxiety over what she was about to do ate away at her. Talking was a way to pass the time productively. Edgar was the only one there to listen.

"I'm going to San Francisco," blurted Rachana. "To see my dying husband."

Feeling a little uncomfortable, Edgar said, "Wow, I'm so sorry."

"It's okay. Thank you, though. It was only a matter of time," she hung her head quietly.

Trying to break her solemn mood, Edgar asked "How long were you two married?"

Rachana answered. "Since 1972. Almost twenty-four years."

Sounding impressed, Edgar said "Wow, that's a long time. Any kids?"

She nodded, as he glimpsed into the rearview mirror. "Two. We have two daughters."

"And where did you two lovebirds meet?" he winked.

"Cambodia, where we are from. I wouldn't say we were lovebirds, though. Our parents arranged our marriage, which is Cambodian tradition. The man pays the family a dowry or offers gifts to ask for the daughter's hand in marriage."

"They still do that over there?" Edgar sounded surprised.

Rachana nodded, "Oh yes, very much so. Cambodia is a very old, traditional, and conservative part of Asia."

Edgar said, "Well over here, the bride's family pays for the wedding. I think I like that idea better. When I went to my own wedding, all I had to do was show up in a tux!"

She laughed. "It used to be similar in Cambodia, except the bride's family paid a dowry to the groom's family. That is, until the women caused uproar about how unfair it was."

Edgar asked, "What do you mean? They have women's rights activists there too?"

Rachana said, "Something like that. I was born close to Angkor Wat. Besides the richness of God's gifts, there were a lot of ancient monuments that our ancestors left for future generations. You may have heard of a great temple there?"

"I'm not familiar with Cambodia, except for what I've heard in the news about the war and terrible things that occurred there," Edgar admitted.

"Let me tell you how it changed . . ." Rachana explained.

"One of the popular tourist attractions in Cambodia is the great Angkor Wat temple near Siem Reap. There is a legend that goes with West Baray, which is quite near the temple. Its significance has everything to do with the reason why men now pay a dowry for marriage, instead of the other way around." She told this story:

"*In ancient times, it was customary in Cambodia for the bride's father to offer a hefty dowry to the family of his chosen son-in-law. The marriages were arranged in a way that a Cambodian father would find a man he wanted for his daughter and offer gifts and money to the groom's family. Rarely did the children get a say in whom their parents chose for them.*

A bride's family had to pay for the wedding, much like they do in the U.S. The women or her family had to give men the dowry and make the proposal.

The new generations of Cambodian women were no longer happy with this arrangement, so they set out to reverse this custom. The women grew smarter and more outraged by this tradition, no longer wanting to be subservient to men. So, the women formed a pact. They thought of a clever contest to challenge the men and change history.

Women agreed to choose the smartest woman among them to be their leader and meet with the male leader. Whichever group—male or female—was able to dig the biggest, most beautiful and most useful lake would win the case. The loser had to do the proposing, pay for the entire wedding, and would be required to pay the dowry. This competition would take only one night to accomplish. All of the women were to dig one lake, while the men would dig their own lake. The men had to dig on the east end, while the women dug on the west end. East Baray was about thirty kilometers from West Baray. The competition was to start at sunset and end upon first sight of the morning star. Neither the men nor women were allowed to communicate with each other during the competition.

The men were happy about this challenge. They knew that physically, they were bigger and stronger and felt it was an easy contest to win, hands down. Plus, the women had all of their children to take care of, even while they participated in the contest. The men saw no way to lose and felt certain they would beat the women to keep the set traditions in place.

However, the women were smart and very organized. The leader of the women's side divided them into groups. A few women handled all of the childcare, while the others were assigned to digging. Both groups began digging and making their lake. The men were so confident in their ability to beat the women that they did not take their digging very seriously.

The men underestimated the women of their time. The women knew they had to outsmart the men if they wanted to win. So, the leader of the women's side instructed a few ladies to make a very long pole by attaching bamboo sticks end-to-end. Then, the women tied a lantern to the top of one bamboo pole and lifted it high into the air, not far from where the men were digging.

Upon seeing the light just above the trees, the men announced that it was time to stop. They thought the morning star had risen and shone brightly overhead. Thinking the contest was over, the men quit. They sat around gloating, thinking they had dug quite an impressive hole and that certainly their lake would be much bigger than the ladies.

Meanwhile on the west end, the women worked through the night while the men socialized. They were on their hands and knees, digging what is now West Baray. By the time the real morning star appeared with the sunrise, the women had surpassed the men. They were victorious! They had outsmarted the men and left a legacy for the next generation of women. From that point forward, the women of Cambodia no longer had to pay the family a dowry. But the men did, and still do until this very day."

"Did that really happen?" asked Edgar, intrigued by her story.

"Many Cambodian people believe it did. But it is a legend. Nobody truly knows what took place," Rachana answered. "If you go to Cambodia you can visit West Baray, the women's lake. The men's lake is nowhere to be found because it never became deep enough to fill with water."

Edgar laughed.

Rachana continued, "Nonetheless, one custom remained, and that is for the parents to choose a mate for their daughters. Both sets of parents meet and negotiate the fee, including how much to pay for dowries, how many guests can attend, how elaborate the wedding ceremony and reception will be, as well as other details."

Edgar asked, "How did you know if you would be compatible? Or even like the person?"

Rachana said, "Very often there were other factors to consider, such as astrological compatibility, family relationships, education, salary, career aspirations, and accomplishments, as well as others. The more wealthy a man's family, the greater ability he would have to negotiate the bride of his choice with her parents."

"Well, you must have liked their choice to have stayed married for so long and have two pretty kids together," Edgar responded.

"In some ways, yes. He was good in the beginning, but not always the perfect husband," Rachana said, as her eyes drifted out the window of the van. She stared at the whizzing trees going by, remembering the day she had married Narin. Before long, the shuttle pulled up to the airport and Edgar helped Rachana with her bags. She gave him ten dollars as a tip and thanked him for the ride.

"Good luck, honey," said Edgar. "I'm sure this is difficult for you. Go in peace."

"Thank you," replied Rachana. "You have been very kind to listen." As she walked inside the airport terminal, she searched for the screen that would indicate her departure. She was on her way to say goodbye to her husband, even though he really didn't deserve it.

Chapter Three

"Tough Decisions"

Truth be told, Rachana's marriage to Narin was one of her greatest regrets. She recalled how upset she had been with her decision, for although it was in Cambodian tradition to marry a fellow of her parent's choosing, Rachana had caused a huge disturbance against marrying the man her parents had chosen for her. She swayed them otherwise, then regretting it after it had been done.

In fact, Rachana had not wanted to marry any man at all. If it had been up to her to decide, she would have stayed happily single and carefree forever. She was content with where she was in life, not wanting a marriage to change anything. Plus, she didn't want to end up marrying a man who was like her father. Rachana was afraid of having the kind of marriage that her parents had endured, one of awkwardness and parsimony, at least from her dad. Even though Lee Sim had plenty of money, he never shared any of it with his family. Not one bit, even when it was most needed.

Prior to marrying Narin, there had been a few parents of sons who had approached Rachana's parents. One candidate in particular had been Lee and Thida Sim's top choice as a future son-in-law for their youngest daughter. His name was Phon.

It was understandable that Rachana's family were eager to get her married off and settled. She was the baby of the house and the last child to marry. The groom's family was obligated to pay a dowry. And the more well-to-do their family, the more money they could offer to the bride's parents. Rachana had rejected all of the men who came before her parents, no matter their financial status.

It was at a time when Rachana had finally "made it" and accomplished her teaching degree. She landed her first teaching job and was enthusiastic to put her education to good use. She didn't want to be tied down. Plus, she was the first of the Sim children who had achieved an education.

Rachana had always been fiercely independent. At the beginning of the school year in 1971-1972, each of the teachers were required to recruit their own students. The parents brought their children to school before the first bell rang, to choose their teachers. Then, the teachers flagged the kids down who looked to be the right age, saying, "You can be in my class!" In Rachana's case, it was the sixth graders.

The tables were arranged under the trees, set from first to sixth grade. By late morning, the crowd slowed down and many of the children had already chosen or picked their teachers. As they sat around a table getting to know each other and enjoying the conversation, a poorly dressed elderly man arrived with a little boy of about six or seven. He approached another table first for the registration; however, the teacher acted very snobbish towards the old man. She ignored him, glancing back at him with a nose of indignity before looking back at the other teacher who she had been carrying on a conversation with.

The elderly man just stood there, holding the boy's hands in front of her. He didn't say anything or know what to do. Not pleased, Rachana jumped up from her seat, calling out to the man. "Come join us!" she said, waving her hands.

As he walked over with the boy, Rachana smiled. Her friendly nature put the man at ease. After a few questions and some compliments, she had cheered him up. Although she could not register the boy because he was younger than a sixth grader, Rachana pointed him to the right place.

A few days later, a stranger came to visit Rachana's home. Thida had gone to the market. So, Rachana invited the stranger into their home to wait for her mother, as was the usual Cambodian custom. The woman introduced herself to Rachana as Mrs. Ung. Never hearing that name before, Rachana looked bewildered.

The woman continued. "I have seen you nearly every day. I know you are a teacher at the school, but I did not realize that you are related to me," said Mrs. Ung. "Just the other day, my husband's cousin stopped by and told me all about you."

Not being particularly curious, Rachana left it at that. She did not know Mrs. Ung and therefore could not possibly have known her cousin.

She figured it was a friend of her mother's and left it at that. From that day on, Thida added Mrs. Ung to her frequent list of visitors.

It turned out that Mrs. Ung lived only a few houses away from the small home that Rachana shared with her mother. The stopovers became more frequent. She put two-and-two together that Mrs. Ung and Thida had other business matters that were confidential.

Then one random Saturday, the elderly man whose grandson Rachana had helped to register stopped by, bringing nice gifts. "Is Thida Sim home?" he asked politely.

"No, my mother isn't here right now," replied Rachana. No one was with her that day. She didn't recognize the man right away, although he looked familiar. "She went to visit my father in Siem Reap, at the farm."

"I see," he said, thinking about what he should do next.

Rachana went on, "She won't be back for a few days. Would you like to come in?"

"Sure, thank you," he said politely, removing his hat as he stepped through the door. Once inside, Rachana fixed him lunch. Although she felt strange dining with the old man, it was a custom not to let visitors return home without feeding them first.

"I have these . . . for you." As he said it, the elderly man pushed some exclusive jewelry to her–a jade necklace, gold bracelet, exotic handbag, vintage pocket watch, and some other treasures. They were all very beautiful gifts.

"What is this for? Who are you?" asked Rachana.

He smiled, "You don't remember me, do you?"

She shook her head.

He continued, "After that day I left you at the recruiting table, I went around to find someone who knew about you."

Rachana suddenly recalled him as the elderly man with the young boy she had helped. "You did that? Why?"

"Because you were the only one who was nice and kind to me," he answered. "So, I want you to have these gifts."

Now curious, Rachana asked, "Well, what did you find out about me?"

He raised his eyebrows, and told her, "I was so surprised when I heard who you were. Your mother and I were best friends at one time. When I discovered that you were Thida's youngest daughter, I realized why you are so sweet and kind. You are the shadow of your mother." It was a very nice compliment to Rachana's mom.

But she wasn't convinced that it was true. Rachana's mother had never mentioned this man. "You're best friends?" she asked inquisitively, as if asking him why he hadn't come around before. If they were indeed such close friends, why had he never come by to visit?

He went on to explain. "Actually, both of your parents and I were best friends. Your father, Lee, and I knew each other back in grade school. We both were married within the same year and used to get together frequently. My wife was very close with Thida, your mother. So was I. In fact, I was there when all of your brothers and sisters grew up, but you were very young when my wife and I moved out of town."

"What did you say your name was again?" asked Rachana.

"Mak Yorn. And my wife's name is Jorani," he stated. Come to think of it, Rachana had heard both of her parents mention them before. However, both of her parents, especially her father, Lee, knew so many people that Rachana thought nothing of it. He was always making deals and had a revolving door of visitors.

Mr. Yorn winked at Rachana and told her, "We did have a vow together before my wife and I moved out of town, nearly twenty years ago." With a very cheerful smile, Mr. Yorn looked straight into Rachana's eyes. "Now it's time to renew our vow."

Not understanding what the old man meant, Rachana let him be. After a little more chatter, he excused himself. "I will stop by your father's place and maybe stay the night with him."

"That would be lovely. I think it would be a nice surprise to both of them. They will certainly be happy to be paid a visit by a long lost friend," she agreed.

With that, Mr. Yorn picked up his hat and cordially said goodbye.

A few days later, Thida returned to stay with her daughter. They lived in a different city because of Rachana's teaching assignment. Being unable to bear life without her mother was impossible for her to think about, so Thida chose to live with her youngest and returned only to visit Lee from time to time.

Rachana overheard her mom talking to a neighbor about Mr. Yorn and his two sons, who were about the same age as Rachana. The eldest of the two sons was once Rachana's classmate in high school, however she had never really noticed him before as potential marriage material. As she was listening in on her mother's conversation, Rachana heard Thida tell the neighbor that the elder son's birthday and Rachana's did not match up well, therefore they could not marry. In Cambodia, astrology was always a major consideration as an element of one's decisions. If the sun and moon signs did not fare well together, then Cambodians believed the couple's compatibility as husband and wife would not fare well either. Astrology played a big role in life decisions.

Upon eavesdropping, Rachana finally realized what her mother was up to. The "vow" that Mr. Yorn spoke of finally made sense. Rachana's parents were cohorts with their best friends, Mak and Jorani, to match one of the Yorns' two sons to be married to their daughter.

No less than a month thereafter, a new lady friend came to visit Thida. It was Mak's wife, Jorani, and she was there solely to do business with Thida. Although she did not stay for dinner this time, Jorani began visiting more frequently thereafter. Wondering what they were up to, Rachana realized their conversations were becoming more and more serious. Every day one or two people from the Yorn family came to visit Thida.

Not long after that, Lee also came to stay with his wife and daughter for a few days. Rachana's sisters also came to visit for the weekend. The small home was now crowded with the entire Sim family—Lee and Thida, with their five daughters and their husbands. The eldest Sim daughter was Phary, then Tina, Rachel, Kalianne and finally, Rachana. She was the baby, even though she was now a grown woman. She was the last one to be married. However, if it were up to her family, that aspect was about to change.

Rachana's tiny house looked like a family reunion. Everyone was happy to see one another. The women were busy in the kitchen, preparing Rachana's favorite food. As she poked her head in, Rachana's mom and sisters said, "Ahh . . . the baby is hungry now!" They giggled.

"What are you all cooking?" asked Rachana, wondering what they were up to and why they were all so secretive. What were they doing here, for real? Besides visiting?

Tina said, "I'm in charge of the mixed vegetable soup. You know I am good at making it. Isn't that right, dear sister?"

"Yes!" Rachana said, licking her lips. "Honey always likes it."

Sister Kalianne chimed in, pretending to steal the spoon. "Yes, I do. Can I have a little taste now?"

Phary interrupted. "No, honey, you should taste my food first. I am the oldest and have the most experience. And therefore, I am the best cook!"

Tina made a funny face. Then Phary gave her baby sister a big piece of fried fish. It was her favorite dish and tasted even better because she had not eaten it for so long.

The family had a grand time visiting and catching up with one another. They had not all been together in the same place for a long time, well over a year. Because of the war, nobody dared to travel. Doing so meant taking your life in your own hands. Bombs went off everywhere, and without notice. People often got robbed and killed when traveling. Just going to visit a relative was a huge risk.

It was 1971, the year after the Cambodian Civil War erupted. The Khmer Rouge teamed up to defeat the Cambodian government, which was made up of the good people of Cambodia. They were known as the Khmer Republic. It was a struggle for power between the communist party and the Republican Allies.

For Cambodian citizens, these conflicts represented many changes in the way they lived, including simple excursions to visit family across the countryside. Everyone used to be kind to everyone else, helping strangers and trusting one another. After the war started, the entire country turned upside down. There were many casualties. People became cautious.

After the Sim family ate a big, delicious lunch, everyone went outside to visit. The next youngest sister to Rachana was Kalianne, who had eight years on her. All four of her sisters now had families of their own. They felt that it was Rachana's time to settle down.

Phary, the eldest of the five Sim daughters, approached Rachana with a big smile. She said, "I have great news, dear sister. Daddy, Mother, and all of us agree that Phon is right for you." As she made the announcement, Phary motioned her hand in a circle to imply the unanimous agreement of their family.

Rachana squirmed. "Who is Phon?" she asked.

"Phon and Sangha are Mak and Jorani Yorn's sons. The youngest one they call Phon. He is about your age, maybe a little younger," Phary answered.

Rachana appeared uncomfortable.

Thida piped in. "They are very nice, very good people. Their family is very loving. We know both boys' parents very well. Although we have not seen the boys as young men, you may have heard the saying, 'You can tell a tree by the fruit it bears.' Besides, both Mak and Jorani Yorn gave us their words of promise. All night long they guaranteed your happiness and told us how happy it would make them if you would accept Phon as your husband."

Not knowing what to say, Rachana just sat there as if someone were holding her tongue. She could not speak. Her mother continued, "At first, Mak asked for your hand for Sangha, his eldest. However, the birth-dates between you do not mesh well for compatibility. So I said no. But when Jorani returned, it was to ask on behalf of their baby boy."

Rachana's father, who had kept quiet for much of the discussion, finally spoke. "My daughter, we are so happy for you. We are going to have two babies in the family! You are our baby. And Phon is the Yorn's baby. It is a perfect match."

Finally, Rachana said, "Oh really? You are all very happy about this choice?" Her entire family nodded, smiling.

Lee exclaimed proudly, "Yes, you should hear how much Mak and Jorani have offered for your dowry! The whole big package! A three-day wedding with unlimited guests for the babies of our families." He beamed. "They asked your mother and me if 100,000 riels would be enough to marry our youngest daughter and, if not, just to let them know and they would offer more. It surprised me. I did not know they were that rich."

Rachana thought about it. "What do they do to have that much money?"

Her father said, "After they moved away from Siem Reap, they got into the rice business. They began buying and selling rice. After just a few years, they made very good profits, enough to build two rice factories. Then they started exporting rice outside of the country. They told us the money they offer for your dowry is for you to keep."

Thida chimed in, as if she didn't want her husband to leave out any of the most important details. "Phon will be paying for the wedding. We hope that you will accept him as your husband. We know his family very well. His father is very good to his mother, and we know that Phon will be the same with you. He will make a great husband and a good father."

Kalianne said, "I believe that too!"

Tina said, "Me too." Everybody else in the family jumped up in spirited unison.

Rachel said, "Oh good, the mission is accomplished! Our baby sister is getting married. I'm so excited!"

"Not that fast, sisters!" Rachana looked confused and less enthusiastic than they were. "I have not seen the man. I cannot marry a guy I haven't seen. And by the way, how old is Phon?"

Tina replied, "He's a little younger than you."

Hesitantly, Rachana asked, "How many years younger, sister?"

She answered, "Only five years younger than you."

"Five!" exclaimed Rachana. "Oh, for heaven's sake! The boy is not fully-grown yet. That would make me a cradle robber. Oh, let his mama help him grow up first."

This time, the eldest sister took a stab at convincing her. Phary said, "But honey, your cousin married a younger man. Phon's sister married a younger man. She is seven years older than her husband. Look . . . even your neighbor and our relative Mrs. Chewy is four years older than her husband. And what does this say about me? I am one year older than Pitch." Pitch was Phary's husband and Rachana's brother-in-law.

Kalianne cut in. "I am a year older than your brother-in-law and we have a good marriage. Phary is right. Everything will be alright. We all know this will work out well for you. Phon comes from a very good family and both families are happy about this. Don't say no. Honey, say yes!" she implored.

After thinking about it for a minute, Rachana replied, "Well, I have to see him before I decide on anything."

Thida took a long, deep breath. Then she addressed her daughter's request. "It may be awhile because Phon is on the other side of the country. He is in the province of Kampong Som."

"Very well then," Rachana said, satisfied that she had stalled them long enough without committing.

A few days later, Rachana found a picture of two good-looking young men on her desk at school. The two were dressed fashionably for the times, but it was not a style that Rachana preferred. She knew the picture was of the Yorn boys. In the photo, Phon was wearing a tight shirt and tight pants with bell-bottomed legs. He was tall like her father, Lee. Indeed, Phon was extremely attractive. All of her sisters praised him, for they knew not the kind of husband their baby sister was looking for. They did not understand Rachana's secret pain that she kept hidden deep within her heart, mostly out of disappointment in her dad.

Rachana's father was wealthy too. Lee was a well-respected member of the community. However, he intentionally kept his wealth to himself and did not use any of his money to take care of his family. Instead, Lee's family had to fend for themselves. Therefore, Rachana did not want to marry anyone who reminded her of her father.

It was a senseless concept and definitely not smart decision-making on her part. In a way, Rachana used it as an excuse to rebel against the wishes of her family. It was as if to spite her father by avoiding his choice in a husband for her. So after thinking about it for a few weeks, Rachana made her decision.

She first told her eldest sister, after weighing the pros and cons for several weeks. "I have made my decision. I will not marry Phon," Rachana disclosed to Phary.

Phary looked surprised, to say the least. "Please, honey, take more time to think. How come you don't want Phon? We are very sure he will be a wonderful husband for you."

"How can you be so sure of this man, when you haven't even seen him?" she inquired.

Phary replied, "Haven't you heard? 'The mango does not fall far from the tree.' Phon's parents are very prestigious and people of integrity. They love us. They also love you, very much. That's worth a lot. They are willing to give you everything you want, if you are willing to marry their son. Please do not throw this blessing away. Besides, Phon is coming to meet you next month. The airlines only have one flight per month for him."

Undaunted, Rachana said, "He will have to cancel his flight then."

Rachana's sisters and mother were heartbroken. Her father was disappointed. Nobody knew or understood her blatant rejection of the best possible choice they could ever have found in a husband. But when Rachana studied Phon's picture, all she saw was her own father. It wasn't that she hated her dad, but she was disgusted by the way he excluded his own family from his wealth and his love.

Because of Lee's stinginess, it had clouded his daughter's judgment and contaminated her mind. Even though Rachana had always been independent and rebellious, this was the ultimate revenge. Sadly, the person it affected the most was her own self. She was naïve—a fool. A very stubborn young girl who did not realize what was best for her.

And so it was that Rachana did not marry Phon, as it was supposed to have happened. Instead, the track of her destiny changed with her decision. One day, a neighbor and relative showed up at Rachana's door. The woman presented her with very expensive gifts, which were wrapped in pretty silks from the marketplace. Outstretching her hands, she said, "My father just returned from Phnom Penh and asked me to bring all of these things for you. Rachana, please take them."

Rachana was surprised. The gifts were very expensive. There was jewelry and a basketful of hard-to-find fruits, candies, and imported treasures.

These gifts were only appropriate for an engagement, or something momentous. "Wait a minute, are these from your parents?" asked Rachana.

The girl replied, "No, Frank will explain things to you. Goodbye." With a big smile, she ran off. Rachana was puzzled, having to wait for the explanation.

Since her own family had no success in convincing Rachana to marry Phon, his parents tried to cleverly maneuver around her by asking one of Rachana's best friends to do the job.

Frank was someone that Rachana went to college with and who knew the Yorns. He was very smart, spoke eloquently, and had a knack for smoothing things out between people. Frank and Rachana got along very well and often sat and talked for hours. They were very good friends. Even Frank agreed with the Sim family's choice in Phon. For days—even weeks—he tried to convince her how happy she would be to marry Phon, but to no avail. Her shield was up and there was no getting through it.

On this particular day, Frank tried another approach. He came to Rachana with a gigantic smile, as if he had just won the jackpot. Seeing this, she knew he was up to something. Her scowl only made him burst into a fit of giggles.

"What is the matter with you, Frank?" asked Rachana.

He played into her curiosity. "Oh, it is a long, long story."

She agreed. "It must be! You have brought me gifts, as if I were going to get engaged to you. I hope there is no mistake about all of this?"

Frank replied, "Oh heavens no. And if I were to ever make such a mistake, and then my head shall be cut off before dark."

They both laughed and sat side-by-side on the deck outside of Rachana's home. Frank avoided talking about the gifts; however, Rachana would not let him off the hook so easily. She asked, "So, tell me Frank. Are these gifts from Phon?"

"No, Phon didn't give these to you," he said evasively.

She prodded. Curiosity got the better of her. "Are they from his parents?"

Again, he denied it. "No, no. Do you think Phon is the only man who is attracted to you?"

Rachana answered, "I don't care about any of the others. Just Phon alone has given me enough of a headache already. I was fine before all of this hassle."

Frank replied, matter-of-factly, "Well, do you want to stay single for the rest of your life?"

Eagerly, Rachana responded, "Yes. I have a secure income on my own, enough to make a good living. I can be independent and happy. It is plain and simple. I don't need to marry someone just to be happy."

"It is not your family's wish. They want you to get married," Frank answered. "Do you realize that?"

"Yes, I do. But nobody asked me what I want. What Rachana wants!" She pointed at herself. "I think there should be a change in the old tradition. It is a new age! New way! New revolution! We should all have the freedom to choose how to live our own life. Don't you agree, Frank?"

"Funny girl," he shook his head. "Don't you care what people think of you, or are you too independent?"

"I know what they are going to think, but it does not hurt me." Rachana was rebellious at heart. "Tell me though, if these gifts are not from Phon and his family, who in the world would buy me such expensive gifts like this?"

Frank went on to explain to the anxious girl. "You knew that I was away for the entire month, didn't you?"

"Yes, I did," confirmed Rachana. "I can tell these gifts are from outside the province. Where are they from? Who gave these to me?" she waved her hands across the gifts, emphatically.

Annoyed, Frank told her, "Be patient. I will get to that very soon."

She said, "Oh, I hope so. I hope this won't cause any more headaches for my sisters and my mother. Please, get to the point!"

Frank said, "While I was away, I stayed with my oldest brother, Cameron. You know him, don't you?"

She nodded. "Yes, very well. I like him a lot. We get along famously."

He went on, "As I was saying . . . while I was away, Cameron's best friend, Narin Long, stopped by. Cameron and Narin have been best friends for a long time now. They went to the same professional school and work in the same field. But Narin has a better job than Cameron. He works for the government, whereas my brother works in the private sector. His salary is half of Narin's. Do you know Narin?"

Rachana thought for a moment before giving her answer. "I've heard of him, but I don't think I've ever met him. I think he left for high school before I was done with elementary school."

Finally, Frank revealed that the gifts were from Narin. Rachana's reaction was one of surprise. Her jaw dropped. "How dare he do that?"

"Hold on," Frank interrupted. "Please, let me finish the whole story."

She listened intently and told him to go ahead without holding back any details.

"Narin is single," explained Frank. "It surprised me. My brother is now married with two sons. I asked Cameron why Narin remained single, and he explained that Narin has simply not found the right woman. So, when I saw Narin I told him about you and everything that is going on with you. He begged and pleaded with me to ask for your hand. I told him that he could never compete with Phon's family, who are very wealthy. Plus, Phon is very attractive and Narin is not."

"He is not?" this caught her attention.

"No, Rachana, he is not. However, Narin does have a better job than Phon. Narin is head of the ministry of commerce. This is something you should think about. You need someone who can provide for you and any children you may have together."

Quietly, she nodded, but not in compliance.

The very next day, Frank came back with his sister-in-law. Although Rachana was unaware of their plan, they returned with more gifts. She wondered how a total stranger could do something for a girl he did not know. How could Narin have already decided that he wanted to marry her? To Rachana, the whole Cambodian custom didn't make any sense. She had a new way of thinking, one that she felt strongly about. Rachana believed that women and men should be able to choose their own mate, rather than having the decision made for them by their parents.

Before they left, Frank told Rachana to consider marrying Narin. He pointed out their friendship and that he had never steered her wrong. Despite her protests, Frank told her that Narin wanted her to have the gifts, regardless of whether or not she accepted his marriage proposal.

Furthermore, Frank mentioned that Rachana had possibly seen Narin at the Formation Pedagogic School in which she had attended at the University, while she was studying for her teaching degree. She had not noticed Narin whatsoever. It was as if he never even existed. She failed to notice the admiration he had for her. Indeed, Narin's crush on Rachana began with that first glimpse of her across the room.

It was true. Rachana was never friendly with strange men at all, especially those who gawked at her. If she knew and trusted someone she was with, that was a different story. She was very down-to-earth and friendly. Yet, with certain skepticism, she kept an aloof distance from those who had ulterior motives.

Frank was there to convince Rachana to marry Narin, nothing more and nothing less. That was why he had brought his sister-in-law, to do further convincing. He studied Rachana's reactions very carefully, almost methodically.

After they all ate some lunch, Frank stood up to excuse himself. He had been waiting for the right time to tell Rachana what he needed to say, on behalf of his friend Narin. At the same time, he betrayed his promise to Phon's mother, who had asked Frank to help her persuade Rachana to marry her son.

"Listen, before I leave today, I want you to know something," Frank spoke seriously. "I know this man very well. For two years, Narin stayed with us. Our family likes him a lot. He is still the same man he was then, which was years ago before college. Narin has not changed a bit and is still very close to Cameron and our whole family. Even Cameron implored me to speak to you. He gave me his word with a guarantee that he will be personally responsible for Narin's behavior. It would make him extremely happy to have his best friend marry someone who means so much to us." With that, Frank reached for Rachana's hand. "You mean the world to us, dear."

She smiled. "I'll think about it."

Satisfied with that, Frank reaffirmed. "Please, just take it into consideration."

Rachana had a tough decision ahead of her. Phon's family was close to hers. Of course, they were rich and able to offer her the sun and the moon. Indeed, what they offered could not be outdone. However, wealth and fame did not always come with happiness, as she had seen from her own parents and their strange relationship. Plus, it really bothered her that Phon was a lot younger than she was.

Frank was very clever. He understood how to manipulate a broken girl, a stubborn girl. He had gotten to her, and he knew it. Rachana was defiant, which he felt could benefit his friend Narin. She was the type who would refuse to marry Phon just to spite her dad, because that was his choice and not her own. Had she seen or met Phon without knowing who he was, Rachana may have actually liked him. She refused to give him a chance just because she was foolish and narrow-minded. She thought because her father horded all of their family's income, that perhaps Phon would do the same.

As he left, Frank urged Rachana to keep the gifts, regardless of her decision. He took full responsibility for Narin and backed him one hundred percent as a worthy marital candidate.

After he left, Rachana mulled over the decision between which of the two men to marry. She knew that if she chose Narin over Phon, there would be uproar within her family. An argument would ensue. Then again, Rachana wanted neither man. She didn't even want to get married in the first place. It was all so confusing.

Realizing there would be a big argument with her parents, Rachana avoided the topic altogether for a few days. She wanted to see none of them. In fact, Frank kept himself out of her sight for a week, leaving Rachana to make her own decision.

Meanwhile, Rachana's mother kept asking her about Phon. She would not let it go. Thida wanted Phon as her son-in-law and knew that he was perfect for her daughter. She knew his parents and felt that all of the qualities were there to make for a lasting marriage, including Phon's ability to provide for her daughter.

Knowing Frank was good friends with Rachana, Thida had asked him to talk to Rachana on Phon's behalf. Phon's mother had done the same. Little did she know, Frank had already worked on getting Rachana's hand in marriage, but for someone else–someone whom she did not know. Frank betrayed Thida by telling her he would help, but persuaded Rachana to marry Narin instead.

After exactly a week passed, Frank stopped by Rachana's house again. This time, she was not as cheerful as she had been on previous encounters with him. It was because she was terribly stressed out over the decision she had been forced to make. She had to give these men an answer, and soon. She had to turn one away, maybe both.

In a low voice, Frank asked, "Have you thought about the gifts from Narin and whether you will marry him or not?"

"Yes, I have." She admitted. It had taken her all month to think about marrying Phon. Hence, adding Narin to the equation had thrown her off guard.

The wedding plans to Phon were already underway, even though Rachana had not yet agreed to it. Her family wanted her to marry the Yorn's son, and that was that. Frank had one last chance to make an impact and to sway Rachana to marry Narin.

"What did you decide?" asked Frank. "Do you need more time? I do not want to rush you; however, I know that Phon is going to be here very soon. And when he gets here, the wedding will take place shortly after that. Have you thought about it? I would love to see you marry Narin instead. He is a great guy. He doesn't smoke, nor drink. He's sweet and kind. You have my word that he will make a nice husband for you. You'll see."

Frank was quite convincing too. Shamefully, Rachana chose to trust him even more than her own family who knew what was best for her. When Frank asked again of her decision, she boldly chose Narin. Her reason for agreeing was rather foolish. Most of it was to escape the spotlight of having to marry Phon. It was also an act of rebellion against her father. Rachana had found a way to escape his grasp by choosing Narin.

Another reason that she reached the conclusion to marry Narin over Phon was because Rachana didn't want anybody else's money, even though Phon's family had offered her the world. Rachana wanted to pave her own way, which she was doing as a teacher. From the time she was a young girl–throughout the teenage years and into her adulthood–Rachana was hard-headed, stubborn, and fiercely independent.

As seemingly stupid as it sounded, Rachana also didn't like the idea of marrying a good-looking young man, because she felt that all attractive men would be like her father. Like the horns of a ferocious bull, Rachana's resolve to push against what was best for her were like spikes charging towards the matador, which was her entire family. They teased and taunted the stubborn bull with a red blanket of enthusiasm, shaking it in front of Rachana's face until she lashed out.

Rachana told Frank she would marry Narin, but deep down she only did so out of impetuousness and spite. It was not so far off from the old Khmer proverb, "You throw out the meat and collect the bones, only to discover the hard bone when you bite down. So then you return to look for the meat." Her hotheaded attitude threw Phon out to marry Narin at the last minute. As she would later discover, Rachana had actually thrown out the meat and instead settled for the dry bones.

"Narin will be thrilled!" exclaimed Frank. He looked pleased that he had won her over. It was like winning a challenging game. Rachana's simple "yes" answer was the only prize.

Rachana added, "There is one small problem. You will have to talk to my family."

Unfazed, he jumped up from his chair joyfully. Frank said, "I get it, I get it. I will go tomorrow to see your father, Lee."

"Good luck," replied Rachana. "You know my father well, don't you?" She knew he would not be receptive.

Frank reassured her. "Yes, I do. Don't you worry; I will be able to smooth things out so that everyone will be happy."

Chapter Four

"Regrets"

Nobody knew why Frank was such an advocate of Rachana choosing to marry Narin over Phon, but then again, nobody could understand why she had agreed to it, especially Rachana's sisters. They knew Narin and had seen him. He was not good looking by any woman's standards. He was short, stocky, and had a dark complexion with unappealing facial features, whereas Phon was tall, handsome, and had a manly physique. They didn't know anything about Narin or his family, while they knew Phon's family very well.

As soon as her sisters found out, the wedding was dubbed "The Princess and the Beast." Why had their youngest sister refused a great husband prospect over an iffy one, at best? They could not understand for the life of them how a girl could reject a man who came from a great family and who was sure to have treated her like a princess. They were all very disheartened.

Nevertheless, the wedding was hastily planned. Unlike the three-day wedding event that Rachana would have had with the Yorns paying, the dowry offered by Narin was a lot less than 100,000 riels. But it was her decision. She had made her choice. All because of her father and the secret resentment she felt for his lack of family support.

It was kind of silly from the outside looking in. Lee had always treated Thida well as a husband. It was just that he kept his money and refused to give their family any, except in unusual and exceptional circumstances. However, Rachana's parents rarely argued and were not mean to her. She was a difficult girl to raise.

On the day of the wedding, Rachana wore one of her sister's wedding gowns. It was gold with sequins and she wore a beautiful tiara in her hair. She looked elegant. The ceremony was fairly big, with 150-200 guests attending. All of her sisters and their husbands and children were there, as well as her aunts, uncles, and cousins. Narin had a few family members there as well, including his brothers, Vibol and Heng, along with their families.

As she prepared on the day of her wedding, she sipped mimosas with her sisters. They tried one last time to reason with her.

"It's not too late!" cried Kalianne.

"Please, will you come to your senses little sister?" asked Tina.

"We all love you and want to see you happy. Age does not matter. Happiness does!" exclaimed Phary.

Rachana was nervous and anxious. Her stomach was in knots. Come to think of it, she hadn't wanted to get married at all. She wasn't even sure herself why she was about to go through with it, but at this point Rachana felt like it was too late to turn back time and she still did not want to marry Phon. Quite honestly, she wanted to be single and make her own decisions. *IF* and *WHEN* she married, Rachana wanted to choose her own husband. However, that was not the Cambodian way.

In contrast, Narin's family was elated, especially his mother, Elita. Elita knew Thida and was pleased with the prospect of having Rachana as a daughter-in-law. Not only was Thida very beautiful and intelligent, but the word was that she took very good care of everyone. Thida was known for being nurturing to her parents, grandmother, in-laws, and especially her children. Basing Narin's choice in a wife by the girl's parents, on all accounts it seemed that Rachana was a dream girl for her son.

Elita knew Lee, too, just as everyone in the community did. Rachana's father was the "go-to" guy for anything and had visitors constantly coming and going. Lee was a loan shark of sorts, except without the fierce teeth. Everyone liked him, although he was reputed to be a shrewd business man.

Nonetheless, by Narin's parent's standards, the couple had all of the elements of success and potential for great offspring. Rachana was a pretty girl. She was skinny, with dark shoulder-length hair and pleasant facial features. Although she wasn't a curvy girl, Rachana was womanly in confidence. She had great poise. People liked that about her.

On that day, Elita came to see Rachana right before the wedding. She wanted to have a heart-to-heart talk with her and to assure her that she had made the right choice in marrying her son. Elita took Rachana's hands in a firm grip and told her how happy she was to have her as part of their family and as her daughter-in-law. She presented the Sims with the dowry that had been offered by Narin.

But as Rachana sat down next to her groom for the hair cutting ceremony, which was the first part of a traditional Cambodian wedding, her heart sunk. She felt as if she were sitting in thick tar, as if she were stuck to her seat not by her own choice but as if everyone had persuaded her to be there. The nervous goose bumps on her arms turned into needles, pricking her everywhere. When she looked at Narin, Rachana was very disappointed. She wished she had seen a picture of him before committing.

Narin was less than average looking. He was sitting there with a big grin–like a giant jack o'lantern–looking strange and smug. At that moment, Rachana knew she had made a mistake. However, the pressure of the crowd closed in on her, in its state of expectancy and awe.

Maybe I could leave him right after the wedding, she thought to herself. *Or maybe I should get up now.*

They went through the cordial formalities of traditional ceremonial customs. The tea ceremony and the pairing ceremony were performed in which all of the family and friends were invited to tie Rachana and Narin's left and right wrists together with strings of blessings. Although everyone sang the traditional wedding songs, the guests were not as happy as they could have been. Rachana looked as if she would burst into tears at any moment.

After the seven rotations and tying of the wrists with ribbons, the newly married couple got up to celebrate their wedding reception in the backyard of Phary and Pitch's house. Narin's father had prepared a simple toast to the bride and groom. Rachana's parents sat quietly. Lee chewed his food with great intent. Thida stared at her plate, mostly shifting her rice back and forth to make it look like she was eating.

Deep down, Thida detested Narin. Although she didn't know him that well, her heart had been set on Phon. Her dreams were shattered by her daughter's rebellion and she was not happy about it at all. Like the rest of the family, Thida could not fathom how Rachana would choose Narin over Phon. In fact, she felt it was insulting of their daughter to have gone against their wishes; especially after all she had done to help Rachana through the college years. Nevertheless, Rachana was her baby, so she largely kept those feelings to herself. In Cambodia, people rarely spoke about their feelings. Children were to obey their parents and respect them, no matter what.

After they were finished eating a wonderful dinner, Rachana suddenly jumped up from her chair and covered her mouth. "Excuse me!" she screamed. She ran for the house, holding the hem of her wedding dress in the other hand. Her sisters jumped up too. They glanced knowingly at one another and then ran inside to find out what was the matter.

Rachana was nauseous. One of her sisters wetted a wash rag and rested it on her forehead. "What's the matter, dear sister? Do you not feel well?" asked Rachel.

Tears welled up in Rachana's eyes. "I have made a terrible mistake! You were right, you were all right!" she sobbed hysterically. "What have I done?"

"There, there, sister dear. You're going to be fine," coddled Tina. "You just need some time to get to know him."

"I don't want to!" cried Rachana. "I want to kill myself! Life is not worth living any longer after this big mistake."

"Take it back!" yelled Kalianne.

"Come, come. Surely you don't mean that?" said Phary.

"Yes, I do mean it. I want to end it all right here!" Rachana yelled dramatically. "Please, I will be so miserable. There is no other way out of this mess than to commit suicide."

"Snap out of it!" shouted Rachana's eldest sister. "Now get out there and enjoy your reception. These people were kind enough to show up to this fiasco, so you'd better show some respect and get out there."

She did as her sister asked. However, when she had the opportunity, Rachana snuck into several of the elderly ladies' bags and took the medicine bottles out of their purses. *Surely by mixing the pills together, it would be a deadly concoction*, she contemplated.

The guests stayed for the entire weekend. Rachana was cordial to everyone, although she seemed very sad. Frank came to her and asked, "Rachana, what is wrong? Are you not happy with Narin?"

"No, I'm not. I can't believe I let you talk me into this charade!" she said loudly. "The only way to get out of this now is to kill myself. I have already made a plan."

"Please, I implore you. Trust me on this. Narin will be good to you. You made the right choice, you just haven't seen it yet," Frank said, encouragingly.

He was extremely stressed out because he was the one who had talked Rachana into marrying Narin. So, not only was she unhappy and talking about death, Frank was also in hot water with Lee and Thida, as well as the entire Yorn family. He didn't know Phon as well as he knew Narin, but from what he had seen, Phon was not such a bad guy. Now he felt guilty about intervening. Frank had changed the course of history and the only people who were happy about it was Narin and his parents.

She dropped the subject with Frank. Rachana knew that he was the wrong person to discuss it with because he was Narin's friend. However, she didn't realize that as she spoke these words out loud to Frank, all of her sisters, mother, new mother-in-law, and cousin, Kim Sivorn, were in the pantry, listening to the whole thing.

On the third day, Elita came to Rachana before she went home.

"Honey, I am going to say goodbye now," said Elita. "I am so happy to have you as my daughter-in-law."

"Thank you, Mrs. Long," said Rachana politely. At least Narin's mother was sweet.

"Please, will you join me on the walk to the bus stop?" asked Elita. Rachana agreed and they began walking. Elita linked her arm through Rachana's and bumped her in the hips, like a friendly gesture. "Listen, I know it's none of my business . . . but I overheard things when I was in the pantry with your family . . . things that don't seem right."

"When?" asked Rachana. She tried to recall the last time she had been near the pantry. It was when she confided in Frank about wanting to kill herself. "Did everyone hear me?"

Elita nodded yes. "I'm afraid so. It makes me sad. Please, honey, stay with my son. He is not a handsome man, this I know. But Narin is a very good man. I know he will be good to you. Please . . . stay with him."

Rachana didn't say anything. She was still shocked about having her whole family overhear the conversation she had with Frank.

"I was so happy when Frank went to see you, after spending time with Narin at the capital for business. You know, in the times we're in now, it's a good thing my son works for the government. It's a good job. It's secure. He will be a good provider. I taught him well how to treat women," Elita said, as she squeezed Rachana's wrist.

She added, "As a daughter-in-law I will love you and cherish you. I can give you my word that if my son ever causes any problems, I will handle it."

As she stared at Elita's worried face, Rachana found her mother-in-law's words to be endearing. They melted her heart. The way she said it and the tone of voice–along with the hopeful expression on her face–was magical. Suddenly, Rachana felt that she could not say no to this innocent woman standing before her. Yes, Rachana was shallow and self-centered, but she did have a conscience. Elita's love touched her in miraculous ways.

Meanwhile, Thida felt betrayed by Frank. He was supposed to have been on her side, helping to talk Rachana into marrying her choice for a special son-in-law, specifically the Yorns' son.

The truth was, Frank had stayed with Narin for two years and knew him better than he knew Phon. It came down to likeability. He knew Narin to be a good man who was kind, sweet, and non-confrontational in demeanor.

The next day, Frank invited Narin and Rachana to his house. As he sat across from the newlyweds, he made small talk. Then he asked, "When are you two moving?"

Narin replied, "I will be going back to the Capital in two weeks."

Rachana answered too. "For me, I have not put in my application with the school yet to be transferred. It will take at least two to three months."

Frank paused for a minute and looked straight into Narin's eyes. "Narin, these few days will take a lot of pressure and hard work on your end to get this lady to be your wife," he said, pointing at Rachana. "You do remember your word, don't you? So you cannot make a fool of yourself."

Glancing at Rachana, Narin responded, "No, I won't make a fool of myself. I will be a good husband as long as I live. I will make her happy. I will take care of her very well."

Then, Frank told him, "On the day of your wedding, Phon stopped by my house. I just want you to know that I had a lot of explaining to do to the Yorn family and, specifically, to Phon. It was not an easy task. However, I did it because I like you a lot. You are like a brother to me. I don't want to take any more heat! After this whole ordeal, I am going to stay in my house like a hermit for a while. Just make sure that you will live your life as you have promised."

"Don't worry, I will." Narin confirmed.

A couple of months after their marriage, Narin came to live with Rachana in her home until she could sell it and move to the Capital with him. He would have to travel to his job for now. Rachana's mother was still living with her, but was contemplating the move back home now that her baby daughter had finally finished college, got a teaching job, and got married. Thida was no longer needed. She also detested Narin, mostly because she loved the Yorns' son more.

True to his word, Narin did return to work at his office job as a government official. Rachana put her small house up for sale. She found a buyer quickly, but in the meantime, she discussed another matter with her mother.

Thida turned to her daughter out of the blue one day. "Honey, I am not going with you. Your father needs me and you know that he would not leave his house and go with us. He will stay there forever. You're married now. You will have a family of your own. I have your dad and all of your sisters. Do not worry about me."

"You mean I am going to Phnom Penh by myself?" Rachana asked, surprised.

"Yes!" Thida told her daughter. "You and your husband."

Looking like she was about to cry, Rachana said, "And you are not going with me?"

"No!" confirmed her mother.

"Then neither am I." Rachana did not want to go live there by herself with Narin. "I refuse to go to Phnom Penh without you. I will just get a divorce."

Exasperated, Thida called another family meeting. All of her daughters came to an agreement. They suggested to their mother that she should go with Rachana for at least three months. After three months, they figured she would surely fall in love with her husband, and then their mother could return to the family home in Siem Reap.

Tina said, "Mother, we know that you do not like this man, but for our sake, please go with her. Otherwise, we are going to have a divorce in the family. You know she'll do what you say."

Indeed, Rachana was a very selfish person. She had ulterior motives in having Thida go to Phnom Penh with her, to live with her and her new husband. Hence, Rachana was very happy that her mother would agree to come, because she had a plan of her own.

So, after they moved to the Capital to live with Narin, he asked his new wife, "What kind of food does your mother like?"

"She loves egg rolls and noodle soup," Rachana answered.

Narin had to work hard to impress not only his new bride, but his new mother-in-law too. Every day he brought Thida her two favorite foods as he came home from work.

Finally one day, Thida told her daughter, "Honey, tell your husband no more of these." She was getting tired of eating the same things every day.

Desperate to continue earning her approval, Narin asked Rachana, "What else could I bring her?"

Rachana thought for a minute and said, "She does like mangoes, yams, pudding, and crepe."

Narin never missed a day that he came home with a treat for his mother-in-law. Over time, Thida began to like him. And so did his wife. He knew very well that Thida was furious over Rachana choosing him over Phon.

After three months, all of Rachana's sisters lost their case. Thida was becoming very fond of Narin, even more so than her daughter. He bent over backwards to do things for both of them. He complimented them, brought them flowers, and constantly told Rachana how lucky he was to have her as a wife.

Then, something funny happened. Rachana began to fall in love with him. Narin made her heart sing. She began to love him more than she loved herself because he gave her the love and respect she so longed for. And Thida loved him too.

From 1972 to 1975–even with a war raging around them–as long as Rachana had her husband and mother with her, she felt content and safe. But the young bride had not yet learned that the rest of the world does not always keep its promise.

Chapter Five

"Spoiled Brat"

As Rachana walked into the stark white hospital, it brought back painful memories. She still had shrapnel in her body from head to toe. In fact, whenever she flew somewhere, it always set off the metal detectors. This last time was no exception. The airport personnel felt bad about searching the sweet and humble middle-aged lady, but nevertheless it was their policy. As soon as they could find no evidence of knives or hair spray bottles, they let her pass. You never knew who could turn out to be a terrorist these days. Even friendly Asian ladies had to endure the price of higher security measures.

Upon arriving in Narin's room, he was still asleep. Rachana stood over his bed, looking down upon her husband. He was gaunt and frail. His sickly body was pale, even though his brown complexion. He was so thin. She had mixed feelings. On one hand, she felt sorry for him. On the other hand, she was still very hurt by all of the pain and grief he had caused their family over the last few years. It was hard to believe it had come to this; after all they had been through.

Rachana thought about the irony. She had not wanted to marry a man who did not provide for his family–as her father had not–but she had chosen a man who ultimately put her through something very similar.

Not wanting to wake Narin, she set her bag down in a nearby chair. Come to think of it, she was exhausted. The trip was tiring and Rachana thought that maybe she should sit down for a few minutes before he woke up.

A nurse poked her head through a crack in the door. "Mrs. Long, is there anything I can get for you?"

"I'd like some tea, if you have any?" Rachana asked, hopefully.

"Sure thing, madam. I'll be back in a few minutes. Try to get comfortable."

The oversized chair was calling her name. While she waited for her tea, she felt her eyelids growing very heavy. Her chin started bobbing up and down. It was becoming difficult to hold her head up and to resist the urge to fall asleep.

The nurse returned with Rachana's tea and an extra blanket. "Is there anything else I can do for you at this time?" the nurse politely asked her.

"One more thing," said Rachana. "Can you scoot this chair closer to the bed? I don't want to hurt my back." "Of course!" replied the courteous nurse. Before leaving the room, she said, "Just press this button if you need anything at all." She showed Rachana the call button on the side of the bed.

Rachana sat in the chair, waiting. She wondered when Narin would wake up, if ever. *Maybe he would die in his sleep and this whole trip would be a wasted effort,* she wondered.

As she fought the urge to doze off, Rachana remembered how her sisters used to sit next to her as a child, whenever she took naps. They didn't have to, but they did it out of love for the baby of the family. When she was a kid, Rachana's body was so weak and frail that they always worried about her. She often woke up exhausted and crying or in a bad mood, so one of her sister was always there by her bedside to comfort her when she woke up.

From the time she was a baby and toddler—and even into her teens—Rachana was a sickly kid and very thin, almost skin and bones. Her hair was wiry and short to meet her thin frame. Rachana never liked to eat much and lacked the energy of other healthy children. She was a picky eater. Being the baby of the Sim family, she had played the helpless role very well. There were eight years between Rachana and Kalianne, the next oldest. Then Rachel, Tina, and Phary were the eldest sisters. There were eighteen years between Rachana and Phary. The Sim sisters and their mother coddled their baby sister, as did her brother when he was alive.

Although people thought she was a cute little girl, Rachana's fiery attitude quickly turned them away. One day, Thida put four-year-old Rachana to bed for a nap after she refused to eat breakfast or lunch. Sister Tina took the naptime duty of watching over her beloved baby sister. Rachana's precious head lay lovingly in her sister's lap.

Tina was busying herself with sewing as her baby sister slept. She used a sharp hunting knife to unthread her blouse. When she noticed baby Rachana waking up, Tina smiled and began teasing her. It was the wrong time to do it. The wrong time for Tina, as Rachana woke up grumpy and was not in the mood for teasing, laughing, or anything of the sort.

Instead, Rachana reached for the knife that Tina had placed on the nightstand. With an angry expression, the little girl sunk the knife deep into her big sister's leg, right on the front of her shin. Laughter turned to screaming. Blood gushed out of Tina's leg as Rachel and Phary came running to help. Rachana screamed too, frightened for what she had just done. Her eyes were as big as a cow's. She had reacted in anger to the teasing.

Even after the three of them pulled the knife out of their sister's leg and cared for the wound, Tina continued trying to console her baby sister. Seeing the blood everywhere, Rachana screamed at the top of her lungs in hysterics. She was scared to death that she had truly injured her sister.

But Tina assured her, "Don't worry, honey. I'm fine! See? All better . . ."

No one ever punished Rachana for her actions, but they should have. She certainly deserved a good whipping. Nevertheless, she was far too spoiled to ever suffer any repercussions for her actions. It was not good to spoil a child, whether she was sickly or not. Unfortunately, nobody realized that spoiling Rachana and allowing her to get away with her actions only worsened her behaviors.

Rachana became a real brat who was never disciplined for any wrongdoing. Instead, the rest of her family often took the brunt and the blame for her actions. They rarely even yelled at her or got mad at her. Rachana was the most difficult and the only one who seemed uncontrollable.

Thida was known to everyone as a kind, patient, and good-hearted lady. She was a wonderful mother, never gossiped about anyone, and people loved her. She was the kind of person who neither agreed nor disagreed. She simply ignored any kind of debate or drama between others and stayed out of their individual squabbles. Not taking sides put her in a position of neutrality; therefore, she was seen as compassionate. When visitors came to the Sim house, Thida greeted them with kindness and hospitality. She often had children holding on to her apron in admiration. Kids had a knack for finding good souls to be around. Her very name meant "angelic girl." If guests dropped by to gossip or talk about others with ill will, Thida disappeared into the kitchen or pantry, usually with Rachana at her heels. She was stunningly beautiful, with long dark hair that was often pulled back. Thida had natural beauty without ever having to get dolled up.

All of Thida's daughters were pretty too. But no one in the family was as gorgeous as she was. Rachana was the least attractive, at least as a child. Her skinny frame looked as if it would blow away with one gust of wind. Some of the members of the community noticed this contrast. In fact, one rude lady blatantly brought it to the little girl's attention one day, as they passed in the marketplace.

Rachana told the woman that her parents were Thida and Lee Sim. The woman told her, "Wow, your mom is so beautiful! How could you look like this? You are the ugly duckling!"

It seemed as though Thida aged backwards. She looked adorable, innocent and trustworthy. She always had the respect of her children and never raised her voice to them with one mean word.

It was too bad that despite her goodness, Thida's generosity was not met by her husband, who offered zero financial support. He was kind to his wife, but firm with their children, especially Rachana, whom he liked the least. He hated to admit how he truly detested his own daughter. "Cha-Cha"–as he nicknamed her–was unruly and mean. As a father, Lee rarely spent any time with her because she got on his nerves and he thought she was a spoiled brat. She interfered with his life just by her existence.

When the mango season was almost over, the trees on their property still bore leftover ripe fruit that had not been plucked during the harvest. The Sim residence was well landscaped, including three solid mango trees that grew right next to the house. It had just the right combination of sunlight and shade to grow giant, plump, juicy mangos.

One day, Phary was looking after her baby sister in the backyard. Phary grabbed a long bamboo stick to pick a mango in front of the house. Five-year-old Rachana stood on the deck, watching her. Phary loved to tease Rachana, which sometimes made her laugh, but often backfired and made her cry. Or even worse, it sometimes made her mad. Rachana's temper was a force to be reckoned with.

Phary pointed the bamboo stick to one of the mangos and asked Rachana, "Honey, which one do you want? This one?"

"NO!" screamed Rachana.

"Is it this one?" she asked, pointing at another ripe mango.

"Yes! That one!" yelled Rachana, pointing at the same one.

"Okay, then I want this one too," teased the big sister.

"Then, that one!" yelled Rachana, pointing to another fruit.

"Nope, this one is for me!" she kidded.

Instead of pointing to the mango that her baby sister wanted, Phary had fun avoiding the fruits and playing a game with her. This outraged Rachana. Her hot temper got the better of her. On the deck, Rachana spotted a pair of sharp scissors that her other sister had been using to prune some shrubs. She picked them up and threw them at her sister, lancing her right shoulder. The scissors stuck straight out of Phary's shoulder blade within inches of her neck. Both sisters screamed.

A man walking by the scene ran to help, as blood streamed down Phary's back and shoulder blades. He helped her take the scissors out with an emergency kit that the Sims kept in their cabinet.

The man shouted at Rachana, "Go to your room! You could have killed her, you little monster!" Even if he was out of place saying it, the neighbor felt that Rachana deserved to be reprimanded for her actions.

Rachana started bawling and ran to her bedroom.

After she was cleaned up and cared for by the Good Samaritan, Phary went to talk to her little sister. She picked up the young child's hand lovingly and said, "Honey, I am doing fine. Stop crying. Everything will be alright." Just like Thida, Phary was kind beyond belief.

Miraculously, the scissors missed killing Phary. They could have punctured her neck, brain, head, or even an internal organ. This was the second incident of fury-induced attacks that Rachana had targeted towards her family. She lashed out whenever she was provoked.

When Lee came home and found out what had happened, he was infuriated. What angered him the most was that no one blamed Rachana. He knew she had done it and wanted to punish her. That little kid needed a good whooping! If it were up to her father, Lee would have already cracked that spoiled brat over his knee and showed her what pain really felt like. That would "learn" her.

Instead, Lee took his anger out on the trees. Even though the mango trees earned their family a lot of money and were already producing fruit, Lee chopped them all down. Those mango trees had some of the juiciest fruit in town. He did it to spite Rachana. By his account, she was the least favorite child.

Because she was never punished, Rachana's anger issues continued. When she was six or seven years old, one day she got into an argument with the neighbor's kids. The two sisters were both a lot older than Rachana. The fight started over something trivial and escalated when the two sisters—who were thirteen and fifteen-years-old—came over to the Sim's house to find Rachana. They wanted to have words with the girl and were brazen enough to appear in the Sim's front yard.

When she saw them walking up, Rachana went into warrior mode. As she came out onto the porch to greet them, she stood between her father's big machete and an axe that was leaning against the wall. Even though her skinny little body could never have lifted either of these weapons, they looked scary to the predators. Rachana's older sisters were already sitting on the deck, keeping an eye on everything.

Feeling protected, Rachana hollered, "Come, you cowards! Come to me so I can cut you up into pieces!"

Although the neighbor girls were five times bigger than Rachana—in both height and build—they were smart enough to stay their distance.

Finally, Rachana's father had a chance to witness her maliciousness with his own eyes and hear it with his own ears. Phary's husband, Pitch, was in the dining room one night, when Lee came home unexpectedly. Just then, Rachana had been cursing at her brother-in-law something fierce, with crazy words coming out of her mouth. Again, he had been teasing her, like the rest. He liked to make her mad just to get a reaction. However, it was no excuse for Rachana's foul words. They were words that nobody ever deserved to hear.

Lee had enough. He yanked the child off the floor and said, "Your time has come!"

Frightened by the anger of her father, Rachana started screaming and twisting. Lee reached for his horsewhip and threw her down on the couch, face-down. Her thin dress was not nearly enough padding to escape the painful lashes of his horsewhip. For what seemed like hours—but was really only a minute or two—Lee angrily lashed the little girl. It seemed like he even enjoyed it.

She cried, yelled, and screamed. Rachana would not shut up, which only made her father more angry. So, he whipped her even harder. Yet, she continued yelling and screaming. "Come on! Kill me! Just kill me so that you can have the whole world!"

The pent-up anger Lee had endured now for seven years since Rachana was born all came out through the horsewhip. He was still mad about the hunting knife and scissor incidents that Rachana had inflicted upon her other two sisters. He was mad about the mango trees too. Even though he was the one who had chopped them down, it was his youngest daughter's fault they were gone. Had she not thrown the scissors, the mango trees would still be there. This time, Lee had caught her red-handed!

As this occurred, Maum and her husband, Paul, happened to come by. Maum was Rachana's cousin and the eldest daughter of Thida's sister, Ella. They were very close to the family and only lived about a mile away, so they came to visit often. Upon entering the room, both Maum and her husband stopped in their tracks. Their warm smiles of hello quickly turned to jaws of surprise. Lee paused, still standing over his screaming daughter with the horsewhip.

"Help!" screamed Rachana. "Dad is killing me!"

With that, Lee put the whip down to his side. He hung his head and looked apologetic, although deep down he didn't regret one single lash.

Maum ran over, grabbed Rachana, and ran off. She put the child in her lap and rocked her, whispering "Shhh . . . it's going to be okay."

Then Maum took her to a store nearby and showered Rachana with gifts. The little girl's whole body was covered with welts, worse than a hive of bees that had been stinging for hours. Indeed, it had stung Rachana badly. Not just her tiny body, but her big ego too. The girl's eyes were swollen and red from crying. But Lee had put a nasty little spoiled girl into her rightful place.

After that day, Rachana learned her lesson. The horsewhip performed a miracle and she never cursed nor hurt anyone else in their family, ever again. The Sim family also learned their lesson about teasing the angry child, so they ceased to provoke her in future encounters. Despite the hurt it caused, Lee had disciplined his daughter on time. He believed that "to save the rod is to spoil the child."

The bamboo that was once crooked had since straightened up. From that point on, Rachana was a more loving sister. She watched and learned from the elders as her role models.

But her father's beating didn't stop Rachana from bullying other children. She had a "my way or the highway" mentality and it wasn't about to change, except with her family. If the other kids in the neighborhood didn't do what Rachana wanted them to do, she got mad. Only when they played by her rules did they all play together.

As an example, the kids often liked to play student and teacher. Rachana wanted to be a teacher someday, so she always played the teacher role when pretending. Whatever she told the other kids to say, they repeated. They were the puppets and Rachana pulled the strings. She was the bossy and demanding puppet master.

Not many children went to school at that time. Only the lucky ones did. It was the fifties in Cambodia, so times were different. Besides, Rachana's father was against her going to school. Lee believed that women shouldn't go to school because they would come home pregnant. Plus, school cost money in books, clothes, etc. He had the money to pay for these things, but he was very stingy and just wouldn't. Some parents sold off their land just to put their children through school. Many times, those kids made nothing of themselves.

However, Rachana really wanted to go to school. She knew she had a better shot at convincing her mother. Thida kept her daughter back until she was bigger and stronger. With a thin frame and sickly disposition, Rachana was not yet ready to tackle the challenges of school. At least, that was what Thida thought.

Against her father's wishes, eventually Rachana did start school at the age of nine. She never heard her parents argue about it, but she knew they had. Thida approached her husband with kid gloves one day and told him, "I'm going to enroll Rachana with the new school season."

"That's preposterous!" Lee exclaimed. "I will not have it. Nor will I pay for it or condone it."

"Why are you so against it, if that is Rachana's wish?" asked Thida.

"When women have an education, they will not respect or be submissive to their husband. They will control the husband and become arrogant and they will try to be the one who wear the pants in the family," he yelled, angrily.

Quietly, Thida said, "Is that how you see our marriage? That you wear the pants and I must be submissive to you?"

Lee retorted, "I'm not talking about us. I don't approve of Rachana going to school at all."

His wife replied, "Well, I disagree. Very rarely do I ask anything of you. But I am asking you now to let her go."

Begrudgingly, he turned his back and didn't speak of it again. He did grind his teeth in his sleep for many weeks thereafter. Rachana enrolled in school and got good grades. Not for her father's approval, but because she enjoyed school and learning.

Thida was a very clever woman and knew how to get results from her husband. He thought he wore the pants, but he never truly did. Even though Thida said very little, she was constantly thinking. She was clever. More importantly, she always stood up for her daughters in doing what she felt was right.

School suited Rachana well as a learning outlet, but the conditions in Cambodian schools during the 1950s were miserable. Because her immune system was so weak and sickly, Rachana struggled to stay alive in a miserable academic environment. The teachers were unbelievably cruel. They beat up students with no mercy. They were crazy. Teachers were allowed to whip and punish students harshly if they felt they deserved it. Just a simple childhood gesture–such as note passing or talking in class– could lead to a brash whooping.

Nevertheless, Rachana was resilient and continued going to school. She became tough and confident. Despite her skinny frame, she was still intimidating. Rachana was spoiled and angry, so even boys at school never dared to say anything to her.

As a child, there had been only one special friend whom Rachana was fond of. His name was Chip. Chip was her neighbor, classmate, and older cousin of two years. They were friends since elementary school. Because she was somewhat of a tomboy, Rachana liked to do "boy stuff." Chip and Rachana went fishing, played games, and walked to school together every day. They were like two misfits put together as friends. None of the other kids ever asked Chip to hang out, except Rachana. When they did spend time together, most of it was used by trying to earn money. His mother was happy about this, because she felt that Chip would have been lazy otherwise.

Some of the ways they earned money were by selling wild herbs they gathered from the fields; Chip and Rachana handpicked them when they were in season and then took them to the market for some of the local vendors to buy. The two also went fishing, fruit picking, or found other ways to drum up money. The only difference between Rachana's money and Chip's was that she kept hers to herself, whereas he was required to give his money to his mother to help their family. Rachana made him carry everything and do most of the harder tasks that she did not want to do herself. Chip was her bodyguard too. He seemed to enjoy the role and didn't mind letting a skinny little girl boss him around. In some ways, he needed it.

Rachana was excited when she finished the sixth grade. Very few students would be able to continue their education into high school. Education was a luxury reserved for the affluent kids. Those who went to school were the first class citizens of Cambodian society.

For those children who were unable to go beyond the sixth grade, they often went on to become the workers of the culture. They were the blue-collar folks who had manual labor jobs or who stayed home with the kids to raise them, while their husbands worked long hours in the rice fields or in the woods. Some parents didn't believe in the need for an education, whereas others simply couldn't afford it even if they wanted their children to go.

Still others didn't go because of the way school systems treated the kids. And some just didn't like school, period. Having an education was not important for them to live the kind of primitive lives that they were used to on the farms. At that time, most of the communities had a system of helping each other. Most were satisfied with that and wanted nothing more out of life. Learning was difficult for those who didn't have the desire to learn.

In contrast, Thida wanted more for her daughter. She had a burning urge in her heart and mind that she had never experienced before. Thida felt that her daughter must go to school and would do anything in her power to make it happen; especially knowing that Rachana wanted the same.

At the end of sixth grade, all of the students who had gone beyond the required grade point average got to apply for a three-day exam. Those who passed the test were allowed to move on and attend high school. That test was the end of the road for some students, because the application itself cost money.

Thankfully, Rachana passed the test. However, she was still not sure if she would be able to go to high school or not. In order to attend high school, Rachana would need a place to live, because the high school was far from home. She certainly didn't dare to ask her parents, because she knew the answer would most likely be no, especially if it were up to her father.

Lee would recite all of the typical excuses: "A woman should not learn how to read or write," he'd say. Or, "Women should not have an education." And the biggest excuse of all, "It costs too much." Rachana knew these excuses well, after overhearing her father talk to her brother-in-law, Pitch.

But Thida had an independent streak of her own. After learning that her daughter earned the award of third place overall in the test grades out of the entire school, she couldn't wipe the smile off her face. Even though she didn't speak much sometimes, Thida was always thinking.

After the school year was finished, Thida began taking mini-excursions out of town more often. She said she was going to visit friends, her sister, her niece, or whomever she pleased. It just so happened that these frequent visits were in the same city as the high school.

When Rachana figured out what her mother was doing, she was quietly excited. She hoped her mother could make it happen, but it was too soon to get keyed up just yet. By now, Rachana was smart enough to keep her mouth shut.

Then, just three weeks before school was to commence, Thida told her husband, "Next week, I need your help. Get a few of your people to help us build a little place for me and our baby to live in. I am going to stay with her for a while to help her until she is comfortable enough on her own."

Lee was quite surprised, for he had not known what she was up to. And Thida was smart for not asking him for permission. Instead, she told him only what he needed to hear. For a wonderful wife who never asked him for anything and who constantly gave, gave, gave and supported every decision that Lee had made, Thida was now full of her own surprises.

Taken aback, Lee replied, "Where is the place at?"

Thida answered, "Next door to the high school." She said it so matter-of-factly and without confrontation.

Lee took a deep breath and looked at his wife with a straight face. He thought for a moment and almost uttered a protest, but then thought better of it. Come to think of it, why bother? Protesting would only get him into trouble and then she might have asked him to help pay for the expenses if he talked too much.

So, Lee nodded to acknowledge that he would ask for a few favors. He knew it would be easy to recruit help, as he had helped so many people financially and with favors or loans. Lee could literally snap his fingers and have a handful of people ready to lend a hand. However, most of the time he kept that power to himself and didn't want to use his connections or influence to help his family. Instead, he often helped strangers.

Thida was glad that her plan worked. She felt that it was meant to be and was happy about a change of scenery in the city. Her plan was to live with Rachana for a while, while her daughter was going to high school until she got settled and accustomed to living independently.

When Rachana found out that she would be able to go—and that her mom was going with her—she was overjoyed! The devoted mother came through and took a stand against her husband's erroneous beliefs.

The next week, help arrived as promised. Thida had gone to get a wagonload of lumber to build the small house that she would live in with her daughter while Rachana attended high school. Help often came from the most unlikely places, and in this case it brought back memories of her darling son, right before he passed away. The people whom Lee had recruited were from the mountains. They were Ponleau's friends.

Chapter Six

"Beloved Brother"

Even before the four girls were born, Thida and Lee had one son. Ponleau was the first child and for a long while, he was the pride and joy of his family, especially to his father. However, Ponleau was severely crippled from having polio at the age of thirteen. Up until that point, Ponleau had been just as normal as any kid, but unfortunately the polio left him unable to walk. However, instead of using a wheelchair to move, Ponleau walked on his hands. During that era, wheelchairs in Cambodia were somewhat scarce.

Undeterred, Ponleau dragged his body and placed all of his weight on his hands to slide around, which he did very well. What people admired most about him was that instead of becoming helpless and vulnerable, he chose to continue living life in a manner as if he could still walk. He did not see himself as being crippled. Ponleau had a tenacious attitude that was contagious.

In fact, Ponleau could gracefully maneuver his body so well that he could even mount his horse. As youngsters, Rachana and Kalianne would fetch and saddle the horse and then lead it to the stairs for Ponleau, making it easier for him to get on the horse's back. Ponleau shared a special relationship with his horse. It was a magnificent white horse with a great disposition and friendly to all children. The horse's name was Hibiscus and the only thing the horse couldn't do was talk. It was unbelievably smart and always looked after Ponleau. If he fell off his horse, Hibiscus waited in that spot until Ponleau found a way to remount. The horse was Ponleau's guardian angel. They went on many journeys together, as Ponleau traveled through the mountains for work. Hibiscus saved his life on more than one occasion.

One night, as Ponleau was returning from a trip, he fell asleep and slid off the horse accidentally, smack dab in the middle of a cemetery. Hibiscus just stood there next to his friend and master. The horse wouldn't leave his side.

Ponleau told Hibiscus, "Go get my family!" and Hibiscus did just that. The horse galloped back to the Sim's house, whinnying as loud as possible to wake everyone up. Of course at first, everyone was excited to see the horse. However, when his family discovered that Ponleau was not riding on the horse's back, they became alarmed. Everyone screamed to wake up Lee and tell him to go find Ponleau. The whole family followed Hibiscus to the middle of the cemetery, where Ponleau laid waiting in the same spot the horse had left him. They all helped Ponleau get back on top of his horse and then walked home, relieved that it was nothing more serious. Hibiscus was rewarded with an extra bucket of grain and a box of corn.

There was also a pet seal that followed Ponleau and Hibiscus everywhere they went. Ponleau trained the seal himself. The three of them–the handicap man, his white horse, and pet seal–were all quite a spectacle, traveling through town. Everyone knew Ponleau and knew that he was Lee Sim's son. They respected and admired the kid for all that he had accomplished, despite being crippled.

Ponleau's family adored him too, especially Rachana. She looked up to him. He was the big brother of the family, but he was twenty-six years old when she was born. Ponleau was old enough to be her uncle or father. He was often a chaperone and babysitter too. Hence, Ponleau was like a father figure to his youngest sister, except she thought him to be much nicer than her own dad.

All through the mountain regions, people knew Ponleau as a modern day trader. Riding Hibiscus high up into the hills of the most rural corners of Southeast Asia, Ponleau was well-traveled and very in-tune with nature. He talked of the great beauty he had seen. The ocean, rivers, lakes, rainforest, lush countryside, rice fields, mountains, and dramatic landscaping were also very rich in fish and wildlife. Before the war, the landscape was unspoiled in its picture-perfect splendor.

Nevertheless, Ponleau made good money by selling the resources that nature bestowed. He brought supplies to the mountains from town for the rural tribes to buy, as well as trading things with them that could be used within his own community. They both had things each other needed or wanted. Hence, Ponleau's cart was full on both his trip there and upon his return.

Instead of his horse and seal, sometimes Ponleau drove an ox and cart to his destination. It depended on his load. He returned to certain places at specific times of the year, so that the mountain people knew when to expect him. And they were always happy to see Ponleau, with his cart full of goods that they would not have had access to otherwise, if it had not been for this service he provided.

One of his specialties was bamboo sticks. The mountain people used them to catch fish in the lake and to make houseboats and floating homes. There was a huge lake with many fish. The people who lived on the houseboats liked to catch and sell them. The Tonle Sap—which translated to "Great Lake"—was also the largest lake in Southeastern Asia, and it was not terribly far from where the Sims lived in Siem Reap. During the monsoon season of June through October, the lake grew to six times its normal size during the dry season. The flow of the water also changed direction, which Ponleau knew and had timed perfectly. The monsoon seasons were difficult to travel in, however many of the mountain people needed supplies, especially for fishing in the floodplain regions of the Tonle Sap. The whole lake was sprinkled with houseboats during these abundant fishing seasons.

Ponleau was a smart businessman, just like his father, Lee. He bought things cheap and sold them expensively. He earned very good money. Had it not been for his handicap, Ponleau would have made a great husband.

Ponleau forged great friendships with the mountain people, which came into play even after his death. The village people remembered Ponleau and helped his family during the reign of terror that was to be inflicted by the Khmer Rouge.

Actually, Ponleau learned the idea of selling bamboo from his father. Lee was also very good at sales. While Ponleau sold bamboo mostly for houseboats and building, Lee sold much of his bamboo to the craftsmen. These artisans made everything imaginable. Expensive furniture, baskets, flooring, trivets, and more were crafted from Lee's great bamboo. The Sim's bamboo stock was just about as sturdy as anyone could find. A lot of times Lee handmade his own baskets to sell. They were durable enough to last for at least twenty years, or more.

However, Lee's main source of income didn't come from bamboo. Most of his wealth was earned from the rice fields in share cropping ownership. All of the rice that the Sims didn't eat or need, he sold. Lee had sharecroppers who took care of his fields, so he never actually had to do the physical labor part of it, except in very rare circumstances when an extra hand was essential. He was the "boss man" and highly reputed in the area to be the guy that people went to for advice on any topic.

Since there were no hospitals nearby, Lee also served as a medicine man for the community. Out in the rural areas, there were no equivalents to prescription medicines or professionally trained health care people to help when someone became ill or injured. Therefore, Lee sold healing elements to people who came to him for help. These natural-based ingredients were gathered by hand from the forest to make medicine. Lee knew which ingredients to mix together to create healing products. It was a talent he was born with. He was skilled in herbal remedies since he was a young man.

Because of his unique ability to heal the people that lived within a ten-mile radius—or sometimes further—Lee was respected by the whole community and even known throughout the city. Aside from the mountain inhabitants, many hunters came to see Lee. They sold him birds for the feathers, which he then used to make fancy capes and costumes for kings and the royalty of Cambodia.

In fact, Lee had more money than he knew what to do with. By Cambodian standards, the Sim family was rich. With as much money as he had, Lee could have opened a business for each of his daughters and still had money to spare. He had hundreds of thousands of riels. From all of his enterprises and connections, Lee Sim was one of the most affluent residents of Siem Reap.

It seemed that all he had to do was speak or open his mouth and everything went his way. Lee was tall, charming, and successful. He was poised and confident. As a businessman, Lee gave great advice and money to his fellow friends and neighbors. Quite oppositely, he was really tight with money whenever his kids asked for something. He did not share it with Thida either. Instead, he hid his wealth from them. Only Lee knew exactly how much money he had stashed throughout the house. He even kept a journal hidden away that offered a daily tally of his riches.

He was generous when it came to others and had been known to loan out as much as 8000-10,000 riels to people who never paid him back. Yet he never gave money to his own children or wife. Thida earned her own money and bought most of the necessities for the kids. It was peculiar considering his wealth and expectations of a man to be the head of household; under most circumstances, a man's family benefitted greatly in his ability as a provider.

Thankfully, Thida was very resourceful and entrepreneurial in spirit. She was able to do what she needed and to make enough money on her own, even without his help. Like her husband, she used many of the assets on the family farm to make money. Exotic fruits were her niche. The Sims had many fruit trees, and Thida picked the fruit to sell. She filled up several baskets a few times a week and took them into the marketplace. There were mango trees, Asian plum, jackfruit, papayas, and pomelo. During the hottest days of summer, all of the neighbors would gather with the Sims under their trees. Their home was a social hub of the community.

Their village was a subdivision of the province of Siem Reap. Everyone knew where the Sims lived and who they were. The Sim's old-fashioned farmhouse had a lot of character. The giant structure was made of old wood, with a gently worn patina finish from years of duress under the harsh monsoon rains. There was a river nearby with many great trees that were over a century old. And they were quite wise looking with their tall posture and whispering leaves. The river offered good circulation to moisten the vegetation and garden, where the Sims grew much of their food. But because of the rising waters during the wet season, the one-story home had been built on stilts.

The front of their house was charming and homey. There were hammocks tied between the sugar palms in the front yard. At one time, the hammocks had stripes, but even those had faded into one color from the sun bearing down on them. Lee tied the swings and hammocks to the trees with big, heavy strings that were strong enough to hold even a grown man. The children ran around, playing tag and other games. There were always crowds of people who came to visit the Sim family for social time. Whenever people sought his advice, Lee gave them answers. He was knowledgeable about everything from spouses arguing to financial matters, self-help topics, or health issues. People enjoyed Lee's advice, because he was well versed in a wide range of topics.

Whenever the mountain people needed to come to town for supplies that Ponleau could not bring, they stayed at the Sim family farmhouse as guests. The Sims were very hospitable and enjoyed their visits. They were not just business relationships at that point, although they all benefitted greatly by helping each other. Over the years, they also became good friends.

So, when the mountain people were asked by Lee to help build a house for Rachana and Thida to live in next to the high school, they jumped at the chance. Doing so put them in Lee's good favor. Ponleau would have appreciated it too, had he still been alive.

Five people came with five wagons of lumber to build the house next to the high school. Lee obliged only because his wife had asked him as a favor, rather than out of any obligation to provide for his daughter. Since Pitch paid for the lumber, Lee did not have to worry about the costs. Nevertheless, with five people and five wagonloads of wood at their site, this was enough to erect the small abode that Rachana would share with her mother for two years. It only took a few days to build. The helpers stayed two or three nights and didn't charge Thida and Rachana one single riel. Of course, Thida fed them and provided shelter for them while they were there.

Besides, spending time with Ponleau's old friends was enjoyable for Thida. It brought back memories of the son who she had lost, the son who she had loved. They all recalled stories of Ponleau while they were there. The mountain people missed him too.

It was a tragic loss when the world took Ponleau away from his family at the young age of thirty-five. While in the mountains, he got bit by a mosquito and came down with malaria. The disease spread quickly. Ponleau suffered for a few weeks before finally dying just before his next birthday. The whole family mourned Ponleau for a great many years thereafter. Everyone loved him so much.

Rachana took it the worst of all the kids, since she looked up to Ponleau as a father figure, one whom she respected much more than her own father. She was only in first grade when he passed away. As the baby of the family, all of Rachana's sisters and brother were nearly grown up just as she was given life.

Ponleau adored his baby sister and treated Rachana like a princess. The rest of the family did too, except for Lee. In her family's mind, little Rachana could do no wrong. The little girl knew it and played them all, often turning against them and being a whiney little brat. If Rachana did not get her way, it was dangerous for everyone.

Although she did settle down more as a teenager, Rachana was still very difficult. If it weren't for Thida, she would never have been able to go to school and experience the blessing of an education. Deep down, Thida wanted an education for her daughter. It was a calling she felt compelled to achieve. Lee had made sure that none of the other daughters went to school. So Thida had to make sure that Rachana had a different future.

However, Thida also supposed the time away from Lee might do their marriage some good. It wasn't that he was a bad husband or that he stepped out on her, gambled, or abused her. What hurt Thida was the fact that Lee liked to make her suffer a little bit with his lack of generosity. She would never have told him how she felt, but deep down she thought it would be nice if he treated her to a few surprises or shared his wealth with his wife and children. Thida was strong and knew she could provide for their kids–and would do so no matter what it took–but she couldn't understand why he gave perfect strangers much of his money instead of supporting their family. Maybe . . . just maybe . . . he would miss her.

After the mountain people bid goodbye, Thida told them to keep in touch. She knew they could mutually benefit by helping each other. She told them they were always welcome to stay there. Whenever they had visited in the past, they always brought gifts to the Sims. Not just for her, but for all of their daughters, too. They were kind people whom Thida was quite fond of.

School commenced within only a few days. Thida found it to be relaxing and quiet at their new house, especially while Rachana was in high school. She never had so much time to herself. So, Thida kept busy by finding ways to make money. Because she no longer had the fruit trees in their backyard to rely on for income, Thida earned riels by cutting wood and selling it in the market. She also made incense by searching deep in the woods for a special tree. She then shaved off the bark to bring home and prep by drying, grounding, and pounding it to make incense. It was a lot of tedious work for just a little bit of money. Yet, she never complained, nor asked for help.

After a year of earning a living this way, Pitch stepped in and paid for everything for the duration of Rachana's high school years. Even though Thida never asked for help, Pitch could see his mother-in-law struggling to make ends meet. He was a noble man and loved Thida very much. She was truly like a mother figure to him.

In fact, Pitch detested the shack that Rachana and Thida lived in and insisted on building a better house before Rachana went into the ninth grade. Her second year of high school was more comfortable as the girl settled into a new routine in a better living environment. Thida went back home to her husband on the family farm, leaving Pitch and Phary to look after the youngest sibling as she finished high school. Thida had high hopes for her daughter to graduate and become a teacher one day, which was what Rachana longed to be.

The second house, although nicer, was further away from the high school. Pitch and Phary had received permission from Rachel and her husband, Len, to build the small place right on their property, since they had more land. So, Rachana lived on the land of her third sister, but the home was provided for by her first sister's husband.

Being a little farther away from school, Rachana pedaled a rusty old bicycle that her father had given her—at least ten years back—as her means of transportation. She didn't mind because she was just happy to have the chance to go to school. Plus, Rachana loved her little house and living so close to her two sisters and brother-in-laws, whom she also adored. Staying in the house by herself gave Rachana a taste of independence. It made her more mature and forced her into being more responsible, since Rachana had to get herself to school on time and fix her own breakfasts and meals.

For the first time in many years, Rachana was very happy. She was coming into her own person, while learning more about whom she was, and what she was meant to be. Pitch especially developed a fondness for Rachana and took over the role of father figure, which Rachana hadn't felt in many years since Ponleau's passing. As a brother-in-law, he was extremely generous and often spoiled the girl.

Rachana couldn't help but to think how kind he was, considering at one time she had nearly butchered his wife with a pair of scissors and then cursed her brother-in-law relentlessly until she had been caught and whipped by her father. Yet to Pitch, all of those past hurts had been forgotten. In fact, he blamed himself for instigating her. At the time he had enjoyed provoking Rachana but with no inclination of the outcome.

Nevertheless, upon seeing his "little sis" ride home one day on her rusty old bike, Pitch felt compelled to help. One pedal was barely turning as Rachana struggled to keep the warped tires on the road. It was transportation, at any rate. But Pitch knew it would be easier for Rachana to go back and forth to school with adequate wheels.

As she arduously pedaled home from school one afternoon, Rachana looked forward to the weekend. Phary and Rachel had told her the night before that their mother and fourth sister, Kalianne, would be coming to visit for a few days. She thought it was going to be a fun weekend for the girls, since she had not seen them in a couple of months. Besides, Pitch had gone to Phnom Penh for a business trip, leaving Phary wide open to spend time with them, "husband-free."

But as she got closer, she saw Phary and Pitch standing together in front of Rachel's house, which was just in front of Rachana's. Her mother was there too, and Kalianne. They were all crowded around something, as if trying to hide it. They smiled too. As they saw Rachana approach, they all spread out to reveal a brand new, shiny bicycle. Pitch had just picked it up in the capital while on his "business trip." This excuse was a decoy story to throw Rachana off.

The bicycle was truly stunning, with a bright red frame and silver handles. Pitch had spent a whopping 4000 riels on the bicycle, which was the equivalent of buying or building a very nice house. It was a Peugeot bike that was only available for sale in the capital of Phnom Penh. Very rare, very expensive, and very smooth riding was this elegant new bicycle for Rachana. Only rich kids owned such a bike.

Rachana accepted it with glee, even though she did not feel as though she deserved the bike. She still felt rather bad about what she had done to her sister years prior, but she was so thrilled that she carried that kindness with her in thought for a lifetime. It was the greatest gift anyone had ever given her.

They all happily embraced and shared in Rachana's enthusiasm. Thida couldn't help but to think of her husband, Lee, who should have been the one buying his daughter a bicycle for school. Instead, he had helped another girl the week prior by buying her a motorcycle, just because he knew the girl's dad. Thida wished her husband would extend the same help to his own family, yet she knew Lee well and that he would not. He was a lost cause that way.

Nevertheless, he was her husband and she accepted him as that. It was only Rachana who did not. Perhaps it was for these reasons that Lee and his youngest daughter never saw eye to eye.

Thankfully, Pitch's business was doing great. He took Rachana under his wing and cared for her just as much as his own family. When he was blessed with extra cash flow, he spoiled them sufficiently. Pitch told his mother-in-law not to worry about Rachana anymore. He would supply her needs. After seeing her report card from the past two school years, it reassured him that Rachana would be able to accomplish something that no one else in the family had done when she received her diploma. In fact, Pitch made sure of it by using his own address for the school to send her grades. He became her appointed guardian, by choice.

Aside from the nice house and an expensive bike, Pitch gave Rachana a weekly allowance. He wanted her to focus on her schoolwork and not on having to struggle to buy food or necessities. There were not many parents in Cambodia who went out of their way to build a nice little house and spend their fortune on an expensive bike and living expenses only for the reward of making good grades. But Pitch and Phary did. Everything was going great for all of them, which only spurred Rachana's desire to study harder. In her mind, it was the only way she could pay them back and say thank you for all they had done.

The school year passed quickly. Before she knew it, summer vacation arrived. Rachana decided to go home and spend time with her parents for those two months off from school.

By then, both Lee and Thida were growing older. Thida was in her early sixties, while Lee was turning seventy. All of their children were married and had their own homes, except Rachana. It was a version of empty nest syndrome they had never before experienced as a couple. They had started their family forty years prior, when Ponleau was born. They loved each other in their own ways. They never argued, even when the kids were little. In fact, they never so much as raised their voices at each other. By anyone's standards, the elderly Sim couple lived in harmony and peace. Lee still earned a good income, but Thida's income was based solely on the fruit trees. It brought just enough for her spending, with no help from Lee at all.

By the time she was a teenager, Rachana saw her mother's struggles from a new vantage point. One day, while her father had gone visiting friends in the village nearby and her mother was at the marketplace, Rachana's curiosity got the better of her. She decided to snoop. She spotted the row of keys that her dad had hanging on the antlers. Even though she thought better of it, Rachana couldn't resist the urge to take the keys and find the one that fit into the china hutch, which was where he harbored most of his secrets. As a child, she had seen her father hide his money there before. Rachana knew it was there, she just didn't know how much.

First, she found her dad's notebook with a log he kept to track his wealth. In it, Lee had handwritten daily and weekly numbers, including a list of people who owed him money and how much they owed. Rachana's eyes grew big and her heart skipped a beat. Her eyebrows stiffened with miffed contemplation. The figure was at least 100,000 riels. That was a lot of money, especially for that era. What made Rachana the angriest about her discovery was the fact that her father had been saving his stash for more than thirty years, keeping it all for himself. He had not spent so much as one riel on himself, not even for food. Thida took care of that.

As she dug deeper, Rachana found the cash box. It was a steel box that locked. Lee was so organized that he kept all of the money separated and perfectly aligned. She barely dared touch it, for fear he would have noticed if one riel was out of place. The five hundred bills were on the left, moving to the hundreds, fifties, and twenties. The one-riel bills were kept in a separate box, of which there were hundreds. She knew he had a lot, but never thought it was this much. Rachana was staggered. Shock and disappointment washed over her in a wave of envy. Not envy for herself, but for her mother who had always worked her tail off to support the whole family.

How could he? she wondered. Secretly, Rachana had a plan for her mother. It became one of the fundamental reasons that Rachana wanted to become successful. She wanted to get her mother out of there and away from having to provide for a man who had been fully capable to provide for his family all along, yet who chose not to.

What Rachana did not realize was that the family did not care about Lee's money. They had already learned their lesson of the whip and had never dared to defy their father. They all just accepted his ways. Everyone kind of knew he had cash on hand, but nobody knew just how much. They were less rebellious than the youngest.

From that day on, Rachana's heart filled with grave disappointment. On one hand, she loved her father dearly. She wanted so much to be loved by him. It was difficult to feel anger toward him, knowing that she had been wrong in prying on his private belongings. So, Rachana felt torn about it.

For many days, Rachana grappled with herself about what she had done. She swayed between feeling ashamed of being nosy and disappointment in her father. Was she glad to know about how much money her father had? No, she was not. She wished she didn't know. It was better that way. The discovery had spurned even more resentment.

She wanted to tell someone. Rachana could no longer stand to withhold the secret of their father. And who better to share his secret with than their eldest sister, Phary? One day, Rachana cornered her sister and spilled her guts about what she had done. She told Phary the truth that she had stolen one of the keys and unlocked the secrets of their father's china cabinet.

Phary turned ghostly pale. She gasped, "Oh, honey! Don't you dare touch that again! If you ever need money more than what we give you, just tell us how much. Okay? If we do not have enough, we can sell the cattle at any time. Don't you worry."

Although she disagreed, Rachana did not protest Phary's request. She zipped her big mouth and tried to forget about what she had seen. But in her head, she didn't have a switch to turn it off. Her whole world came crashing down on her as she mourned the loss of her father's love. Instead, there had been Ponleau and Pitch to teach her the real love of a father, one by blood, and one by marriage.

Suddenly, Rachana questioned her whole existence and why she was put on this earth, if not with her own father's approval. Now she knew of his deepest secrets.

Chapter Seven

"The Secret"

As she commenced the next school year, Rachana began with a troubled heart. She kept wondering how her mother could live as peacefully as she did, when her father kept all his money to himself. Not just kept it, but spent it on so many other people besides his family. Lee handed out loans of ten thousand or twenty thousand riels as insignificantly as a bowl of rice, while Thida continued working, trying to make ends meet to support them. Perhaps she did not realize his wealth? Surely she could not be that gullible.

Rachana surmised that her mother must not know, because if she did, Rachana knew that her feelings would be hurt. Then again, maybe Thida was content living in oblivion and not discussing the Sim's financial matters. She was a traditional Cambodian wife who never pried into the affairs of her husband.

At that time, Cambodian women were the rulers of the household. The men's role was to be providers. As normal households functioned, the husband was the primary worker and brought the money home to his wife, who took care of the family. The wife raised the kids, did the shopping, and managed the monetary matters. Men looked for a good wife who was smart, ambitious, and who could manage money well. If he was lucky, his wife made sure they all lived well and saved as much money as possible. On the flip side, a Cambodian man who married a woman that knew nothing would often become nothing. He would be unimportant and would likely struggle through life if he had a wife who misled the family, or if he did not live up to his role as the provider.

Thida did not know how to read or write. The women of her time did not have the same opportunities as the Cambodian children of Rachana's time. Although it was still difficult to achieve an education, it was at least possible for those who were smart and lucky. Not knowing how to read or write, Thida would not have been able to understand Lee's notebooks even if she had seen them with her own eyes. The numbers and notes meant nothing to her. They were nothing more than ink scratches in a book.

Considering this fact, Rachana became even more bothered. She obsessed about what she saw in the china hutch because the more she thought about it, the more unjust it seemed on her father's part. She was angry that he had been taking advantage of her mother's generosity and kindness for their entire marriage. There was nothing to indicate any unfairness on Thida's side, only goodness. She wondered, *Even if he doesn't love me, how could he have not at least provided for my mother?* Rachana simply could not grasp her father's behavior or reasoning behind it.

Her head hurt from thinking about it so much. Rachana's headaches worsened by the day. She put her own mother under the microscope to try to find any fault she could that would lead Lee to do such a thing to his own wife, yet she could find nothing. Hence, Rachana began feeling sorry for her mom. Her heart opened up more and more in love for her mother, as Rachana wracked her brain to find the answers to her father's secrecy.

By all accounts and even to others, Thida was quite angelic. She had a beautiful personality and pleasant features. Her face was lovely and nice to look at. Even more than what people saw on the surface, Thida had a heart that was pure and simple. She loved her children with all of the love she had to muster, and then some. Thida would have made any sacrifice to keep her daughters–and one son–out of harm's way. She was born with a magical touch of perfection that did not take sides, nor feel envious, mean, or even angry. Thida lived every day with a quiet smile and pensive nature that was cautiously outgoing. She let many people into her heart. But only those who were most special did Thida make an extra effort to go beyond the call of friendship, motherhood, or Good Samaritan.

Thida's radiant beauty was magnetic. This fact may have saved her during the regime. Even killers could not look into Thida's eyes with ill intent. Even tigers in the woods could not rip her to shreds. She was instantly liked by anyone who met her. It was her aura, like a bright white glow that enveloped her entire being. She never had to try hard to be good, she just was.

Quite the opposite, Rachana had always been a scrappy-looking girl. Her thin frame and sickliness was unappealing. Standing next to her mother, who was gorgeous, Rachana knew she was different. She was the ugly duckling next to a beautiful swan. Even most of her sisters had acquired their mother's natural good looks and wholesome presence.

Whenever Rachana brought some friends home from high school, they always fell in love with Thida. From an outsider's perspective, Thida was a wonderful wife, aunt, sister, mother, and daughter-in-law who took care of Lee's parents and her own father, as well as being a caretaker to her grandmother before they all had passed away. Thida was also a wonderful grandmother to all of her daughters' children too. Come to think of it, nobody on the planet had a single bad word or complaint about her. She never badmouthed anyone either. As long as she was alive, the only words ever uttered from her lips were the good qualities she found in everyone. She saw the best in people. The bad, well, she just swallowed it up into a sea of forgiveness.

There wasn't a time when Rachana could remember as a little girl that she wasn't holding on to her mother's apron. She was constantly on her mother's heels, even as Thida did the cooking, gardening, or visiting with company who stopped by. Because of the age span with her siblings, Rachana didn't have many little kids to play with. Kalianne did play with Rachana until she was six or seven, but then as she became a teenager the playing time was less and less frequent. Yes, Rachana's sisters loved her and spent time with the baby of the family. But it often meant having to participate in adult activities, if she wanted someone to hang out with.

Thida also had one younger sister who she had a strong bond with. Ella lived about ten miles away with her husband and five children. They were five years apart in age. It was a three-hour walk to Ella's house, so their visits were only occasional. All of the cousins–both Thida and Ella's children–were very close and loved playing together. Rachana truly looked up to her aunt, as did everyone. Even Lee had a soft spot for Ella. She knew how to butter him up and often teased him with her jovial sense of humor. Lee was always very friendly to her, even though Thida usually kicked him out of bed whenever Ella came to visit for an entire week. The sisters were so close that they enjoyed sleeping together and whispering into the wee hours of the morning. From dusk until dawn, they acted like two little kids telling secrets under the blankets.

Because modern transportation was expensive and more often used in the big cities, the rural people of Cambodia used small scooters and motorcycles, wagons pulled by bulls, or they simply walked. Since the Sims lived on the farm, it was more common for Ella and her kids to come visit them in Siem Reap, rather than asking Thida and her clan to come to her. If Ella had not come for a long time, Thida sent Rachana to get her.

All of Thida's girls loved Ella very much. Appearance-wise, Ella was quite the opposite of her lean big sister. She was actually pretty fat; however, unlike some customs that scorn obesity, the people of Cambodia considered being overweight as a sign of health and wealth. Their simple philosophy was that if someone was fat, then they must be rich enough to have plenty of food. Working hard in the fields or elsewhere kept most people trim enough. Those who could afford not to work hard must be wealthy and able to eat well.

Although she was never officially diagnosed with any health problems, it may have been Ella's thyroid that caused her to be fat. This was a theory, of course. Her family lived well enough financially, but they were not rich.

Instead of being teased about being chubby, strangers exclaimed, "Applaud her! Her husband is a good man. He must bring money to her so she can eat well!" In a country where people were skinny, Ella stood out as different.

One of the best benefits of Ella's visits was the fun she brought with her and the spontaneous generosity of Lee. It was during Ella's visits only that Lee gave his wife an allowance to "just have fun with." Although not in his character to do so, it was a gesture that was warmly appreciated by Thida. With her allowance in hand, Thida and Ella set out for the marketplace every day of her visit. They splurged on a great breakfast, and then spent the morning shopping. They came home with groceries, supplies, and special things. Then they cooked a delicious meal in the afternoon and frolicked in the kitchen, reminiscing about old times. Thida and Ella never tired of each other and spent every second together laughing, tickling, hugging, and talking. For the duration of her visits to the Sim home, the two were inseparable.

On one of Ella's visits, Thida splurged on a new sarong for Rachana. She had found it in the marketplace and both she and Ella had agreed that the color and style suited Rachana perfectly. It was fashionable too.

As Thida handed her daughter the sarong, Rachana's eyes lit up like stars sparkling in the sky. Rachana was thrilled and immediately wanted to try it on. When she did, she felt like the skirt needed an extra touch. So Rachana found the old sewing machine that had been sitting in the pantry, collecting dust. She went to work modifying her new sarong, like a frantic seamstress.

After putting on the finishing touches, Rachana tried on her new sarong. The skirt looked beautiful as she stared at her reflection in the full-length mirror. It was something she had wanted for a long time, yet never dared to ask for. She never bothered her mother for such things, knowing that Thida already had enough on her plate to account for. What's more, Rachana loved the way she had sewn it. It was the new style for young girls to wear.

She walked down to the kitchen, where Thida was busy laughing and cooking with her sister. Rachana wanted to show off her new favorite outfit. Like a proud peacock spreading its wings on stage, Rachana twirled around with her skirt flaring out behind her. She expected a big applause. However, she was disappointed by her mother's reaction.

"Oh, no honey! Why are you dressed like the maid?" asked Thida, in a hesitant tone of voice. Rachana hung her head and dropped her hands down to her side, feeling dejected.

Sensing the child's disappointment, Ella said, "I like it dear. It's very becoming."

Thida shook her head, as if in disapproval.

Ella stepped in to the girl's rescue. "A maid? What makes you say such a thing? The sarong looks good on her. Why don't you just let her wear it like that?"

Seeing the tears well up in Rachana's face, Thida lowered her voice and said, "If you really like it, you can wear it like that. But it does make you look like the maid."

With that, Rachana wheeled around and ran to her bedroom, dragging the heavy sewing machine in with her. She redid the whole sarong the way her mother had given it to her. But she cried as she let out the seams and threads she had just sewn. Yes, Rachana cried hard. She wanted to wear the modified skirt so bad, but nothing in the world—no style, no clothes, and no skirt—could turn her against her mother's wishes.

After a good hour of sobbing on her pillow, Rachana got up and wiped her tears. She had cried enough. Then she joined her mother and aunt in the kitchen, as if nothing ever happened. Rachana did not even let on that anything was bothering her. She did it out of love for her mom and not because she was afraid of her authority. If there was one person who could put Rachana in her place, it was Thida. Yet, she did it in a way that Rachana respected, without having to scold or spank her.

Her mother was one reason why Rachana was committed to work harder in her last year of high school than she ever had. The love she had for her mom gave Rachana the power and strength to focus. Thida had no idea of her daughter's plan to get her away from Lee. In fact, she seemed content enough with the situation. It was Rachana who was bothered by her father's ways. No one else seemed to mind, nor dare to question it. Lee acted like a king and expected his wife and daughters to treat him as such.

Going to classes were difficult, though. Rachana's headaches worsened. Every day by 9:00 a.m., she could barely hear or open her eyes. The migraines pounded her like a sledgehammer knocking down a wall of cement. It was difficult to listen to the teacher or to see the blackboard. Rachana sat in the front row, holding her head with both hands while she closed her eyes. Her grades plummeted.

Even Rachana's professors noticed the difference. They encouraged her to see a doctor. She didn't have money and didn't want to ask Pitch for it, so Rachana bought an over-the-counter pill that was fairly expensive. It did slow down the progression of the headaches, but only for a couple of hours at a time. Meanwhile, Rachana told no one in her family how miserable she was and how severe her headaches were.

Sadly, by the middle of the school year, Pitch's family business went sour. He had owned a fish exporting business with his two brothers. They bid on having the exclusive commercial rights to fishing in the whole lake of Tonle Sap. The lake was substantial in size and yielded abundant fishing. The only other people allowed to fish there were the people who lived on the lake, which meant they had been the only commercial fishing operation to have been granted access for the past three years, with a possibility of an extension granted. During those three years' time, the brothers made money hand over fist. Exclusivity had its perks. That's why Pitch had been able to build Rachana a small house and buy her an expensive bicycle. By society's standards, he earned very well.

However, once the three-year government contract ended, so did the flow of money. The lake may not have dried up, but for Pitch and his brothers, the cash flow did. To make matters worse, the eldest brother controlled the finances. They had made approximately one hundred million riels over the three years' time. However, the eldest brother gave only three million riels to the middle brother and one million to Pitch, who was the youngest. It was not fair, because the other two were the reason the business had flourished. They had worked the hardest, while the eldest brother handled the paperwork and financial matters. He had been very irresponsible with the money and had purchased many things. Two houses, two buses, and one brand new jeep for "the business," or so he claimed. These alone cost him nearly seven hundred thousand riels, which he lied about to the other two brothers. Unfortunately, they could not fight with him because everything was in his name. Sadly, they had to accept what was given to them as their business folded.

There were also changes in the political climate, which disrupted the economy. A war was about to transpire, but the people of Cambodia did not entirely know or understand what was happening. They just lived. They went to work and then went home to their families. Most people just lived in a cloud of oblivion.

Not long after losing his business, Pitch fell ill. Phary spent all of the family's resources on his medical care. He did recover, but by then their family was nearly broke. As a result, Rachana was displaced. At that time, she was moved from her beautiful little house that her brother-in-law had built for her. Phary and Pitch had to move in there and sell their bigger home to downsize because of the extreme deduction in their income. Subsequently, Rachana was moved into a home with strangers. Pitch had promised to take care of her, so they rented Rachana a room with some friends of theirs. But he struggled to make the rent due to a lack of work and insurmountable medical bills.

Then, the sisters received word that their father, Lee, was sick with the fever. Phary went to be there for him and to help their mother. However, Rachana could not afford to take any days off from school because it was the end of the school year and there was a big exam to take. It was the most important test of her entire high school career and the reason she had gone through so much for her diploma. That piece of paper was Rachana's whole future, so she had no way to escape. If she did, her entire years of high school education would have been in vain.

But as bad luck would have it, two months before the big exam, Rachana awoke with a sharp back pain that left her crippled in bed. The ache was so unbearable that she could only speak, but couldn't move. When it rained, it poured. All of these problems came at once. As a result, she missed an entire month of school because of the migraines and back pain. It was mysteriously stress induced. The combination of not eating well, the stress of her brother-in-law and father, the strangers she lived with, the anticipation of her final exam, and most likely needing glasses were all compounded to give Rachana some serious health problems.

To try and make up for lost time, Rachana's professors tried to help her catch up by dictating the information to her as she furiously tried to write it all down in her notebook and remember it. There were no photocopiers or books to highlight, only a pencil and notebook to acquire the knowledge. Students had to be very quick and often met during breaks to share what they had missed with one another. They all wanted to pass and to graduate.

It was difficult under the circumstances, yet Rachana was determined to do it. For her mother.

There was a lot of studying to be done. Missing one month from school represented a huge setback and ultimately put Rachana at the end of her rope. Despite the migraines, the back pain, the broken heart from a dishonorable father, and the pain of seeing her beloved brother-in-law, the one thing that saddened Rachana the most was witnessing her innocent mother endure the facts that she did not know about. It was all more than she could bear, and Rachana didn't know how to let it go. Being out of school for one month was the straw that broke the donkey's back.

Unfortunately, Rachana flunked the final exam in high school. It was the ultimate humiliation. She had been eager to prove to her father that what he believed about women was very wrong. To her, it was a tragedy and would make Lee all the more resilient in his beliefs that women should not get an education.

With so many things going on around her, Rachana had reached her most difficult days to endure. It seemed to her as though the whole world was collapsing around her with no way to make it better. And the headaches kept pounding with a painful vengeance. The pain and hurt Rachana felt over her father's unfaithfulness to their family ate her alive. She could not forget what she had seen or what she knew.

After flunking the last exam for high school, Rachana went home for three months of summer vacation. She did so with shame. She dreaded seeing everyone and what they would say or ask; or not say or not ask. Either way, it was embarrassing.

When she arrived home from school, her father was still sick. Thida took great care of him. She was a faithful, loyal, caring wife and mother. Why couldn't he see that?

Rachana was even more confused. What she saw Lee doing to her mother was wrong and unacceptable. Part of her wanted her dad to recover from his illness, but another part of her thought he deserved it. It was an internal rival between love, anger, and jealousy. She was envious of all the people who had benefitted from Lee's loans while the rest of the family struggled to get by on many occasions.

But it was not just the money or the greed that infuriated Rachana. There was something else she knew, something that she did not dare to share with anyone. It was something so terrible that she could not confide in one single person about it. She had known about it for the entire school year and had speculated that knowing this terrible secret was causing her craziness and perhaps even causing her severe headaches, back pain, and sudden bouts of illness.

Why couldn't all of these disturbances have happened later, after I got my diploma? Rachana wondered.

She had to get her mother out of there. Rachana knew that if Thida knew what she knew, she would be devastated. Not just because of all the money her dad had tightly locked away. It was because of the other things he hid from her.

Chapter Eight

"Loan Shark"

uring the summer vacation from school, Rachana locked herself away in her room or sat outside in the backyard alone. There was a curve on the riverbank that she was particularly fond of, where she liked to think and daydream. Every morning, Rachana brought a few notebooks along in her satchel and carried them with her to the river-bank, where she would study and write and think profusely.

Mostly, Rachana was upset over all of the situations that she could not control. She was an angry teenager. Yet, she was still determined to bounce back from her setback. She decided one day to pick herself up with joy and to study even more in preparation of the next school year. She knew not what it would bring.

Day by day, Rachana held on to the beauty of the nature surrounding her. The combination of the scenery and solitude helped her focus; doing it with joy and peace made her feel more at ease. Hence, the migraine began to dissipate as well. It was a miracle that nature healed Rachana's throbbing headache.

The beauty of the river, the bamboo, the palm trees and fruit trees, the green grass, the wildflowers, and the birds made Rachana's heart sing. These things restored her soul and healed her body in God's hands.

Thida gave her daughter a mat that was handmade from palm leaves, along with a towel, sack of notebooks, and writing utensils. This time, Rachana demanded of herself to stay out of trouble and remain focused on what she needed to do. Never before did she have so much joy in her heart. Nature was alive and spoke to her.

The bamboo trees attracted many different kinds of birds to make their home. They reminded Rachana of Ponleau. Some days, she swore that her beloved brother was speaking to her through them. The birds made music in a hardened heart and healed the girl's broken soul.

For those three months, Rachana took only a few days off from studying to visit her brother-in-law. He was so happy to see her. She told him all she had done to refocus and rejuvenate her energy channels positively. Pitch was pleased with her. He asked Rachana to visit more often, if not at least to visit with her nieces and nephew. She politely declined, explaining that playing with the children would interfere with her studying. Pitch understood and was proud of Rachana for her dedication.

Still, Rachana never heard any words of encouragement from Lee while she stayed with her parents for the whole summer. Sure, he was recovering from an illness. However, Lee truly did not care about his daughter's goals and didn't want to bother himself by asking about them. He had to keep his distance to keep his money safe.

Rachana's expectations of her dad could never be met. She continued holding on to the hope that he would one day become the father she had always wanted him to be. Alas, he would not.

Honestly, Lee could have put ten children through school and college easily if he had wanted to. Children were completely dependent on their parents' support academically and otherwise. That was why only rich kids with caring parents were those who had the chance to attend high schools and universities. These were the parents that understood and wanted to see their children have a good life, perhaps even a better life than they had experienced growing up.

By the time Rachana was scheduled to return to school, she had memorized everything in the notebooks. So well, in fact, that she could recite everything by heart. She felt secure in her belief that she would pass the test this next time. Rachana was now healthy, both in mind and in her soul. At least as much as she could be, if it were not for the dark thoughts she felt about her father.

This time though, Pitch no longer had a steady income because of his brother's cruelty in destroying their family business. Now, Pitch's only source of income was his herd of cattle. It wasn't worth nearly as much, but the assets from the milk and beef was enough to feed their family and pay for one employee to care for the livestock. Rachana had a fixed allowance that varied from week to week, depending on how well Pitch and Phary did in earnings with their herd of water buffaloes and cattle.

There was an instance in which Rachana's brother-in-law was unable to sell the livestock on time for their rent.

Pitch asked Rachana with much sorrow in his voice, "Honey, do you think you have the courage to ask your daddy for the rent this month? Just for this month?" As he looked at her with sadness, he continued, "I'm so sorry to put you through this, but just for this month only. I am sure a lot of people will show up at my door later next month, because the season is coming."

Secretly, Rachana was happy to go and ask her father to fulfill Pitch's request. She wondered how Lee would respond and whether he would own up to his responsibilities as a father. Rachana didn't let on any of this to Pitch. She simply replied, "Don't you worry, I'll give it a try."

The next Saturday, Rachana made the trip back to her parent's house from school. On the afternoon of her arrival, she fixed a special sugar palm ball and jasmine tea that she had brought back from the city. From the kitchen, she peeked out the window to see her father outside, sitting at the table on the deck. He was visiting with some friends. Rachana thought it was a good time to ask her dad, since surely he would not be able to deny her request in front of his friends. On one hand, she was eager to ask him, but on the other, she was very worried about his reaction.

So, Rachana brought the plate and tea outside in a pitcher and set it down in the center of their table. At first, Lee was very happy with the tea. He was proud after everyone praised him for having good children.

After she served them, she asked nervously, "Daddy, I need money for the rent this month, could you please help me out? Just for this month?"

Rachana hoped that he would not say anything harshly in front of a crowd. She was very wrong. After she said it, Lee looked immediately away from his daughter in silence. Her heart sank like a big anchor thrown deep into the sea. Rachana sensed that his silent reaction was not a good sign. She stared down at the floor, anxiously, breathlessly. Everyone at the table turned to Lee, expectantly, wondering how he would react.

Lee took a deep breath and said, in front of all his friends, "As you have all heard, I built a nice house for her. She doesn't like it, she moved out. She wants to rent a place instead. She does as she wants. Now she wants more money." As he said it, Lee's hands flailed in exasperation. His face was red with fury.

Suddenly feeling uncomfortable, Lee's friends dropped their heads down in silence. They knew that Rachana was a good girl. They knew she was going to school and trying to better herself. They knew she tried to please her father. Now, they felt embarrassment and pity for her. One by one, people got up to leave.

After everybody was gone, Rachana sat in front of her father and began to cry. She cried like a baby. The tears would not stop, rolling uncontrollably down her cheeks, like ink dripping from the top of a pen.

Lee was the King of the Jungle. No one dared defy him. He said what he wanted to say, even though it was all a lie. Lee did not build that house for his daughter. Pitch had built it, with his bare hands. He had also paid every penny for it.

After he humiliated her, Lee went into the house. He came back outside as his daughter still sat sobbing in the same chair. He dropped fifty riels on the table in front of her and walked away without saying a word. Rachana could not even muster the words to say thank you.

In fact, she was mortified by both the lie he told and the disgrace that he had caused her in front of complete strangers. Lee's actions cut her deeper than the wound from the scissors she had thrown at her sister years ago. It was the sting of shame. Nevertheless, Lee remained the ruler of the house, which he did with an iron fist.

Rachana dared not tell a soul about the incident. The next morning, on a Sunday, both of her parents got up very early to go to the Buddhist temple. The Sims were devout Buddhists. Traditionally, the two stayed overnight until Monday morning. This time, Rachana got up with them at the same time and carried their bedding to the temple. Then she rode her bicycle back to her apartment, without even saying goodbye.

The school year went by at a fast pace. Anytime Rachana was stressed out, she thought about the squirrels and birds at the river. It was nature that carried her through the studying and brought her happiness to get through school. This time, Rachana passed the test with great grades. Her whole family was thrilled and made plans to attend her graduation. She was the first and only Sim to receive her diploma. Not surprisingly, Lee did not come to the graduation. Rachana was not expecting him to. Her sisters did not even bother to tell him she had made it. Lee was not concerned.

Now that Rachana had earned a diploma, she needed even more financial support if she was to continue and go to college. She still dreamed of becoming a teacher. The next step was to apply to a number of professional schools throughout Cambodia. However, there was one problem with this. Rachana had to travel to the Capital of the country to put in her university application, and then wait to take the test. The test sometimes took one, two, or three days, depending on the major. Doctors and political students required extra days of testing.

Another dilemma she faced was the need for money for the bus fare, living expenses, and for the test itself. All of these things were expensive; hence, why the rich kids were the only ones who could afford to go to college.

This time, Lee blatantly avoided his daughter. He suspected she would hit him up for travel money. He had overheard the conversation between Thida and Phary, although he never asked about it. They didn't know he knew.

Phary and Pitch were the greatest supporters of their little sister. They were her number one fans and advocates for her education. Rachana did not even have to ask them for what she needed. Pitch told her not to worry about the cost; they would provide her with the means to go to Phnom Penh for the college admissions test.

Phary asked Rachana one day, "When are you leaving for Phnom Penh?"

Rachana answered, "If all goes well, in two weeks."

Big sister said, "Just get yourself ready, I already told mother to go with you. I will not let you go alone." With that, she handed Rachana two thousand riels. It was a lot of money.

As a big smile came across her face, Rachana exclaimed, "WOW! I am so very happy. It will be a mother and daughter vacation for two months to see the Capital of the country! What a double blessing!" She hugged Phary with a giant embrace.

On the day that Rachana was to be leaving, Pitch pulled Rachana aside. "I want you to apply for the College of Teaching only. We don't expect you to pass the test the first time. I will provide financial support, even if it takes you five times. Please . . . I don't want you to go into any other professional field. We know you can do this and it is your destiny."

It was true. Teaching was Rachana's dream ever since she was a little girl. She still remembered a lot of occasions in which she played teacher and made her friends pose as students. Although she didn't have a lot of friends, there were her cousins and nieces and nephews too.

Of course, Chip was always by her side as well. He was her only constant friend throughout grade school and there were not many others. One of the reasons why Chip and Rachana got along so famously was because Rachana was so bossy, while Chip was so compliant. He always caved in to Rachana's wishes and did not have much of a mind of his own, which she did. In that sense, the two were polar opposites. It was the leader with her follower.

Chip was kind, gentle, and sweet. He always let Rachana have her way. For example, if the two went fishing with other friends, she made him carry the bucket and fishing net. Everyone else struggled and grew tired, but Rachana had her puppet to string along with Chip to do the work for her. It didn't matter how tired he was; Chip never said no to Rachana's requests. Therefore, he was also her best buddy.

In fact, Chip and Rachana went fishing quite frequently. She used live minnows as bait and a bamboo stick as her pole. When one day Rachana got a big bite, her pole suddenly slid through her fingertips and dipped down towards the water. Afraid to lose her big catch, Rachana yelled to Chip to help her. He was within earshot and came running to her aid. She couldn't bring in the fish because it was much too strong and heavy for a little skinny girl.

Chip pulled the fish up for her effortlessly. It was the biggest fish Rachana had ever seen. Of course, she took the credit for the catch too. As they walked home, Rachana dragged the fish on the ground all through the mud and the dirt.

Chip's mother yelled at her from the porch. "Cha-Cha! What do you have there? Did you catch a blind fish? How did you get a fish so big?"

Thida was also overjoyed with her daughter's big catch and made spicy coconut soup with the fish for the whole family that night for supper.

Chip helped Rachana in other ways too; some that he was not proud of. As a prepubescent girl, Rachana was somewhat of a bully. Aside from the incident with the neighbor girls she had scared off from her family's property, there were other times the wiry little girl showed off her mean spirit.

One girl in particular became the target of Rachana's bullying. Even though she was bigger than Rachana, Chip served as her bodyguard and secret service agent. Together they stepped on the girl's heels and kept asking her for money, although at any time the girl could have easily taken Rachana down if it had come down to a good cat fight. But the girl was too afraid to stick up for herself. Rachana intimidated her through Chip, because he was stronger than either of them.

On a separate occasion, Rachana made a loan to another classmate. A humble girl named Kara borrowed eighty cents from Rachana one day, which turned out to be a mistake on her part. The verbal contract was to pay double by the very next day. But by the next day, Kara did not have the money to pay Rachana back. So, the new amount owed became the eighty cents plus one riel in interest. On the third day, the girl paid Rachana one riel, but by then she owed her three riels. So, Rachana told her that the one riel is just the interest for that day.

It was cruel, but Rachana had devised the loan to accumulate interest daily, instead of weekly, monthly, or yearly. Every day, Kara had to pay one riel so the interest would not go up. So, each day, after she received her one riel of allowance, Kara had to remit the coin to her bully. Sometimes Kara got hungry, so instead of giving it to Rachana she used her money to buy lunch. On those days, the amount owed to Rachana grew by one riel.

As the bullying progressed, the eighty-cent loan became twenty-eight riels. That was a lot of money for a kid. On the day Rachana had designated it to be due, Kara still didn't have the money to pay the debt. Rachana made Chip step on her heels and interrogate her all the way to school. Kara was afraid, yet she had no need to be. Secretly, Rachana was just a coward who could not have bullied the girl on her own because she lacked the energy and strength to fight. She was nothing more than a skinny little girl who used Chip as her intimidator.

Finally, Kara wanted to rid herself of the nightmare that she had put herself in. She wished she had never borrowed the eighty cents in the first place. Eventually Kara stole the twenty-eight riels to pay Rachana back for the loan, finally freeing herself from the bullying.

Amazingly enough, the girl was too embarrassed to have ever told her parents or another adult. Then, after Rachana got the twenty-eight riels, she asked Thida, "Mom, may I go shopping today?"

"Yes, what would you like to shop for?" her mother inquired.

"Material for a new blouse," replied Rachana.

"For a blouse?" She had never heard of her daughter asking for new clothes before. Thida had always supplied for her needs, as well as those of the other children. No one ever asked because they didn't want to burden their mother for such things they desired. They knew how hard she worked for what few things they had.

"Yes, Mother, I have twenty-eight riels," said Rachana. "I know that will be more than enough money to buy the material, plus pay for the seamstress."

"Of course! But where in the world did you get all that money?" her Mom asked, curiously. During that time, children did not have many ways of earning money, nor did she give them an allowance.

"Kara paid me back the loan today." Rachana made the statement in the presence of her father. There was a big surprise on both of their faces.

"Loan? What loan is this?" asked Thida, troubled.

After Rachana explained truthfully what she had done, she wondered if they would be mad or proud. Actually, her parents were both astonished. They had never heard of such behavior like this before. Indeed, they were not proud of what Rachana did to poor Kara. Both Thida and Lee told Rachana to return the money back to the girl, but she protested.

Rachana exclaimed, "I did not ask her to take that loan. I warned her again and again that it would cost her so much if she did not pay me back on time. She agreed, and she swore an oath. We had a pact and she broke her promise and did not pay me back in time. So, she had to pay the price."

Lee and Thida looked stunned. Who was this devious child that stood before them?

"No, Mommy, I won't give her back the money. It is my money. It was originally out of my own savings. The day she borrowed it, I did not have money for my snack!"

Even though they disagreed with her, Rachana had a point. And every day thereafter, whenever Rachana asked her mother for money, Lee would say, "Hurry up honey, before Cha-Cha hikes up the interest!"

Eventually, Rachana was ashamed to hear them say it. She came to regret what she had done to the girl and bullying her. It was not a classy thing to do. In actuality, Rachana liked to earn her own money the right way. Even if she had to work very hard and earn very little, she was proud of her accomplishment. She felt the difference in earning money honestly instead of dishonestly. Ultimately, she did not own up to this until well after the fact, although she learned her lesson and did not bully any more kids thereafter.

During the months of May and early June, Rachana did have a chance to make money the right way, by working for it. Within the rice fields, there was a special wild herb that grew everywhere in the fields. For the children who were eager to make money, it was an opportunity to do so. In the afternoons, they picked the herbs and stored them in water. Although it didn't pay well, Rachana welcomed the occasion to earn some of her own money.

Every morning, she woke up early and walked with Chip to the market. It was one giant open-air farmer's market, where all of the vendors offered fresh produce, fabric, handmade goods, and everything under the sun. Of course, Chip was in charge of getting up on time and going to Rachana's house to wake her up too. Had it not been for her human alarm clock, she might have overslept. Chip never went without Rachana. It was an order.

On the way to the market, if somebody stopped the kids to buy their herbs, Rachana sold hers first, not Chip. He was required to stand and wait for her in the distance. It was Rachana's rule and Chip obeyed. At the market, they always stayed together. It was too easy to get separated and Chip and Rachana were still children, even though they had become mature enough to go without their parents.

Whenever buyers came to Rachana, it made her very happy. However, when they came to Chip instead, it made Rachana madder than a hive of angry hornets. She was very jealous whenever he did better than her at anything. So every day, she made more money than Chip and she was thrilled about that. It wasn't because she was any better or worse at selling, because the marketplace was just the luck of the draw. Rachana made the stack of cards work mostly in her favor. She was greedy and unfair to Chip, yet he continued to befriend her and stick by her side.

After returning home from the market, the two ate lunch and went off to the fields to harvest more herbs. It was another day and Chip was the only friend who was willing to go with Rachana. Yes, he would have rather been home playing with the other boys in the neighborhood instead of harvesting herbs. Instead, he was stuck with Rachana. She was the only one who dared to boss him around. Plus, it was a bonus that Chip's parents were pleased with him for bringing home a little money instead of just idly playing around. Whenever he hung out with Rachana, he either brought home fish or money. So the pressure from his parents and big sister to hang out with Rachana was also there. On the rare occasions he chose to play with the boys instead of working with Rachana, his family never let him hear the end of it.

On a similar note, whenever Rachana brought along a few of the other girls she knew for herb harvesting, they ditched her by midday. Only Chip was left standing by her side, because none of the other kids could tolerate Rachana's rules. One rule was that whenever all of them found a corner of the field that was full of thick, tall herbs that were ready to be picked, she would quickly use her feet to draw a circle around them, as if to claim them for her own. Rachana told them, "All of the herbs in this circle are mine. No one can pick the herbs inside the circle."

Another rule was that whenever they all played games, she was the authority figure in any role-playing. If they played school, Rachana was the teacher and they were the students. If they played work, she was the boss and they were the employees. If they played restaurant, she was the chef and they were the wait staff. If they played house, she was the rich homeowner and they were the servants and butlers. It was either do things Rachana's way, or leave.

Even when they left, Rachana didn't mind because Chip always stayed behind. She liked having him all to herself. Even though most of the girls were bigger and stronger than Rachana, for some unknown reason, no one dared defy her. She had a reputation, despite her frail appearance.

Now that she was applying for college, that ruthless girl seemed far removed from the person Rachana was now. She regretted some of those choices, but she had a chance to make things right with people.

Regardless, Rachana was thrilled to hear her brother-in-law's intent for her education and their offer to provide unlimited financial support. Rachana now knew that teaching was not only her dream; it was their dream for her future too.

There were two colleges of teaching institutes within the entire country. One was centrally located within the capital city of Phnom Penh. The other was about twenty miles just outside the city outskirts. Rachana chose the one on the outskirts because she didn't want anything to do with the cousins whom she knew that were living in the capital. They were wealthier and very arrogant. Besides, they liked to stir up trouble.

Nevertheless, Rachana flunked twice. That only left her with one option if she was to get into teaching school. The Baccalaurean premiere party was an exam held only within the capital.

Pitch and Phary sold another pair of livestock to pay for the trip. However, his buyer was unable to pay right away. The customers said they would pay in two weeks. It would not be too late, as it still gave Rachana plenty of time to take the Baccalaurean exam. She told her brother-in-law, "When I go to the capital this time, I am going to apply for every job that opens. And I will not come back until I have good news for you. They have a great need in women's nursing, with not enough women who have a diploma to fulfill the need."

Rachana had heard this from other strangers in Phnom Penh. Even though nursing was not her aspiration, she was willing to do whatever it took to get a career that earned a good income. There were fifty seats open to lady candidates in the nursing field, yet only thirty women who applied. Therefore, the hospital took all who applied, whether they passed the test or not. It was unfortunate, but Cambodian tradition still held women back behind the kitchen door. By Rachana's generation, more and more women stepped out of the kitchen to participate in the evolving modern world.

The day after speaking to Pitch about nursing, a strange idea came to Rachana's mind. She planned to face her father one last time. She thought about giving him another chance to step in and fulfill his role as a father and his duty as a provider.

Rachana felt compelled to awaken him, but for the right reasons. Lee had become so lost. The lines of right and wrong were a blur. His priority should have been his family, but instead it was strangers and outsiders who didn't care for him like his wife and daughters did.

Even though Pitch had guaranteed to satisfy his sister-in-law's financial needs for school, Rachana did not feel right in accepting it. She knew he needed it to support his own family. Instead, she felt determined to find another way. Phary and Pitch had done enough already. It was Lee's turn to help. More than ever, Rachana was driven not just to attend teaching college but also to truly make something out of her life. She refused to come home empty-handed. It was time to take the challenge, because this was her last chance.

So, Rachana went home to visit her parents, looking for an opportunity to discuss things with her father. As she walked up the front yard, Lee was sitting on the porch with Thida. He was so relaxed, so peaceful.

Rachana's mother initiated the conversation. "Baby girl, I missed you! I am so happy that your brother-in-law let you come home. How are they?"

"They are good, Mom." Rachana replied. "I missed you too." She hugged her mother tightly.

Thida added, "The other day I was visiting them, Pitch told me that he will keep you there because the children are so excited for you to come home. They asked me if they could see you again before you leave."

"They had me for a few days already. I wanted to see you too. You two are my parents and not them." As she said this, Rachana glanced at her father.

Thida replied, "Well we are going to see each other for two months, aren't we? The last two times I went with you, I really enjoyed visiting all the in-laws. They were excited to see me and I was so happy to see them. I will bring a lot of palm fruit for them. That is all they have asked me to bring this time.

"Yes, Mother, I know they like those," Rachana confirmed. Lee's parents lived in the capital, and Thida loved visiting them while her daughter was busy trying to accomplish the world. By now, they were quite elderly and not able to move around much.

The trio then walked upstairs. It was a beautiful late afternoon. The three of them spoke about many things. Before long, Lee was comfortable and in a very good mood. Rachana seized her chance.

She smiled at her father and reached for his hand. "Daddy, can I please have three thousand for this trip? I know it is a lot, but this time when I go to the capital, I will apply for more than one position. I am going to take many tests and stay there until I finally get a good job. Whatever job I get, it will be a good one because now I have two certificates." Then, Rachana held her breath, waiting for his response.

With thoughtful hesitation, Lee said, "I am sorry, Cha-Cha. I do not have money left at home. I lent it all to several people."

As her face grew hot, the joy, peace, and laughter they had just shared came to a screeching halt. It became a quiet afternoon. Rachana retreated to her room. Before she jumped to conclusions, she wanted to learn the truth. Mostly to make sure that she did not falsely judge her dad. He was a man who had bought a motorcycle for a stranger, a girl who was the daughter of a hired worker of his. Yet for his own daughter, Lee would reject the opportunity to better herself. She was his flesh and blood, how could he deny her this? How could he live knowing that his son-in-law was caring for his own daughter, and that Pitch was struggling to do it?

He had more than enough cash on hand to have helped many times over. Rachana knew it. To her, these facts made little sense. She was disappointed, yet not terribly surprised.

For two, three, and four days thereafter, nothing happened. By the fifth day, Rachana turned to her favorite place on earth for guidance–the riverbank. She talked to the squirrels, birds, wildflowers, and the bright blue sky. They listened, as they always did. She dangled her legs down into the water. The coolness of the river felt nice on her hot feet, which were calloused from walking.

As she sat there staring, she observed the nearby ducks. There were a handful of them feeding. They were busy working hard to eat and the ducks did not share. Yet, other types of birds she observed retrieving bugs and worms to share with bird friends and relatives. Rachana supposed that birds were a lot like people. Some were selfish. Some were kind. And the selfish ones always expected the kind ones to share with them. They thought the world owed them everything. Within that moment, Rachana realized that the way she felt about her dad was mostly her own problem. She expected too much from her dad. He was just not capable of sharing with the people who loved and took care of him, whereas Rachana's brother-in-law bent over backwards to help her even though he had his own family to support. She felt like a burden to Pitch, even though he never minded helping and always offered it to her. He was a generous bird.

Why am I such an encumbrance to him? Rachana wondered why her father had never accepted her. In contrast, Rachana's mother was a staple of beauty, doused in goodness and careless naivety. She would give anyone–especially those she loved–anything she owned. Rachana wondered why her father's selfishness didn't bother anyone else in the family as much as it bothered her. She had seen with her own eyes and had harbored his secret now for two years. It was the secret she kept forever and that ultimately made her lose respect for him. What Rachana had discovered when she opened that china hutch was more than just her father's gobs of cash. His secret life was locked in there like a lost pirate treasure.

Even though it was wrong for her to have snooped through his private belongings back then, what she found was shocking and led to the distress of her migraines, back pain, and even flunking her test for the diploma. That whole school year was a direct result of the pain that tore at Rachana from the inside out and that had taken her a whole summer of vacation to get over.

With her own eyes, she had witnessed Lee with two other women, on two separate occasions. Rachana had even seen him giving them both lots of money. But it was the notebook in his hutch that confirmed it. To one mistress, Lee gave nine thousand riels. To the other, he gave four thousand. Rachana kept this shocking secret with her for a lifetime. It was one of the underlying reasons she wished to remove her mother from his presence, even though Thida seemed quite content living in oblivion. She wanted so badly to tell her mother, yet didn't want to hurt her. Rachana knew that knowing something like this would crush her.

More than anything, Rachana was appalled by how unfaithful her dad was and how ungrateful. On one hand, she wished he would get caught.

On the other, she didn't want her mother to feel pain. Therefore, Rachana was torn. It infuriated her that this rotten man was her own father. He went on through life, successfully undetected by his loving, innocent, naïve, and wonderful wife. Lee even hid his secret from his four other daughters. The only one who knew what he had done was Rachana, the educated one. She had always been the troublemaker. She had always been the free-spirited child who disobeyed.

It was better when Rachana didn't know what her dad had done. The knowledge drove her crazy. It made her sick. She suspected her discovery had been the reason for her migraines, illness, and flunking the exam. Instead of unlocking the hutch to find treasure, Rachana had found skeletons. She was the only one nosy enough to dig into Lee's private business. Everyone else knew better.

Although she had given her father multiple chances to come through and change, he did not. Rachana decided that it was time to go and leave this life behind. She couldn't wait for a fresh beginning and a new shot at achieving something in life, something she had dreamed of doing since childhood. Suddenly, the doorway to the outside world seemed narrow. What was she to do? Rachana kept all of the pressure on her shoulders.

Deciding there was no good solution, Rachana walked back to the house. As she got closer, she saw her father leaving the house in the opposite direction. The door swung shut loudly as he left in haste. Lee had not seen Rachana approaching. His back was to hers. She could tell that he was going to visit his friends in the next village based on what he brought with him.

Creeping quietly back into their house, Rachana spotted the whole bundle of her dad's keys dangling on the antlers. They had previously been hidden away, but Lee must have thought that Rachana had left, so he hung them back up in their normal spot. He must have noticed something out of place that first time she had snooped. Now he was wiser and removed them whenever she came by for a visit.

Suddenly, the temptation of adrenaline kicked in. Rachana's heart started beating wildly. It was louder than a grandfather clock in an empty room. She crept into the house cautiously, like a tiger stalking through the cattails. After all, she knew that Thida was still inside.

Once again, Rachana carefully took her dad's keys that were hanging on the antler hook. She quietly unlocked the china hutch and pulled out the boxes that were still inside. Like last time, the naughty daughter wondered what she would find.

Nervously and quietly, Rachana started counting the one hundred riel bills from each thousand bundle. Lee kept his money so neat, and all in tidy bunches. There were one thousand riels in each stack. He was very organized. She could tell that he loved his money because every bill was so crisp, as if it had just freshly come off the press. It was a shame Lee refused to spend any of it on his family.

After she counted out three thousand riels, Rachana arranged the money exactly as she had seen it and then locked the door to the hutch. Then, she hung the keys on the same antler and walked into the kitchen, where Thida was fixing eggs for a late morning breakfast.

"Mother, I am leaving for Phnom Penh now."

"Why now? What happened?" Thida asked, concerned by the change of plans. "We do not have the money yet. Plus, I have not packed. I am not ready!"

In all seriousness, Rachana pulled out the stack of riels that was tightly wrapped with a rubber band. "Mom, look! I have the money. I stole it from Daddy."

Suddenly feeling nauseous, Thida asked, "Daughter, how did you do that?"

Almost proudly, Rachana explained, "Dad forgot his keys. And this time, I must go to Phnom Penh alone. I am leaving now."

Pleading with her, Thida cried, "No! No! Please . . . put it back, honey, please! You cannot get away from him. Please put it back. Your brother and sister told you that they would give us the money. You know that. Why would you do this? You will hurt your brother-in-law more than anybody else. Do not do that to him. Pitch loves you. Both he and Phary care about you so much. Pitch will be very upset. Not to mention your father!"

"Don't worry, Mom, everybody will be alright," reassured Rachana. "Mother, do not worry about me while I am away from home. I will take care of myself. I will make you proud of me."

Her mother shook her head desperately, as if she were afraid. Thida didn't know what to do. Rachana felt bad turning against her mother's will, as well as her brother-in-law's generosity. As she slammed the front door behind her, Rachana didn't know what came over her, except retribution. It was time her dad knew who she was. She felt like her father owed it to her. He owed their family. She felt like this was the only way to make him pay. *Why should Pitch have to suffer in taking care of his own family when Lee had enough money to have helped everyone many times over?* She was disgusted by her father and took the money out of spite and anger. Besides, he lied and said he didn't have any. She really needed the money and it was just sitting in the closet, never to be spent in this lifetime. It was only going to be wasted on strangers.

Thida didn't know these things. Instead, she didn't understand why her baby girl would blatantly go against her father like that. For the last few years, Rachana had never shown any signs of being the difficult and mean spirited child that she once was. Rachana had become peaceful and obedient ever since she started school. She seemed to appreciate things more, especially her family. So, how could she do something like this?

No one else dared to defy Lee the way that Rachana did. He was someone people looked up to. *What had changed her?* Thida wondered what would happen. She hoped that her husband would not notice, although she suspected that he would. *Was it for her father's approval that she did these things? Was it for attention or the lack thereof?* Even admonishment was at least acknowledgement.

Rachana ran and jogged much of the way to her sister's house. She took the shortcut. As she ran, she felt much like a convict. She imagined what it was like to be a prisoner escaping from prison. Because that's what she was right then. She was a criminal. She couldn't help it. There was a devil on one shoulder nudging her along, while the angel on the other side (who looked a lot like her mother) said, "No! Don't do it! Please, there's always another way!"

Her mother's pleas were to no avail. Rachana took the money anyway. She didn't dare to look back, thinking that Lee might be running after her by now. Upon arriving at Phary's house, Pitch announced to the children, "Hey everyone, honey is here! Honey is here!" Rachana was out of breath from running.

Looking a bit worried, Pitch asked her, "What happened to you? You look like you just got away with murder or something!"

"Yes! I did." Rachana was only half kidding. "As a matter of fact, I am going to leave for Phnom Penh right know."

"You mean it? But we do not have the money yet. You just got here!" Pitch exclaimed.

Rachana told the truth. "Yes, I do have the money. I stole some of Daddy's money. He has more than anyone knows about," she admitted.

"You did what?" Pitch gasped in shock.

At the same time, Phary said the same thing in unison with her husband. "You did what?" They looked at each other and at Rachana, dumbfounded. Even Rachana's little nieces and nephew came around to stare at her.

"Yes, I took three thousand riels," she replied. "I need to move fast before Dad gets here."

Both Rachana's sister and brother-in-law were very upset. They begged her and pleaded with her, taking turns trying to talk some sense into her insensitive choice. Phary said, "Honey, please listen to me. We do not need Dad's help. Please stay away from his money. Please do not create problems. You need to give it back to him."

Unfazed, Rachana replied, "Well, you do not know this, but our father has so much money. Much more than any of you can imagine."

"We do not care how much he has," Phary said, sternly. "Please give it back to him. He will be mad, yes. But not as mad as if you did not return it with an apology."

Angrily, Rachana rebutted. "No! He bought Mr. Doda's daughter a brand new motorcycle. Why not me? What has he ever done for me? His own daughter? Who is she? Is she related to him? No! She is not. Who am I? Am I not his child? Who is he responsible for? Me or her? She has her own parents. If it were not for you both, I would not be where I am today. And who does he think he is? Is he not my dad? This time I will make him know who I am!"

"But it is his money, honey please!" Phary pleaded.

"No, I have made my decision and I am very sorry to both of you," she firmly replied. "I won't give it back to him. After all, he is my father. He has taken care of many other people and even kids who were not his. Why not me? Or you? Or any of us? Why not his own flesh and blood? I will open his eyes for all of us. For all of us girls that he did not provide for!"

"What makes you do this to us?" Phary asked, disappointed that she could not get through to her little sister. Of course, Rachana could never reveal the other things she knew about their father. Like the money he had given away to his mistresses.

"Please do not worry about me while I am away. I promise I'll be a good girl. I will take care of myself. I promise I will come back with good news. I will not disappoint you," she reassured Phary.

Again, Rachana left for the city with a troubled heart and sadness on both sides, from her mother, sister, and brother-in-law. Even though she had done bad things, never before had Rachana ever been this bad, this wicked, this stubborn, this disobedient. Rachana surprised her whole family and even her own self by her defiance. The decision to do it had been so spontaneous and unplanned that even she had no idea that she could ever have done such a thing. Yet, she did.

True to her word, Rachana remained in the city until the school announced all of the candidates who had passed the test. Thankfully, Rachana Sim was one of them. Aside from the great news of her passing grades, she also was offered a job. However, Rachana decided to choose the continued pursuit of teaching that she knew she belonged in. This time, her dream would come true. She had overturned yet another hurdle.

As she made the walk home to see her family again and to give them the great news, Rachana couldn't have been happier. She didn't even feel bad for Lee. Come to think of it, the only person she felt bad for was her mother for having endured the many years of deception.

Rachana told her brother-in-law and sister of the great news. They were thrilled and very happy for her. The kids were happy to see their auntie too.

Then, Pitch took a deep breath and said, "Listen, you have no idea how worried we have been for you. After you left, there was a lot of explaining to do. We played dumb. This matter is between you and your father," Pitch said, referring to the stolen money.

"Yes, it is. I'm glad you did not get involved," she agreed.

"Now you know you can't go home, right?" Pitch asked Rachana, more as a telling statement than a question. "You have to stay here with us. It would not be good for you to go there."

"Yes, I know," Rachana agreed once again. She didn't want to go back anyway. She didn't want to see Lee ever again, at least not for right now.

Chapter Nine

"Forgiveness"

The whole thing was blown way out of proportion. There were many close relatives who were angry with Rachana for what she had done to get to Phnom Penh, but at the same time they were proud of her achievement in passing the difficult exam. Now she would become the only member of the Sim family with a college degree.

Although Phary rarely spoke much of her own upbringing and relationship with their father, she too had experienced a closet of disappointments that she kept closed. Phary took after Thida in that she pushed aside her resentments and just accepted the way things were. She left well enough alone to keep life undisturbed. In contrast, Rachana had always been hotheaded and tenacious.

So being the peacemaker that she was, Phary called upon her eldest daughter Ashley for help in patching up the relationship between Lee and Rachana. One day, Phary and Ashley set to work baking an afternoon's worth of goodies that were to be sent home to their parents. There was also something special that she bought in the marketplace. Phary knew that her father loved a certain food from France. Because it was only available through one particular vendor in the entire Western region of Cambodia, Lee appreciated it very much. Phary knew it would take a lot of effort to coax him back into letting Rachana return home, even just to see their mother.

After "the incident," Lee had arrived at Phary's house in hot pursuit of his wayward daughter. By then, Rachana had already fled to Phnom Penh. He had tried chasing her and was hoping to catch her visiting Phary and Pitch before she left for the capital. Lee was dripping head-to-toe in sweat from walking so far, which was quite a feat at his age. His face was flush and he looked as if he might pass out. When he came upon their yard, Lee yelled, "Where is that little brat? When I get my hands on her, I'm going to whip her ass for good!"

What Phary didn't learn until Rachana's return home two months later was that Rachana had, in fact, asked for the money from her father prior to stealing it. Nevertheless, it was too late to go back in time. That's why she summoned Ashley, who was also very close to Rachana.

"Dear, would you please take all of these goodies to Grandma and Grandpa so that we can keep your aunt here?" Phary asked her teenage daughter. They had made a delicious tray of sweet treats to bring Lee and Thida.

Overhearing her and seeing the tremendous buffet of goodies, Rachana said, "Absolutely not!"

The other nieces and nephews all volunteered to go with Ashley as well.

"No, it is not right. I should go. This does not involve you or any of the kids," Rachana told her determined older sister.

Phary said, "Oh, no! You cannot set foot near their house."

"Why not?" asked Rachana.

Next, Pitch interrupted. "The same day you left, your father was here. About two hours after you set off for Phnom Penh, he arrived madder than I've ever seen him. He asked where you were and we invited him in to serve him a drink. He was dehydrated and red-faced from chasing after you."

Phary continued where her husband left off. "I told Father that you had left a long time ago without any explanation, without even saying goodbye. I told him that you had gone straight to Phnom Penh instead of stopping at Rachel's house to spend the night. I didn't want him to catch you there. I asked him, '*Please Daddy, I will take full responsibility. Please do not do anything yet.*' "

Pitch added, "Do you know what he said, Rachana? He said he would beat you up for good. So, for your own protection I would not go there to visit if I were you."

Rachana looked away, as far away as she could. For a moment, it was as if she was watching the whole scene replaying on a movie screen. She could picture Lee's face as he whipped her with the horsewhip. Yet instead of having fear, it gave her courage.

"Not this time," Rachana said quietly. "I appreciate your willingness to take the blame, Phary. But I am not a four or five-year-old anymore. I am fully-grown. I can walk faster than Daddy. I can outrun him easily and am also a lot smarter than I was twenty some years ago."

With that, she stood up and announced, "I'm going home. I will face him."

Phary pleaded, "No, you cannot go! What am I going to do if a grown lady gets beat up by her father? I cannot let this happen to you. You mean so much to us. How can we bear the shame? And you, how can you escape the shame? Please do not let this happen. You are safe here. Your nieces and nephew look up to you. If this happens, it will cause a lot of problems for the whole family. Please sit back and take more time to think!"

Seeing their worried faces, Rachana said, "I am sorry. I have to explain what transpired. Before I took Dad's money, I did ask him for it. But he lied and said he had no money left to give and that he had loaned it all away. I knew better and that he had not lent out even a fraction of it. I also knew that he was lying. It upset me, partly because I heard that he had just bought a motorcycle for the neighbor's daughter."

Phary and Pitch were stunned. They thought that Rachana had taken her father's money without asking first, although, it still didn't justify her actions. Rachana went on, "Without both of you, I would be in great need. I cannot finish school, nor would I have been able to attend school in the first place. It is because of your goodness and love that has brought me this far. So, when Daddy told me that he had no money in the house, it pushed me to the edge. I have watched him closely. I know every place he puts his money, and I know every lucky person who got a piece of it. I admit . . . I looked through his notebook. He never believed in women's education because he was afraid of this. He doesn't want us to know how much he has. He wants us to be compliant and subservient. Our father doesn't believe that women should be empowered," Rachana stopped, pointing at Phary, herself, and even Ashley, who was still in the room.

"I took his money not only because I needed it, but to make my point. You have been so good to me, and I shall never forget it. But I had to let Daddy know that we are not as stupid as he thought." Again, Rachana pointed to all the females in the room. "And now I have proven him wrong in everything he has said or done. I'm going to prove to him many more times whenever I get a chance. And when the time comes, I have decided that nothing can stop me."

Phary didn't know what to say, except, "So now, what is your plan sister?"

"When Daddy asks me if I stole the money, if he is in the house then I will run down to the bottom of the stairs, shouting . . . '*Daddy, do you remember when I asked you for money and you said you had nothing left? How could I have stolen money that you did not have?* '"

"Besides," she added. "Do you know how old our father is? Lee is old. He can't even walk straight. How can he chase after a twenty-year-old girl who is as healthy and strong as an ox?"

Everyone laughed out loud. Her words put Phary's family at ease. They all visualized Lee with his walking stick, with no way to catch up to his daughter to beat her up.

"Then, I will run back here to your house. But if Daddy is in the front yard when I get there, I'll be sure to stand a few feet away from him and say what I need to, in case I need to leave quickly. He can't harm me. I guess we'll take it from there," Rachana sounded committed to her plan.

Phary was not so convinced. She asked Rachana one more time if she was sure of her willingness to face Dad. Once again, Rachana confirmed it. She reassured Phary and their family not to worry.

With that, Phary sent the gifts and fruits with Rachana to use as a peace offering. She warned her baby sister always to be on guard. Then Rachana made the two hour walk back to the Sim home. It was a home that she was fond of and not fond of, both at the same time.

Upon arriving from the long walk, Rachana found Lee weaving a basket under a fruit tree in their yard. No one was there visiting with him this time, although very often there were neighbors or friends who came over. Lee's beautiful baskets were the expensive kind, the kind that lasted twenty or thirty years even if used for the heaviest of objects. They were designed to carry heavy things with as much strength as a wooden barrel. He earned very good money for his baskets, in part because of the strong bamboo he used to make them, combined with his expert craftsmanship.

Before he noticed her, Rachana stopped to study her father. The years had given him a few wrinkles, but he was still quite a handsome guy. Deep down, in many ways she was even proud of him. Lee was very handy and good at what he did. He was also very creative and talented, which she admired. He was tall, smart, good looking, and charming. Her father was also very well respected in the village. The fact that he knew how to do many things well made him seem like the perfect guy, if it were not for that one missing element from his mind to be a caretaker for his family.

Alas, Lee did not understand his duty as a husband and father. There needed to be boundaries and guidelines, with the family being at the fore-front of them. Yes, it was a good asset to be kind and helpful to everyone; however, by ignoring his family in the process, it had caused deep wounds and emotional scars that would take many decades to heal. Because in the end—when there was no longer a need for material goods—the last breath was the most priceless treasure left. Only then, maybe he would realize the value in having special people who were there to hold his hand and take care of him, or to say they loved him. They were his family.

After putting all of the goodies on a serving tray that she retrieved from the pantry, Rachana made her presence known. She stood before Lee, putting everything that she had brought from Phnom Penh in front of him. Kneeling, Rachana said, "Hello, Daddy."

"Cha-Cha! You are home?" he asked.

"Yes. I brought gifts," she humbly offered.

"How was the test, honey?" Lee surprised her with a kind phrase.

"Daddy, I passed the test! I will be a teacher in one year. They will give us a salary when we start school. It won't be a lot. They will pay six hundred riels a month. But I will be able to live on that." Rachana was eager to get on his good side.

After all of her worry, Lee was amazingly sweet and tender towards her. He had never been like that before. As they conversed, Lee spoke in a gentle, loving voice that Rachana had so yearned for throughout childhood. She could barely believe her ears. She had wanted him to pay attention to her so many times. Rachana had never satisfied her craving for her father's attention. This special moment was a double blessing from heaven. First, in passing her test. Second, in hearing the shockingly affectionate words from her father.

After they visited for a while, Rachana skipped out of the house with tears of joy. She gleefully ran all the way to the beloved riverbank and cried tears of happiness in finally feeling the love of her father. She lifted her young face towards the sky and stretched her hands up to the clouds. Oh, how she wished and hoped to experience that feeling again and again for as long as her father was alive.

Expecting to have been greeted by a horsewhip, Rachana released the anger she had built up within her soul. It was a lifetime of resentment that had caused her sickness and pain within her heart, as well as migraines. Now, finally Lee had changed his heart with unexpected turnabout. It was the most surprising thing Rachana had ever experienced in her entire life.

She didn't want the clock to move one second forward, nor one second backwards, for fear of losing this moment of glory.

Suddenly, Rachana loved her father. She adored him and the way he looked. She was even proud of his talents and his influence on the community. She accepted his ability to help others in handling their needs and disputes. People came to him for different reasons, from seeking advice to buying products. Lee was always eager to help. What had always been resentment suddenly turned to pride. She thanked the heavens for this blessing.

For the next two weeks, Rachana stayed with her parents before returning to attend the new school on a quest to achieve her teaching degree. This time, she enjoyed her surroundings and pondered whether she would ever return to Siem Reap to live. Deep down, she felt a connection with the place. But in her heart she did not feel that it was the place she would return to live forever. It was where she was born and raised, yes, but it was not the place her soul was calling her. At this point, she still had no idea where she belonged.

Each day she took in the beauty and rested, knowing that hard work and plenty of studying was in store for her when she returned to college. As Rachana strolled around the yard under the fruit trees or by the riverbank, she recalled many wonderful memories of her childhood that were sprinkled throughout the property.

Like her elder brother Ponleau, Rachana had favored an unlikely pet. One of her fondest memories was of her childhood pet. Hanky was a docile bull, which suited Rachana's personality in the analogy of strength and one to be feared. Although he wasn't the traditional pet such as a dog or cat, Hanky was very special to Rachana, and was her best buddy as far as pets go.

Rachana gathered some pretty black-eyed Susan's and placed them lovingly on Hanky's grave under the special plum tree that he had been buried under. People had often told her that the bull understood everything Rachana said to him, and she believed it to be true. The bull and the young girl shared a special connection; the strong ox who was a reflection of how Rachana saw herself to be, despite her skimpy physique.

Upon visiting Hanky's grave, the memories flashed back like he was there with her. Hanky was not an aggressive bull. He was very smart. The only thing he couldn't do was talk, although Rachana could understand him just perfectly. Whenever she stood or walked next to him, Hanky never strayed off. In fact, he would have rather starved than to leave his young human companion. Their relationship was undoubtedly unconventional, especially to those who saw them walking or sitting together. Rachana often talked or sang to Hanky, or sometimes she just calmly patted him for what seemed like hours. All she had to do was place her gentle hand on his neck and he would lower it enough to breathe his hot bull breath into her ear, as if to tell her how much he enjoyed her companionship.

After Hanky died, Rachana used to climb up into the plum tree and sit on the branches over where he was buried. She still wanted to spend time with him, at least in spirit. It was the only tree she had ever been willing to climb, having always been afraid of heights. She bent the lowest branch down low enough to lift herself up into the tree, sometimes bringing her journal or a book to read for hours. Now she was much bigger, and so was the tree. The branches had grown past her reach.

Even though Hanky's grave had long since grown over with moss and weeds, Rachana remembered her favorite pet as if they were still together. During this visit, she felt a wave of tranquility and blessings. She was grateful for having four sisters who loved her so much. They had cared for her as if she were a fragile sheet of glass. Rachana had been raised without want or worry, being able to play or go fishing whenever she felt like it. She knew she was a difficult child but felt fortunate to have been brought up in such a loving family.

The return home for Rachana was one of reflection, mixed with happy and sad memories combined. Sad, because she had a plan in her heart that nobody knew about. And happy to have gathered the good memories that she could cherish. She was also happy to have made amends with her father. The two weeks passed by quickly.

Once again, Rachana found herself in the big city of Phnom Penh, all alone and striving to make a better life. She studied every day and kept her nose buried in the books.

At the end of the school year, her grades were tallied. All of the names of students who attended the university were posted on a board for all eyes to see. Each student was listed in order according to the grades they made. Low and behold, Rachana had been ranked fifth out of the whole school. That gave her the choice to teach in any province she wanted, except for one. That one province had a need for only one teacher and the number one student accepted it.

Instead, Rachana chose Siem Reap to be closer to home. However, the very day before the decisions were to be finalized, Rachana walked down to the Mekong River with a distant cousin whom she had made acquaintances with since living in the city. As they were sitting on a bench and deeply engrossed in conversation about life, a handsome guy in a preppy shirt approached the two girls. Strangely, he acted like he had met her before. Shortly after saying hello to them, he singled out Rachana by saying, "So, have you decided where you will choose to go tomorrow?"

Taken aback, Rachana replied, "Do I know you? Or do you know me?"

Kindly, the guy smiled and said. "Why yes, I am Eli, from the very next classroom to you. I see you every day. Didn't you ever notice me at all?"

Blushing, Rachana said, "No, I am sorry, I did not."

"C'mon, really? You don't remember me even though we passed by each other at school every single day?" Eli said in disbelief. "I was in algebra. You were in history."

"No, but now I know," said Rachana. "You look familiar."

"You were in classroom seven, and I was in six. You sat at table three, by the window. I kept my eyes on you every day. I even know where you live and whenever you go home to visit," he added. "Doesn't that mean anything to you?"

Rachana looked straight into Eli's eyes with a lot of judgment upon him. Whether it was because she was so intent on her schoolwork or because she just disliked men–particularly any who had expressed interest in her–she disregarded them, especially the good-looking ones. Using her own mother as an example, Rachana knew that most handsome men were unfaithful or did not look out for their families, which was not the kind of guy she wanted to date or consider for marriage. So, she just focused on her studies and rarely paid men any mind.

Then, Eli stared at her expectantly. He was still waiting for her answer to his question. Rachana did reply. "Well, I'm going back home."

"To Siem Reap?" he asked, but it was more of a statement.

She nodded.

"Can I please ask you to choose Svay Rieng, my hometown? I can guarantee you will have a room to stay with my family and my two sisters will be at your service. My family has heard a lot about you from me, so they would be thrilled to have you as our guest."

Inside, Rachana silently fumed. But instead of flying off the handle, she said nothing. So Eli continued. "You will be comfortable there. My parents and my sisters will provide everything. I promise. I ask you this because I know that with your grades you can choose anywhere you wish to go. But I can't. My grades were not as good as they could have been because I focused mostly on preparing for the second Baccalaurean exam. I want to be a high school professor."

Eli had mistaken Rachana for the caring type of girl. It had taken all of the braveness he could muster to approach her that day. He knew it was the last day and therefore his last shot to ask her out or he may never see her again. Eli had revealed a secret crush on her. And he was definitely an attractive guy, as well as smart. Unfortunately, for Eli, he had chosen a woman who was filled with anger towards men, particularly the best-looking ones.

Yes, Rachana was very sweet and friendly to those whom she knew, but to strangers she was like the Queen of Glaciers, icy and cold and separated from the rest of the world by a big space. Plus, her stubborn attitude was resilient and tough to break. She was difficult to get to know, but once people knew her, she was a sweetheart.

Rachana answered, "No! I have a loving family in Siem Reap who can hardly wait for me to return home. And I miss them too."

Eli implored, "Listen Rachana, I don't want to lose you. I mean, I would really love to get to know you. The other day I pointed you out to my brother when you were walking from the market. He agreed that you were pretty and smart, so he encouraged me to ask you out. I brought him here with me just for this reason."

Rachana glanced toward the trees, where another guy was sitting next to the walkway. She was not even flattered, nor amused. With a very dry smile, Rachana stood up and said, "I appreciate it, but no thanks. Goodbye."

With that, she walked off, leaving the fellow sitting there alone. It was the last time she ever saw him. He reminded Rachana of her father. Eli was tall and handsome, with a nice smile. However, she had made a personal vow to never marry anyone that reminded her of her dad. *It wouldn't work*, she told herself.

The sickness of predetermined judgment clouded any reasoning. It haunted her for many years thereafter. Eli had been the first guy to express his interest in courting her, but he was not the last. And Rachana's anger towards her father had never left, even if she was unaware of it. Her heart was not soft enough for a spirit of forgiveness and she assumed any guy who wanted to get to know her would hurt her, just as her father had done. It wasn't until many, many years later that God stepped in to heal her heart and allow forgiveness to shine through.

Chapter Ten

"Goodbye"

"Mrs. Long? Mrs. Long?" A hand touched Rachana's shoulder as she was slumped over the edge of the hospital bed. "Mrs. Long, your daughter is on the phone."

"Huh?" Rachana lifted her head and adjusted her eyes to the white room. For a moment, she was discombobulated. She focused on the man in the bed in front of her. It was her husband. It was Narin. She squinted as her focus became clear again, like wiping the glass of a windshield just after it rains.

"Mrs. Long, I think you must have fallen asleep," said the petite nurse. "Your daughter Sophea is on the phone. She is very worried and called you several times. Would you like to take her call?"

"Yes, of course," Rachana said. "Thank you."

Rachana looked at the red dot flashing on the square white phone in the hospital room. She picked up the receiver. Sophea was waiting on the other end. "Mommy! Is everything okay? I have been trying to reach you. You were supposed to call me when you arrived in San Francisco."

"So sorry, honey. I must have fallen asleep. What time is it?" she asked.

"It's ten o'clock in the morning," replied Sophea.

"Oh my goodness, I have been sleeping for nine hours!" exclaimed Rachana.

"How is Dad?" Sophea asked.

"I haven't spoken to him yet. I'm not sure if he knows I'm here," Rachana whispered as she looked at the man who was barely breathing in the bed. The white blankets covered him exactly the same as when she had arrived, as if Narin had not moved. But the machines were still on. He was still alive.

Almost as if hearing her voice, Narin lifted his hand. His eyes were barely open as his hand scrunched up to reach towards the sound of his wife's voice. "I have to go, dear," said Rachana. "I think he's awake." "Please, Mommy . . . please call me back and let me know what is going on," Sophea implored on the other line. "I will say a prayer."

"Thank you. I will call, dear. I am fine," she agreed.

Rachana rested the receiver back into the cradle on the phone. She slowly approached the edge of Narin's bed. "You came." He murmured. "I didn't think you would."

"We have been through many things in this life together. Of course I came to see you through to the other side," Rachana said, standing just at the edge of his bed. She gazed upon his face. He just blinked.

"Funny, your brother never came," she went on, rather matter-of-factly.

Narin struggled to breathe. Vibol did not love him or he would have been there by his bedside. Instead, her brother-in-law's ulterior motives had not come to fruition after all. God had other plans; therefore, Narin was not at home and couldn't continue on with his lie of being uncared for by his family.

She touched his blanket. "Are you cold or anything? Shall I get a nurse?"

He could barely nod in acknowledgement. Rachana pressed the call button and within a minute, a nurse came into the room to check Narin's vital signs. She turned to Rachana. Under her breath, the nurse whispered, "You'd better say anything you need to say now because his vitals are declining. With all of the chemo he's had . . . it's bad. He's not going to be here much longer."

Rachana bowed her head down as a few tears rolled down her cheek, landing on Narin's hand. He twitched. The nurse placed a hand upon Rachana's shoulder and squeezed it gently, as if to comfort her. She was not new to death, working in the cancer ward of the hospital. But it was still difficult to see, especially for the families. "I'll be out here if you need anything else," the nurse said, compassionately. Rachana nodded in understanding.

After the nurse left the room, Rachana lifted Narin's hand. "You make me an unhappy wife," she began crying harder. "You were a good husband once. And in the Killing Fields you took care of me. You took care of us."

Narin could barely speak, but he could hear her and he listened. Rachana continued. "After we got to the U.S. you turned on me. You made me very disappointed. But, I forgive you. I will help you through to your last breath. I won't leave you or desert you. I will not let you die alone."

It took everything Narin had to mumble, "I'm sorry."

"Better to say sorry to Jesus," she whispered. She sat by his side for the afternoon. He drifted in and out of consciousness. Unexpectedly, Vibol did arrive at approximately 2:00 p.m. Rachana did not acknowledge her brother-in-law with even so much as a polite hello. As far as she was concerned, he didn't belong there.

When Narin opened his eyes to see his brother in the room, he turned his head away. He was ashamed of what he had done to his family and for letting greed and deceit come between them. Vibol took a seat after greeting Narin. He stared at him.

Finally, Rachana spoke. "It's best if you wait outside," she said quietly. Vibol stood up and left the room. He went to sit just outside in a nearby waiting room.

Rachana reached for her bible. She read the words of God to Narin, just to soothe him. She purposefully chose Psalm 28, a psalm of David:

1 *To you, Lord, I CALL;*
you are my Rock,
do not turn a deaf ear to me.
For if you remain silent,
I will be like those who go down to the pit.
2 *Hear my cry for mercy*
as I call to you for help,
as I lift up my hands
toward your Most Holy Place.
3 *Do not drag me away with the wicked,*
with those who do evil,
who speak cordially with their neighbors
but harbor malice in their hearts.
4 *Repay them for their deeds*
and for their evil work;
repay them for what their hands have done
and bring back on them what they deserve.
5 *Because they have no regard for the deeds of the Lord*
and what his hands have done,
he will tear them down
and never build them up again.

6 *Praise be to the* LORD,
   for he has heard my cry for mercy.
7 *The* LORD *is my strength and my shield;*
   my heart trusts in him, and he helps me.
   My heart leaps for joy,
   and with my song I praise him.
8 *The* LORD *is the strength of his people,*
   a fortress of salvation for his anointed one.
9 *Save your people and bless your inheritance;*
   be their shepherd and carry them forever.

After reading the bible to her husband, Rachana said, "Tomorrow you will feel much better. I will take you home."

Narin smiled, just a little. Rachana patted his arm and gripped his hand. "Friday we will go celebrate Neary's award," she said optimistically. She knew he would not be able to go, however she wanted to comfort him in some way and reached for any way to console him. Narin seemed happy to hear her words. He smiled a bit, for a second time.

Then she said, "It's okay, husband. Just close your eyes and go to sleep." She sat with him and didn't speak for the longest time. Silently, she prayed for Narin. She prayed that God would take pity on him and forgive him for his actions and lack of faith. The only time Rachana rose from his bedside was to use the restroom and to call Sophea and Neary to let them know about his progress.

The clock ticked like water dripping from a faucet, breaking the silence of a quiet room. Finally, Narin just stopped breathing. Their life together as a couple was over.

Rachana felt both relief and grief, all at the same time. She was not unfamiliar with death. She had seen more than her share of death, enough for a whole lifetime. At least now, Narin was at peace.

Chapter Eleven

"Silent Relief"

There were only a handful of people who attended Narin's funeral. Of course, Rachana, Sophea, and Neary were there. So were Vibol and his family, and the professor who knew him, plus a couple of his only friends. The funeral was held at their church.

Sophea and Neary were there for moral support of their mother. Both were very upset by their father's antics of the last few years. It was very disappointing to be rejected by their father, as Rachana had also experienced growing up. It was also ironic that she had married someone who had done the same, although in a different way than Lee. Rachana had tried so hard to avoid marrying someone like her own dad, yet it was inevitable.

Now at least, both girls hoped their mother would finally have the peace that she deserved. As a mother, Rachana had always done her best and looked after the wellbeing of her daughters, first and foremost. At times, it had been difficult teaching them when they were younger, even though she had been formally educated and held a degree as a teacher.

As a child, Sophea blamed her lack of desire to learn on her teacher. Because the teacher was not pretty, Sophea refused to pay attention in class. She sat in class with her back turned, swinging her legs back and forth in defiance. Whenever Rachana took a break from teaching her own classroom, she went down to her daughter's classroom to spy on her. If Sophea saw her mom staring at her with a scowl, she quickly turned around, pretending to pay attention to the teacher. Or if the class was reciting something and she spotted her mother's eyes on her, Sophea opened and closed her mouth, pretending to recite. However, because she never paid attention in class, Sophea truthfully had no idea what they were doing.

Sophea's learning difficulties continued even when they were transferred to the Philippines for eight months, before arriving in the United

States. By then, she was seven years old. At first, Sophea had a pretty teacher. She was a model student who did exceptionally well in school. Then, in the middle of the school year, the curriculum changed teachers to another ugly one. Once again, Sophea quit paying attention in class.

"Why, Sophea? Why?" Rachana pleaded with her daughter. "Why were you doing well in school before and not now?"

Sophea replied, "The new teacher is not pretty. It looks like she has a mustache. I don't care for her class."

Frustrated, Rachana gave her daughter math books to work on because that was all Sophea would do. Otherwise, she just sat in class in her own little world. She found math to be so enjoyable that she finished the sixth grade math book in the first grade. By second grade, it was a repeat of the year prior. The young girl just sat in class and worked on math books. Fortunately in third grade, Sophea finally got a pretty teacher. Her name was Mrs. Tyler and she was a natural beauty, both inside and out. She had a great way with kids. Finally, Sophea started paying attention in class and interacting with everyone.

Neary had difficulties learning too. Rachana often tried to teach her youngest daughter the times tables while Neary hid underneath her desk and cried because she didn't want to learn. In fifth grade, Neary had a big science project that was due the next morning and she hadn't even started it yet. So, her older sister stayed up until 4:00 a.m. to do the project for her baby sis. Neary got an A+ on that project, although the teacher was quite suspicious of the neat handwriting. Neary's handwriting was always more scribbled and messy.

Neary didn't begin improving until she started middle school. "Your big sister is in high school now," Rachana explained to her youngest daughter. "She's busy with her own homework, so you're going to have to start helping with the chores around the house."

"Okay, Mommy," Neary acknowledged her request. So, by sixth grade Neary learned to wash the dishes, clean the kitchen, and help with the cooking to allow Sophea more time for homework.

"And don't forget to wash the vegetables that you'll be putting in the soup for dinner!" yelled Rachana to her youngest daughter. Neary complied. She stood on the stool and scrubbed the vegetables hard with soap and water, trying not to break her concentration. In fact, she scrubbed them so well they were absolutely ruined. She had scrubbed the skins right off.

Rachana had to throw away all the vegetables and they had something else for dinner. Neary was no slacker and took every chore she was given to the best degree of excellence she could achieve. Not long after she began contributing more to the family. Neary also started applying herself in school, maybe because she felt more self-worth, or maybe because she was just growing up.

Neary graduated both middle school and high school as the valedictorian. Both girls had college tuitions paid for entirely by scholarships. In fact, Neary got practically every scholarship the community had to offer, leaving very little for anyone else. Throughout those years of both her daughter's education and even while Narin was busy being a professional slacker; Rachana always used her summer vacation to work in the fields to help with the harvests. They were living in Oregon then.

In theory, Rachana believed that if she instilled a strong work ethic within her two daughters, then she could also show them how valuable it was to have an education. They worked alongside the migrant workers, picking strawberries, blueberries, raspberries, blackberries, and black cats, which were used to make ink. Not realizing they were not meant for eating, Sophea did try a few black cats and quickly discovered how bad they tasted. But, the most difficult summer job was the garlic harvesting, which required sitting in the dirt along the thick rows of garlic and stuffing the garlic into big sacks that were designed for keeping them fresh. The girls all came home with dirt all over them, from nostrils to fingernails.

In the winter, Rachana and Narin rented out patches of land up in the mountains to harvest bear grass. Sophea and Neary trimmed the bear grass of its dead ends in the evenings as a way of earning extra income. Even though they didn't have to do this, Rachana killed two birds with one stone by teaching her daughters the difference in having to do manual labor over having a skilled profession from a degree. "Educated people work hard in a different way," Rachana explained to her two girls.

And Rachana was never a stranger of hard work, having watched her own mother do so for many years and living through the Killing Fields; and even when their family first arrived in the United States. Rachana took hard labor jobs when they first arrived. Her first job was working at Corvallis Manor Nursing Home, where she was paid a minimum wage of $3.50 per hour. The language barrier posed a difficulty for her at first, especially whenever the old fellers tried to talk to her. She couldn't understand them very well. A couple of them mumbled or hissed words that Rachana could not relate to.

Later, she got a job as a housekeeper at Good Samaritan Hospital. The starting pay was $5.00 per hour. Rachana was excited about the pay increase. She worked at the hospital five days a week. On her days off, she cleaned houses for the doctors and professors. Rachana often spent her whole Saturday or Sunday working for only $7.00, $8.00, or $12.00 per house, but it was enough extra income to buy the groceries with. For $15.00 she could buy two bags of groceries that would feed her family for a whole week. Two nights a week, she also took her two girls to clean a thrift shop for extra income. The Long family performed yard work for these affluent families as well. They pulled weeds, raked, mowed their lawns, and kept things watered.

Just like Thida, Rachana became the family provider. All the while, she was very careful with money. After one year in the United States, they bought their first car. It was a brand new, tan Nissan Sedan. The Longs paid for it with the cash they had saved up.

In the summer, they picked berries. Rachana gave four-year-old Neary a shiny quarter to play with, since she was too young to participate in the berry plucking. She wanted to keep the little girl busy to avoid distractions and inquisitions while they picked as many strawberries as they could.

Indeed, little Neary busied herself for the whole day, not making one peep except the humming of contentment in whatever she was doing to stay amused. At the end of the day, the Long family gathered at the car after a long day of work, only to discover what Neary had spent the whole day doing to keep occupied. The whole car looked as if a cat had scratched the paint off the entire bottom half of their vehicle. The toddler had used the quarter she was given to scrape the paint away, without interruption.

That fall, the Longs got the farmer's permission to glean their harvested garlic fields of any leftovers. From that, they were able to gather an additional two truckloads of garlic that had been missed in the first harvest by the farm's migrant workers. Rachana and Sophea cleaned the garlic, loaded the pickup truck, and drove to Tacoma to sell it at the apartments. This yielded a good profit. Then when winter came upon them, Rachana and Narin left the kids home to go to the mountains, where they picked bear grass and took that to Washington State as well.

These extra money making opportunities helped the family stay ahead and save enough to buy their first house after three years in the U.S. They had enough for a 30% down payment of the purchase price of their new home. This too, was because of Rachana's thriftiness and intelligence in how she handled money. Perhaps it was a trait that she had inherited from her father.

Things were going well for the Cambodian family. Since their arrival in the U.S., they had managed to get jobs, put their children in school, buy a new car and house, and were living as a comfortable middle class family. It was every immigrant's dream to come to the U.S. and become successful, especially after enduring such horrendous atrocities in the war.

But along with the acquisition of new material things came the eyes of greed from Narin's brother, Vibol, and his wife. They were jealous of his brother's family and their apparent success. This spurned their desire to brainwash Narin against his family. Vibol wanted what his brother had, but the only way to gain access to it was to remove Rachana and her daughters from the picture. He tried to do it by turning Narin against them. And it worked.

Sophea already felt apathetic towards her father. Even as a young child in Cambodia, the secrets of Narin's abuse were locked tightly behind the lips of her childhood. Sophea was much too young to comprehend why, yet too brilliant to overlook the knowledge that her father's occasional beatings of her mother were not okay.

The abuse started when Narin's family told him that Rachana was planning to divorce him, right after the war had ended. By then, their family had already survived the Killing Fields. They were all lucky to even be alive. Divorce was not something Rachana had even considered since having their two children. They had already endured enough suffering and had made it through the worst together. That's why it came as such a surprise when Narin unsuspectingly hit his wife for the first time.

But young Sophea remembered it vividly. Her father came home from visiting his family and saw Rachana nursing baby Neary. She was still a newborn. When Narin saw her in this vulnerable state, he beat her up after an argument for which Sophea did not recall the reason for. Rachana was defenseless and held on to her infant daughter for dear life, hoping her husband would come to his senses. He did not. He struck her several times, before finally leaving in anger.

Sophea never understood or knew the reason for her father's behavior. Being only five, she was too young to comprehend such things. But children remember traumatic events and Sophea loved her mother more than anything in the world. She recalled seeing the tears on her mother's cheeks and the welts on her face from being punched. That was when Sophea turned against her father and began hating him. It may have also contributed to her lack of attention in the classroom and her struggles with school.

Now, as she looked down at her father's urn, Sophea remembered other awful times as well. The bad times outweighed the good with her dad. Narin once beat up her mother when Rachana refused to go to the bank to take out a $10,000 loan that he wanted to send to his brother Vibol, who was then living in the refugee camp in Thailand. By then, Sophea was in the fourth grade and the Longs lived in Oregon. These physical altercations worsened as Sophea became of an age to understand that it was not okay and downright unacceptable. Plus, the school systems within the U.S. were better at educating children against domestic violence. They taught the kids that it was wrong and that they should intervene.

One day, Sophea recalled police officers coming to her school to talk to the students. They told the kids that if they ever saw abuse or violence in their home, they were to call 911 immediately to ask for help. So, that's exactly what Sophea did. The next time her parents got into a huge fight, she called the police and they promptly came over and arrested both of her parents. Sophea and Neary were escorted by children's services to stay with a foster family for the weekend.

After that incident, every time Narin raised his hand to hit his wife, Rachana yelled, "If you hit me this time, you are not going to jail for the weekend! You are going for life!"

That was effective in stopping him. However, Narin found new ways to abuse her. Instead of physically using his hands, Narin used psychological tactics. He quit working, as his brother suggested. The only work he did were odd jobs, like yard work for cash under the table. He saved all his money and opened up a savings account with his brother. He never contributed to their family, just as Lee had never contributed, either. At one point, Narin and Rachana had a joint checking account together. He secretly cashed money out of their funds daily, until she caught on.

Narin didn't like his family much, especially his troublesome eldest daughter. He never forgave Sophea for calling the police on him. She never regretted doing it either, because she knew he was very wrong to abuse their mother. Narin also despised the fact that his daughters did well in school. Many times, he said to Sophea, "You will never amount to anything." However, his curse and harsh words only fueled her purpose.

Throughout high school and college, Sophea begged her mom to divorce their dad. "Neary and I will take your side if you have to go through divorce court."

"I can't. I made a vow to God," Rachana dismissed the suggestion. However, Sophea felt that their family could earn a living and have a better life if they could get away from his destructive behaviors. Narin's continual quest to destroy them all was something she strongly disagreed with.

Yet, Rachana continued to make excuses for him, even though she was unhappy in her marriage. "I have no other family in the United States," she justified. "I have to stay with him. I just don't believe in divorce."

It was a cop-out that was based on fear. Sophea surmised that if her mother had actually divorced him, their family would have been happier. But just like Thida, Rachana stuck by her man and turned the other way whenever she was mistreated. Both Lee and Narin filled their daughters with resentment, anguish, and disappointment. Two generations of young women had been affected emotionally. It was a shame, but not so uncommon among the many thousands of women who didn't have the courage to stand up against the actions of their husband's abuse.

Even though Sophea stood by her mother's decision no matter what, she was secretly thankful that her new life without their dad could now go on. Maybe there would be a happy ending after all. Sophea felt relief that he was gone. He had put them all through living hell.

Narin's abuse had not deterred either of his daughters' desire to become successful in life, although there were hardships to endure along the way. They had inherited their mother's fierce determination and yearning to learn.

As the funeral droned on, Sophea wrapped up her malicious thoughts about her father with an imaginary ball of twine. It was time to let it go and move on to positive things that were happening for her. It would take her mother some time to heal, but Sophea knew that she would eventually be fine. Without Narin working hard to destroy their lives, maybe things would be easier for all of them.

Sophea had also heard the stories Rachana told about "the one who got away," speaking of Phon. She had told her daughters about the tough decisions she was faced with and her mistake in marrying their father.

"My mother was right," Rachana regretfully told them one day, as she talked about the day she married Narin and the events leading up to her decision. "Always listen to your mother. I wish I had."

The minister wrapped up the funeral with a final prayer as everyone bowed their heads in respect. As the small crowd gazed down upon Narin's urn, they all had different thoughts. Sophea's relief was her mother's grief. Neary, too, was relieved that a new chapter of their life was about to begin. Vibol was only there for show, perhaps so that he could slap their family with a mysterious lawsuit later on by playing the role of a helpless, mourning brother. The professor glared at their family for most of the time she was there. She thought they had abused him and she had fully intended on prosecuting Rachana and her daughters to the maximum in order to send them to prison. And Narin's friends stared off, as if lost in thought about something else.

Everyone was there for different reasons. Life would go on one way or another.

Chapter Twelve

"First Class Citizen"

Tears welled in her eyes like chunks of ice melting from a glacier that had spent a day in the warm sun. Rachana squeezed both of her daughters' hands as they sat next to her, listening to the eulogy at Narin's funeral. It was a small ceremony amongst people she did not know well. If it were not for both of her daughters' presence, Rachana would not have even felt comfortable being there at her own husband's funeral.

She cried not for love lost, but for those enduring memories of what they had gone through together in their early years of marriage. Hers were much more profound, and perhaps one of the biggest reasons why she had stayed with him right up until his very last moments on earth. Yes, Rachana knew he was a scoundrel. She had basically told him so in the hospital. Narin hadn't always been rotten though. In a way, she had always clung to the glimmer of hope that he would return to being the loving husband that he once was in the first few years of their marriage. Like most abused women, she held on to the mistaken belief that he would one day wake up and change. However, he never woke up and never changed for the better. He only changed for the worse.

What she thought about now was not the abuse or the last few days, weeks, or years of their partnership. Rachana's thoughts traveled back to those days of fear in Cambodia.

Long before she had even met Narin and before the war broke out in 1970, life in Cambodia had been pretty good. In fact, there were a few years when she really came to know herself and was doing what she felt that she was put on earth to do.

After she received her teaching diploma in 1966, Rachana returned to her parent's house in Siem Reap for the summer vacation. At the state level, the graduating teachers had one more chance to choose among the different schools that they wanted to teach at. The school closest to the Sim's home back in Siem Reap was taken by another lady who had better grades than Rachana. However, this did not bother her because Rachana had decided not to return to her hometown anyway. The truth was, she had really grown tired of her father and did not want to live near him ever again. She had had enough of his ways.

Her grades placed Rachana next in line to choose a teaching position, so she picked the city of Kralanh. It was 70 km away from home. She was excited about that. She briefly remembered a guy named Eli who had begged her not to go there. She wondered for a second or two how her life would have fared if she had accepted his offer. Would he have been a better man for her than Narin? There was no way to go back in time and know.

All she knew was that she had made a mistake in choosing Narin. And instead of getting out of the mistake, she compounded it further by choosing to stick to the mistake for the rest of her life. It was one mistake after another and a downward spiral that she refused to walk away from.

Before all of that, living in Kralanh gave Rachana a chance to see something new. Finally, she was given a fresh new start at life. She was no longer reliant on anyone else to take care of her. She brought her mother along with her and two nieces, who were Phary's daughters. Thida always went with Rachana when she enrolled in school or when she moved to a new city for a teaching job. However, Thida didn't seem to mind the opportunity to experience other cities and enjoyed the fact that she could see and experience different places. She made new friends along the way. Both mother and daughter were very happy living in Kralanh.

Rachana loved the town, the people, her new job, and her new students. They were all so nice and loved her too. Many brought little gifts and handmade tokens of appreciation, such as fruits, eggs, vegetables, or small baskets of goodies. Although she was the toughest teacher in the school, she was also the favorite of the students.

Within her circle of teachers, there were four women who became close friends of Rachana's. One of them was her classmate and best friend from high school, Lana. There was also Lynn, Maly, and Em. All five ladies were single and got along better than rice and porridge. For Rachana, it was heaven on earth. Thida also thrived and made new friends in the city, which occupied her time while Rachana was teaching during the weekdays.

Rachana's group of girlfriends also loved Thida more than they loved even their own mothers. They gravitated to her kind heart and warm spirit. On their days off, all of the ladies did everything together. They went shopping, had picnics, went boating, attended the cinema, and hung out with each other in every spare moment. Their teaching careers enabled the young women to afford a nicer lifestyle than they had been accustomed to. They were all best friends. They had finally become "first class citizens," which was a term used for the educated society of Cambodians. They were all professional people in white-collar professions.

Rachana was proud to be the first one within the Sim family to achieve this status. It was the best time of her life. She was free, single, happy, and surrounded by great friends. She wished those days had never ended!

In 1969 just before the Cambodian Civil War broke out, Lana and Rachana went sightseeing to visit the Angkor Wat temple together. Lana had overcome a tough childhood, having lost her mother at a young age. She was also suffering from a broken heart. The boy she was in love with was not available for marriage because his parents were against their relationship. Instead, he had wed another girl they had chosen for him. Lana was devastated by the hurt of losing the love of her life. So, Rachana's way of cheering up her friend was to go on a mini-vacation with Lana for the weekend. Their friendship and support of each other was astounding.

Rachana reassured Lana by agreeing that boys were bad news, therefore they should both just stay single for the rest of their lives. Rachana wasn't in any hurry to marry either. She saw how much happier her mother was without Lee.

When Lana and Rachana walked across the dirt causeway to the Angkor Wat for the first time, it looked like a giant castle. Because of its mystical presence and great beauty, the ancient twelfth-century temple had many admirers and tourists. The fortress was designed to represent the splendor of the ocean and mountains of Mount Meru, which was a home to the Gods in Hindu mythology. A manmade moat surrounded the entire structure. Built in classic Khmer architectural styling, the great temple was rich with history and many secrets. At one time, the Hindu people believed the Angkor Wat to be the center of the Universe.

Also called the "home of the Gods," the elegant exterior of Angkor Wat was decorated with 2,000 heavenly angels carved dramatically along the eaves. To Rachana and Lana, the angels looked like real women. Some seemed to be dancing, smiling, giggling, or peering down shyly at the tourists. The angels leapt out of the wall, just as they had done for close to 800 years since the temple was built. Even at the time of the girls' visit, the Angkor Wat was still considered to be one of the seventh great wonders of the world.

The two young women walked around the neighborhoods of Angkor in awe. Both fell in love with the whole bustling community and dreamed of living there. Rachana was certain that her mother would love to live in this city. Located in the Siem Reap province, Angkor was still within reach of the rest of their family, while being far enough away to seem exciting and fun.

Lana elbowed Rachana as they walked and pointed to a few empty lots for sale. "Look, we could buy some land and build houses next to each other. We could live side-by-side forever!"

"Oh, what a fantastic idea!" shouted Rachana. The girls jumped up and down giddily. They were thrilled to see the land for sale.

"I think this is a sign from up above," Lana cried, enthusiastically.

"My house will be white and eggshell blue with drawings of birds on the side," Rachana dreamed out loud.

"Mine will be pale yellow with mango trees in the backyard," described Lana. Pretending they already lived there, the two girls vowed to return to buy two parcels of land adjacent to each other so they could always be nearby and stay friends forever.

"But you must bring your mother," added Lana. "I just might have to adopt her. She is the closest to a mother that I've ever had." Lana was very fond of Thida. Ever since her own mother passed away when she was only three years old, Lana never had experienced the joys of having a mother to care for her, especially one as beautiful and nurturing as Thida.

Their plan to buy the real estate was only delayed by the fact that the two girls would have to wait for the school transfer applications to open, which was not until April. But before the applications were ever available, the country was at war and the two girls' plans were postponed.

It was March–April of 1970 that the Cambodian Civil War escalated. Although they had already been battling alongside the war in Vietnam, it was during this time that the communist Khmer Rouge and their allies teamed up against the Khmer Republic, who was the government forces of Cambodia. The communist parties had been trying to revolt for years. They had become greedy and brazen after winning many battles.

Most of the citizens of Cambodia didn't fully understand the reasons behind the war, but hearsay of the gruesome atrocities that were underway made everyone terrified, and rightly so. The fighting brought massive casualties and a downward spiral to the Cambodian economy.

Not long after the war began in 1970, Rachana and her core group of friends were split up. Their happy days and dreams of buying land were over and replaced with uncertainty. Little did any of them know, it was the beginning of a decade of fear. Rachana moved her mother and nieces to a teaching position that was closer to home. The move came with a bigger salary in a bigger city. However, Lana never liked the city; it was too social for her taste. So she stayed behind, which saddened Rachana.

Rachana hugged Lana goodbye. "I'll miss you so, so much. You are my lifelong friend!" Rachana told her. They each went in separate directions. At that time, she could not know that it would be the last time they would ever see one another. Rachana learned later that Lana had died of an irreversible illness that same year.

The job Rachana had taken was in the state capital. It was only 16 km away from the Sim family home. However, the war made traveling difficult. Sure, the people were free to come and go, but they risked being shot by the Regime. Pol Pot and the communist leaders of the Khmer Regime wanted to crush the Cambodian government and that included anyone who worked for them or who was educated. The "first class citizens" were at the highest risk of death.

These ruthless dictators also recruited the primitive people of Cambodia to comply and participate in their widespread plan to rule the country by promising them power. They were the very same type of people who had helped Ponleau on his journeys to the mountains for trading. They were the uneducated people who lived off the land, the simplest of folks. Through ignorance and brainwashing, these people were recruited to become enemies of their own people.

Nevertheless, it was very dangerous to travel in between any towns while these conflicts occurred. Thida and Rachana only saw Lee when he came to visit. Thida stayed with her daughter full-time, making things very hard for her elderly husband. Lee had taken his wife for granted all of those years. He had barely known what the inside of a kitchen looked like and was now forced to cook for himself.

Instead of feeling any sympathy, Rachana was glad to have removed her mother from the situation. As far as she was concerned, Lee did not deserve to have a wonderful wife taking care of him. He had been born into a wealthy family with fifteen maids who served him hand and foot, then had married a fantastic wife who took care of his every need. Thida was a great cook, so Lee ate well every day. Lee had found the gold nugget among wives. She never questioned him, was always sweet and cheerful, hardworking, smart, beautiful, submissive, and content to put more than her fair share into the marriage. Lee was blessed. But he did not appreciate the blessing.

Rachana believed that those who abused or ignored the blessings they received in life should have them taken away. So, that is what she did. She took her mom away from her dad to come live with her. Rachana knew how to appreciate her mother and treat her the way she deserved to be treated. Lee held too much power in the family. Essentially, Rachana took away some of that power by having an education and an income from teaching. It gave her the freedom she wanted and a say in the family matters. Now, her father no longer held the reins of the Sim family.

However, Rachana was not entirely spiteful and did offer Lee the chance to move in with her and Thida. He chose to stay in his own home, close to the people he knew. Perhaps he felt as if they loved him more than his own family.

What a mistake. *How could outsiders love you more than your family?* Rachana wondered. *Who takes care of you when you are sick or too old to take care of yourself?* The outsiders had their own families to tend to. She had no sympathy for him. She would not send her mom back to live with him. He was the one that made his own life miserable. He made his own bed. He might as well have slept in it. Lee was even more stubborn than his daughter.

Things got so bad for Lee that Phary put her own house up for rent in order to move in with their father and take care of him. In contrast, Thida thrived and was happier than ever. She enjoyed living close to Rachel and Kalianne too. They were close enough that Thida was able to visit and spend time with her grandchildren every day while Rachana was at work. All of her daughters were thrilled to see their mother so happy and surrounded by her grandchildren. They all loved her immensely and wanted the best for her. Rachana also made sure she was the best-dressed woman in town. She gave her mom money to go to the market every morning to buy anything she wanted to eat, wear, or buy. Whatever Mom wanted, Rachana provided. Thida was showered with gifts and lacked nothing. She was happy and grateful.

It was not long thereafter that the saga between choosing Phon and Narin happened. Although Rachana was content being single and didn't feel like she wanted or needed a husband, her family had other plans for her. As Rachana looked upon Narin's urn, she remembered the pressure that she had felt to choose a man to marry. She had tried so hard to choose someone who was not like Lee, yet had made the wrong choice in men. One split second decision ended up being the mistake of a lifetime. It was a lifetime of regrets.

Maybe that was why Cambodian parents were called upon to choose the best partner for their children? Rachana silently wondered. It was a fine example of how a rebellious nature could lead to outcomes that affect entire families. *Mother was right*, she thought, *I pray my daughters don't make the same mistakes I made.*

By all accounts, Narin had seemed like the best candidate at the time. After they married in 1972, the two settled in together and Rachana grew to love him. She went from being addressed as "Miss Sim" to "Mrs. Long" by her students. She especially liked the fact that Narin was able to support them, which her father had not done for them. The steady job working for the government offered him a weekly paycheck, plus a monthly salary. He also had a daily allowance for petty expenses.

The rest of the population was not so fortunate. From 1972 until the fall of Cambodia in 1975, the war created a great depression for the entire country. Inflation was rampant. People could no longer provide for their families, especially those who held professional positions like teachers, bankers, businessmen, and others. The price of rice and meat skyrocketed. Some people spent an entire month's salary on a bag of rice. If it hadn't been for Narin's job with the government, Rachana would have been in the same boat.

This affected even people within her own family. Rachana's cousin, Kim Sivorn was Thida's sister's youngest daughter. Kim was only one month older than Rachana. Thida and her sister Ella had been pregnant at the same time with both girls. Because they often visited each other while the girls were growing up, Rachana and her cousin Kim were also very close friends.

Unfortunately, as the war escalated, the rationing caused starvation among many families. Kim's husband Thom did not have a very good job and they were unable to feed their family of seven. Knowing that Narin worked for the government and made a lot of money, Kim leaned on

Rachana to help them. She did so, willingly. Rachana gave them food and money and took care of them every day. She felt lucky to have a husband who earned enough to support them all. It also made Rachana feel good to help her own kin, just as Phary and Pitch had done throughout those years of high school and college. Even though she knew that Kim and Thom wouldn't ever be able to repay them, she didn't mind assisting them in all their needs.

However, everything was about to change. The cloud of darkness crept in. You could feel it in the air, like a thick panic of anticipation just before an accident. The looming mood of gloom was thick and heavy, like a locomotive racing toward a thin helium balloon just before it bursts.

Chapter Thirteen

"Sudden Change"

For many generations, April was the happiest month for Cambodians, Laotians, and Thai people. It was a time to celebrate the New Year with the biggest festival of all. Most people believed that God sends a new angel with each New Year to govern all the people on earth. As part of that tradition, everybody cleaned their house and put their lives in order. People believed that having a dirty house invited the devil, whereas a clean house was blessed by the new angel.

April marked the new year for farmers as the best time for a vacation after the harvest. With the grain all packed away in the barn and the hard work finally seen to completion, the farmers could finally enjoy the fruits of their efforts just before the monsoon season and heavy rains began.

Cambodians often used this time to travel, see their families, and do chores. Because after a few weeks, the planting season started up again. School was closed for a whole month. Everyone who wasn't cooking their favorite foods, picnicking, or playing traditional Cambodian games were often vacationing across the countryside. April was traditionally a time when people visited famous monuments like Angkor Wat, West Baray, and rainforests or waterfalls.

Right before the New Year celebration on April 13–15, the biggest celebration in the country was conventionally set up with a fairgrounds-like atmosphere in the middle of the farmer's fields. There were big movie screens with free movies in the evenings. Traditional dances, comedy shows, entertainers, and singers performed for all of the people who came. All of these shows were entirely free of charge.

It was also a time when a lot of the young men and women fell in love. The rest of the year, usually they avoided each other because of the strict customs that discouraged interactions between them. A young lady was expected to behave herself and not look at any man with flirtatious intent.

She had to avoid being seen alone with any young man. If she fell in love with any fellow before her wedding, she brought shame upon her family.

However, during the New Year's celebration, the young people had a little more "room to breathe." Not complete freedom, but a chance to interact with one another without watchful eyes the whole time. Regardless, it was always a festive occasion for the whole country.

But this was not the case on April 17, 1975. A cloak of darkness enveloped Cambodia during the New Year celebration. The entire country turned upside down. Some people were celebrating when it happened. The whole country was shrouded after the Khmer Rouge took control from the Khmer Republic. After five years of dreadful fighting that began in 1970, thousands of lives were lost and the ruin of the economy resulted in a new government takeover.

On that day, Pol Pot took over the leadership of Cambodia in a style that combined Marxism with agrarian socialism. It was a model based on Maoist China, which was against anyone being educated or having power. Therefore, most of his prime targets were not the ethnic minorities, but rather the native Khmer people themselves. Anyone suspected of being connected with the overthrown government may as well have been wearing a bull's-eye on the top of their head. As well as anyone who held a diploma of any kind or who held a professional career. Narin and Rachana were both. Bankers, teachers, lawyers, and doctors all fell within that category.

Narin had been working for the Cambodian government from the beginning of their marriage. And Rachana was a teacher. Both of these professions were considered to be intelligent jobs that were not allowed by the Khmer Rouge. Therefore, the educated and government sectors of Cambodia crumbled under the new infrastructure, with the first class citizens moving instantly to third class. Yet the good people of Cambodia were unaware of this plan.

They were taken by surprise with no time to act, nor prepare. Innocent people paid the price without knowing what was going on. Just before lunchtime, Pol Pot's new regime ordered immediate evacuation of the cities. Soldiers went from house to house, on every street, and in every neighborhood with guns, forcing people to get out of their houses without delay. No one understood what was happening or why they had been ordered to leave. They had no choice. They complied.

Panic ensued. Some people were separated from their families. The word spread all the way down to Rachana's house. She could see the armed men with tough-looking suits and boots coming. She quickly gathered everything she could. She packed every good piece of clothing they owned, like the silk and satin. She grabbed a mosquito net and blanket and loaded it onto the bicycle. Rachana also grabbed two large buckets, a set of dishes and a large pot, but she forgot the spoons and forks.

"Hurry Mom!" Rachana yelled to her seventy-four-year-old mother. Thida was quite healthy for her age and was a big help with baby Sophea. They got everything ready in a hurry, but could not yet leave until they were told to do so. They had to wait for the gunman to appear and give them orders. Bombs exploded nearby, startling them as they heard the marching of people coming in droves.

Rachana felt blessed that her whole family was with her on that day. Some were not so lucky. She heard some mothers crying and many who were worried about their loved ones. When the Regime came that day, the people were only given two choices. Get out, or be killed. The unexpectedness of it was something that shocked everyone. People had gone about their day as if nothing bad were about to happen. They did not know. They were not given a chance to say goodbye to loved ones, to pack, or have any plan to find each other.

Some people were at work. Some were out of town. Some had gone to the marketplace to run errands. But they couldn't wait for each other; they had to leave when the soldiers arrived. The people were only allowed to gather what they could carry and were ordered to follow the crowd immediately. As a result, many families lost contact with each other.

A neighbor from down the road showed up at Rachana's doorstep. Nearly breathless from sprinting, the teen kid said, "One of your best friends, Em, sent me to get you. She is very ill."

Rachana turned to her husband. "Narin, don't leave without me, okay?" He nodded. She set down her things and ran down to Em's house as fast as she could.

"Em, Em . . . what is wrong? You are sick?" Rachana asked her friend as she reached for her hand.

"I am. I don't think I can make it," Em said, gasping for air.

Rachana warned her. "This is not a game! This is for real. The gunmen are coming. You must pick yourself up and get ready now. They will not let you stay here."

"Where are they going?" asked Em with a perplexed expression.

"People are hitting the main road. But if you delay for even one second you will get the bullet!" Rachana pointed a finger at her heart, as if to prove her point. "I have to go now. I have to get my baby and my mother. I need to go, Em. Please, listen to me."

Rachana knew there was no time to waste and that she couldn't afford to be gone long. To lose her baby and her mother would have made life not worth living. Rachana ran back into her yard just as the group of soldiers arrived at their house. It was already dusk. They were very intimidating. She turned to one soldier and asked, "Comrade we are ready. Where are we going?"

"Just follow the crowd." He was rude and mean.

Rachana persisted. "For how long, Comrade?"

Still brief, he fibbed. "Just temporarily. Only three days. Then you'll come back."

Even before that day came upon them, Rachana had hidden all of their silver in the man-made pond that was in front of their house. With the economy having been so desperate during the war, there were more crimes and thefts committed. People sold much of their gold, silver, and valuables just to put food on their tables.

Thida placed one-year-old Sophea in the baby carriage. Narin loaded up a motorcycle with kitchen supplies, along with a one hundred pound bag of rice. It would be enough to feed the family for a whole month, plus the baby's needs. Meanwhile, Rachana packed the bicycle with suitcases that she had hastily put together. She was prepared for a time such as this, although most people weren't and had no idea what they were in for.

They left home just as the sun was setting, like a luminous fire of doom. By then, the masses of people were crowded in the street. Like sheep on their way to the slaughterhouse, the people of Cambodia just followed the herd. It was so crowded that everyone had to take very small steps, walking shoulder to shoulder. Relatives kept each other close, holding on to a piece of clothing or a hand. Otherwise, their family members would have easily dissolved amidst the crowd.

Thankfully, Rachana and her family were together. She was with her husband and mother, who carried baby Sophea close to her breast. By then, Thida had given the carriage away because of the difficulty in maneuvering it through the crowd. Occasionally, they all whispered to each other as a reminder to stay close together.

For a fleeting moment, Rachana thought of their dad. Phary had moved in with Lee to take care of him the last couple of years, but Rachana and her family lived way across the country in the capital, where Narin worked.

All night long, they heard people yelling out names, hoping to find their lost family members. The crowd continued trudging along, from dusk until dawn. After walking for about twelve hours, by daybreak the huge stampede of citizens had traveled approximately two miles. "Where are we going?" some yelled. Others kept quiet. They all wondered what was to become of them and what was happening.

When the sun rose, Rachana noticed how close they were to her cousin, Kim Sivorn's, home. They had walked about two miles, which normally would have taken only a couple of hours but because there were so many people moving in slow motion, it had taken six times longer. Cousins Kim, Thom, and their five children were still home. They cooked a quick breakfast under the house, trying to avoid being seen. After Kim and Rachana's families all ate, they stuck together and got back on the road to join the rest of the crowd.

Thom knew the area quite well. The new people joining them along the way were people who had just been rounded up by the soldiers. Many scrambled to gather a few belongings and valuables. They crammed suitcases full with clothes, money, and anything they could grab. The gunmen said very little, except, "Get out!" People asked what was happening and if they would be allowed to return? But the gunmen lied and told everyone the same story. "In three days you can come back."

Three days turned into a long two weeks. Everyone was confused. *What was going on? Where were they going? What was happening?* Nobody knew.

The crowd continued walking and eventually reached a big town. Whenever a small handful of people stopped, the entire herd stopped with them. Everyone camped under the stars for a few days until the gunmen came back around to say, "Move, move, move." They all followed each other; they were the lost following the lost.

Some starved to death within only a few days. They were those who had not anticipated the change and who were unprepared. Some simply lacked the resources to have stashed away extra supplies. With the downturn in the economy, many citizens had struggled for the past few years.

Others killed themselves because they were afraid or tired or lost without their families. The walk alone was more than many people could bear. Rachana witnessed a mother with just a purse and her little boy holding her hand as they passed by. They were skin and bones. People who didn't have supplies starved to death. Nobody could share. They were only able to live off whatever they were able to carry. So a few of the not-so-smart people simply put their money in a wallet or purse, thinking they would buy some food along the way. If only they had realized just how long it would be before they were to ever see a marketplace again, then perhaps they could have planned better. Hence, the money in the woman's purse was useless and she could not do anything to feed her toddler. It was tragic.

Some people started bartering gold or jewelry in exchange for food. A young, wealthy Chinese entrepreneur who had three big bags of money with him committed suicide, because he could not do anything with his money. Rather than starving to death as some did, he simply took his own life.

Many more people died of dehydration. Everyone slept on the hard ground at night, with bumpy pebbles pressing hard against their backs. The herd continued walking, passing through vast plains under the roof of an immense sky. The outdoors lacked protection from the elements. These new orders from the Regime represented a tremendous change for all of the people of Cambodia.

As they traveled down the dusty roads of the recent harvest, most people were quiet. They barely dared to speak. The general feeling was one of hopelessness and despair. People were depressed. They missed their homes, their belongings, and their lives. They missed their loved ones. *Where were they going?* Nobody knew. The smell of death drew near as some chose to end it all without ever even reaching the destination.

They had not yet learned that the Regime was sending the entire population on a forced march to work in the fields or in the forests. One of Pol Pot's plans was to redevelop the country's entire agriculture system based on an eleventh century model. Therefore, Western medicine was to be abolished, temples destroyed, libraries demolished, along with anything that resembled Western ways of thinking.

The cities and towns were emptied out, losing all of the busy energy that made them so alive. Instead, the people were all jammed on the main highway, bumping shoulders just to get a space big enough to take a few steps. They walked under the scorching sun by day, through the jungles, plains, and rice fields that had just been gathered. Their road was one to destruction, one of misery and exhaustion.

When the sun set, everyone stopped to unpack and find a place to rest for the night. Some who still had food cooked dinner. To those who were getting down to their last rations, the smell of food drove them crazy. A few fights ensued as a result of desperation. Nobody could predict the next day, whether they would live or die.

Rachana was thankful that her husband had packed a hundred pound bag of rice. They knew how to make it last. They still walked with the Sivorns, although Kim had become quite cold to them lately. Rachana chalked it up to the stress of the circumstances and the uncertainty that was felt by all. Considering their situation, Rachana felt safer traveling in numbers. Kim and Thom had a family of seven. Thom's brother and family of three were with them too. With the five in Rachana's party, that made three grown men who were there to protect them all. One of the men often slept with one eye open to make sure there were no thieves to steal their food in the middle of the night.

Every time the stampede of people came upon a village, they were quite happy. They walked straight through the center, hoping to find others. Sadly, every town had become a ghost town. People were stunned. *How long had the people been emptied from the villages? Where had they gone?* No one knew. They just kept walking.

Finally, they all arrived in Sandan, which was Thom's birthplace. All of the houses in Sandan had disappeared and were left in crumbles, destroyed by the war. He was saddened by the state of the place he had remembered with great fondness. It was severely damaged from the bombings.

There was one big house left partially standing, although in very bad condition. A few families had gathered at the house. Some were upstairs. Others were under the house. Rachana's family got a little spot underneath the house that was shared by four other families. Nobody knew what to do next. Everyone felt hopeless and distressed, especially Rachana. Not just because of the displacement, but because the person in whom she thought she could trust had turned on her. Cousin Kim now treated her with contempt, despite the many years of help Rachana and Narin had offered to their entire family. Status no longer mattered. Everyone was of the same status. They were now third class citizens, no more important than the very dirt they walked upon.

There was a Khmer saying, "The crocodile soon bites the hand that feeds it." Now that the Longs were unable to feed her family, Kim rejected them. It seemed she had been using them the whole time. Family no longer mattered. Rachana overheard Kim and Thom arguing one evening.

"I do not want her to stay in this village with us. We will have to feed her and her whole family. Look at her. She is so weak that she can't even carry her own baby. How can she make a living? It will be you and I feeding her and her family!" Kim said to her husband.

Thom replied, "Have you already forgotten what she and her family have done for us all of these years?"

Yet, Kim had no conscience. "I don't and won't accept her. That is that!"

Upon hearing this, Rachana decided it was time for her family to leave the area. She knew they would be in great danger if Kim ratted on them. By now, people had heard rumors of the killings of many professional people and were advised to remain anonymous if at all possible. So, for her family's safety, Rachana planned to break away from the Sivorns without telling them of her plan. She decided that Kim could no longer be trusted. If she told the new Regime that Narin had worked for the government, they could all be killed.

Narin talked with Thom in private. Thom had been grateful for all they had done to help his family. Since they were in his hometown, Thom knew of a boat he could borrow to take them cross the Mekong River. Rachana's plan was to journey back to their birthplace and to hopefully reunite her parents. Even for her mother's sake, she knew that Thida was worried about Lee and wondered if he was okay. His health condition was not as strong as hers and she wondered about his wellbeing.

The Longs left without saying goodbye to Kim. Thom told his wife that he was taking them on the boat. It was risky. Kim didn't even come to bid Rachana and her mother goodbye. The same woman who had come to Rachana's house every day to eat her food and take extra money for her daily needs now despised her. Rachana was of no use to her anymore.

Right before they set out, Thom and his brother came to see them off. They handed Narin a plastic tarp to use as cover when it rained. In the past, it would have been thrown away, but under the circumstances it was a priceless item. The monsoon rains would be coming any day. And when they did, it would open up a whole new set of difficulties in traveling and staying alive. The heavy summer rains were often accompanied by hail and sometimes down-poured for many days on end. It was no time to be outside without shelter. Along with it, there was flooding and mosquitoes, which were known to cause malaria. The tarp was a welcome gift and nice gesture on Thom's part.

Rachana cried a mixture of tears over the loss of her cousin's love and out of gratefulness in the gift from Thom. "I cannot accept this gift, for it is too precious," she wept. "You need it for you and your family too."

Thom wouldn't hear of it. He looked at their family sympathetically, knowing the Longs were unprepared for any hardships. "We are staying here now and you still have a long journey to make. Please take it."

It was May of 1975. They had been traveling for an entire month. The river was swollen, making it unsafe to go across in a small boat. But they had no choice. Their hearts were heavy. Their future was uncertain. They could no longer think. Thom rowed the boat to the bank across the strong current and helped them to unload.

The goodbyes were tearful, mixed with fright and disappointment. As Rachana turned her back on Thom to leave, it was a face that haunted her for thirty years. She could clearly see the sad look in his eyes. After they walked a short distance and were nearly out of sight, she turned back one more time to see him still standing there on the boat, staring at them as they walked away. Thom was sure they would not survive. The weak and unprepared were the prey of the hunters. Not just the new military, but also the dangerous wild animals that lived in the woods. It was the last time that Rachana ever saw him again. Thom was one of the millions of innocent Cambodians who were killed.

After travelling for a couple of miles, Rachana was even more afraid when she realized that her husband was now the only male in their group. Her seventy-four-year-old mother was stronger than she was. Rachana had been skinny and scrawny her entire life, even more so now with a lack of good nutrition.

Thida carried little Sophea, who was only a year old. They all slept on the side of the road, along with other random travelers. On those nights that it rained, they sat up and held the plastic tarp over their heads as cover and for protection of their belongings. They were so grateful to Thom and his brother for giving it to them. The tarp was very useful.

The Longs didn't realize that they had not even gone through the worst yet. It was only one month into the new order of the Communist Regime. They were all vulnerable as they reached their new destiny. It was the Killing Field.

Chapter Fourteen

"The Devil's Checkpoint"

The Longs were now on Highway Seven. After a few days, there were more tag-a-longs that joined up with their group. Rachana was spotted by one of her students, who approached her.

"Oh, I am so happy to see you," said the young girl. Her name was Sasa. "Would you like to come meet my family?"

Happy to finally meet up with someone she knew, Rachana agreed. Besides, it was better to travel in a bigger group than to go alone. The sparse crowd was not enough to protect them from any harm. They were just happy to travel with another family.

The next day, their group arrived at a big, beautiful Buddhist temple. By now there were about twenty who had joined up with them. From afar, they could all see that there were a lot of people gathered there. It was human instinct to seek companionship, as traveling solo even with family was scary. But when they arrived at the grand door of the temple, they saw the new regime had taken over the whole place.

With guns in their hands, the intimidating soldiers directed them to walk in. Everyone spent the night there, camping out on the floors of the temple. There were at least a few hundred people, maybe more.

In the morning, Rachana ran into another one of her students, a young lady named Justine. She was overjoyed to see Mrs. Long and without thinking she yelled, "Hello teacher!" right before the eyes of the gunmen. It scared Rachana to death. If the gossip she had heard was true, Rachana didn't know what could happen to her.

Justine didn't realize that her friendly greeting could have been a death sentence on the spot, just by addressing her as "teacher." Quietly, Rachana whispered, "Please, do not call me teacher again. From here on out, my name is Cha-Cha."

The girl nodded. Having a grassroots name made her sound less educated. Only hillbillies and backwoods people had names like "Cha-Cha."

The Regime served all of the people rice with sweet and sour fish soup. While they hungrily enjoyed their breakfast, the administrators went around with notebooks to write down everyone's professions. They did it in a manipulative manner so that people were honest. At that point, the citizens were unaware of what was to become of them. Having a good career should have been an asset instead of a liability.

One of the leaders took the microphone. He bellowed, "Attention everyone!" as they all looked up from their breakfast. "You will all be regrouped and taken out on the farms to make a temporary living until the new Regime gets settled in. It is VERY important for each and every one of you to give an HONEST report of your profession. That way, you can still retain your previous job!"

It was a lie, but it worked. Everyone was as honest as could be, both out of fear of getting into trouble with the intimidating soldiers or of losing the opportunity to return to their professional jobs.

There were desks lined up with administrators. The weary travelers all stood in lines, waiting for their turn to talk to the serious-looking members of the new order. When Cha-Cha and her family reached their turn, the young lady with the notebook acted very different with them. She had a nice smile and gently asked them each the same question that she had asked everyone else who had already gone through the line. "What do you and your husband do for work?"

Cha-Cha was honest. "I am a teacher and my husband works as a government employee."

Strangely, the woman kept grinning and only wrote their names down. She did not write anything else. "Thank you. Please, go sit with that family," she instructed, pointing to Justine and her family.

There were only three families in their section. The remaining teachers were sent to sit in one spot. The policemen were in another group. The military and government people were in a third group. All of the professionals were categorized in the same manner and placed within their appropriate clusters, along with their families–men, women, and children too.

Cha-Cha kept looking at the young lady who had assigned them to the corner. She was disappointed that her whole family had been shunned to the section of the unemployed. Cha-Cha was worried that they would be left out and unable to get their jobs back ever again. However, she was too afraid to question the administrator's decision or to disobey. No one dared to ask why. After the grouping of each family was finished, each soldier took charge of a group and ordered them to get up. They all left. The group of teachers went one way. The group of government employees went in another direction. The lawyers and policemen followed a third soldier, and so forth, until all of the individual clusters had left.

The only group remaining was Cha-Cha and Justine's families. Then someone declared over the microphone after all the parties had left, "The rest of you, go to your own destination!" With that, they were free to go. They could go anywhere they wanted.

The Longs were upset, particularly Cha-Cha. They all felt scared and abandoned. They stood up and got back on the highway. By then, they were all very weary from walking and traveling. Narin and Cha-Cha were not strong people. Plus, they had a seventy-four-year-old elderly woman to consider and a small baby, which slowed them down considerably. So Justine's family walked ahead of them, soon leaving them behind altogether, although they did so in kind regards.

The highway was beaten down and the Longs continued walking at a slow pace. They knew that the road would eventually lead them to Siem Reap, where Thida hoped to find her husband and where Cha-Cha hoped to find peace at her birthplace. *Why did that lady exclude us?* Cha-Cha wondered. It was mysterious salvation.

As she would soon discover, those small herds of people were taken to their deaths. If the woman had sent Cha-Cha and Narin to their respective groups of professionals, they would have all been killed. The Regime had no need for the educated people anymore. Yet somehow, God saved them that day through the kindness of one woman.

The Regime had made mass graves for people in the middle of the Killing Fields. Groups were lined up and beaten over the head once or twice with a rock, shovel, gun, or tool. They were then shoved into the hole, whether they were dead or alive. Many innocent people were killed in this manner.

Others were shot with a bullet to the head. Some were burned in chambers filled with gas. But Cha-Cha wouldn't learn of these atrocities until much later. Instead, they continued walking as their lonely family tried to make it home.

Leaving that place, they were separated from Cha-Cha's other student, Sasa and her family. During the interviewing process, Sasa's family had been put into a different cluster, according to her parent's professions. Sasa's group was the first to leave. Her father was a soldier in the military under the Cambodian government. Their group was the first to go, although no one knew where they would be taken.

A few days later, it was a pleasant surprise when Cha-Cha and her family caught up with Sasa. Everyone was happy and Sasa's parents hugged them all. That was when Cha-Cha learned what had happened to the rest of the groups.

That first night after leaving the temple, Sasa's family had secretly overheard one of soldiers speaking to a fellow Comrade. The new Regime's intent was to kill the whole group. They were talking about their plan to do it very early the next morning. The new orders were to kill all of the professionals and there was to be no one left alive who was affiliated with the former powers of Cambodia, especially within the government and military professions. So in the middle of the night, Sasa's family ran away. They had nothing to lose by fleeing, since their destiny had been with death.

Sasa asked her former teacher, "And how did you get here? We thought we would never see you again."

By then, Cha-Cha was unnerved and trembling after hearing what was happening in her own country. "It is a long story and I do not want to talk about it." Silently, she was thankful that the lady who had checked them in had spared them by sending her family to the group of unemployed people.

The Longs stayed together with Sasa's family and felt safer. Now there were two men and seven women in their party, plus the baby. They had lost track of time. No one knew what day it was. What month. All they knew was whether it was day or night.

They continued on, hoping to get to the town of Siem Reap soon. Some people they passed on their journey told them about a big checkpoint for the Regime up ahead and to be well prepared. Kampong Kdei was a long bridge just within the Siem Reap province. They had walked 254 km from the capital of Phnom Penh. It seemed as though they were getting close.

About two miles from the bridge, they all decided to rest and camp right next to the street. They would get up early to get through the checkpoint. Suddenly, in the middle of the night flashlights shining in their faces rudely awakened them. They were soldiers. One of them grabbed

Cha-Cha's suitcases and started rummaging through them. Whatever they found that they liked; they took. One soldier found Narin's overcoat.

"You must be a government employee!" he yelled to Narin. The coat was a dead giveaway, as it was easily identified with a logo worn by many government officials.

Cha-Cha cut him off quickly, before he finished his sentence. "No, Comrade. We are farmers. This thing I traded with a man to use for my baby as a blanket. You can see it has to cover the baby." She pointed at Sophea, who was lying next to her grandmother.

"It is mine now," he proclaimed.

The soldier was not convinced, but after they took what they wanted, they left. The Longs were frightened beyond belief. They all stayed awake until morning. All of their belongings had been dumped out onto the ground, so they had to repack everything to prepare for the danger that was ahead. Cha-Cha rearranged one of the suitcases and Narin took the other. Suddenly, he froze. His eyes grew bigger than car headlights as he dropped his jaw in utter disbelief.

"Honey, did you know that your diploma is in here? The savings book and bank statements too?" he asked his wife.

Cha-Cha's hair stood straight up. Narin put the items in his pocket and they rushed to make some adjustments to protect themselves. Both were quiet, as they knew they could have easily been killed last night. They shook their heads, wondering how the soldiers had not seen their paperwork after dumping everything upside down. Within their stuff were red flags of danger that could have clued the Regime into the fact that they were both educated and could read.

Even her name, Rachana, was a dead giveaway. She was safer hiding behind the nickname that her father had given her, which he still called her right up until the last time they had seen one another. Cha-Cha.

Narin asked, "What shall I do with these?"

Cha-Cha suggested, "Why don't you say you need to go to the restroom and walk ahead of everybody? Behind the bushes in the rice field and under the water, push them in as deep as you can. They should be safe there."

Narin did as his wife told him. Then they all nervously approached the devil's checkpoint, which was also set up for the big headquarters of the state. The Regime were now settled in the town there, with the houses still standing and everything intact. However, all of the people had been evacuated and the new powers had essentially taken it over.

Before the war, the city had been a thriving marketplace. Unbeknownst to many Cambodians, the people from this town had been living as prisoners of war since 1971. The Khmer Rouge had taken it over a long time ago and had settled there to carry out their plans.

Cha-Cha and Narin had lived in the capital when the Prince was still in charge of the country, until that dreadful day of darkness in April of 1975. The communist headquarters were in a different location. The Khmer Rouge had already chased most of the citizens of Kampong Kdei out to the forest. It was easy to see why the Regime had made their headquarters in this nice town. It had a modern highway, bridge, grocery store, shopping place, etc. Location was everything, including a main crossing point for people coming and going.

There was no way to avoid going over the Kampong Kdei Bridge, since it was one road that merged. This passageway left people vulnerable, since there was no other way around it. The Khmer Rouge had designed a checkpoint for people to stop and go. They were like trolls on a bridge who carried intimidating weapons and wore grim expressions. Whether they found anything on their person or not, the soldiers detained people for different reasons. Some were sent to the forest. Others were not so lucky and were killed if they did not pass the interrogations.

Cha-Cha's family walked toward the checkpoint. They were afraid. Hell was right in front of them. Life and death stood face to face with them, depending on how they played their cards.

Life was very fragile now, just barely more significant than a wrong word across the tip of your tongue. The gunmen handed each family a mat made of palm leaves for them to empty all of their belongings onto. They dumped out their bags and suitcases. One soldier came around to sort through everything, while the other stood guard with his gun. The Long's surprise visitors the night prior had been sent by the devil, but their discovery of the paperwork had saved them by getting them better prepared for this moment.

The interrogation was very serious. The family was ordered to sit in the middle of the street. The soldiers made sure every word was recorded. The Long's biography was recorded in the book of death. The devil was deciding life or death for them. They were asked difficult questions and were studied thoroughly for any misleading facial expressions. The mean-looking gunmen tried to get people to crack.

After the interview, Cha-Cha's family was held there for a few days. They became prisoners of war in their own country. It was not safe to talk or even to breathe. They sat in silence as they awaited the verdict, feeling much like a defendant who awaits the outcome of a jury. Their lives were in someone else's hands.

If the soldiers found anything, they would take people away individually. It could be a certificate, diploma, bank statement, or even a business card. It could be as simple as a pin to celebrate an achievement, anything. Then they would know you were not a farmer. They would take you somewhere and kill you.

Three days later, in the very early morning, Cha-Cha noticed people starting to walk back onto the highway. It seemed promising. They all got up and gathered things together. They were ready to move. They didn't care about washing their faces or combing their hair. They just got up to go. *To where?* They didn't know. They just followed the leader.

When they got to the highway, there were thousands of people marching. One of the Comrades who was the head of security spoke out loud to Thida. "Aunt, where is your birthplace?"

Cha-Cha's mother answered quickly. "Srok Puok!"

"Oh! Sorry Aunt! You have to go according to our plan, just for a while. You will be alright." The soldier addressed her as one of the elderly, who the Khmer often referred to as "Aunt."

Cha-Cha whispered, "Mom, do you recognize him?"

"No Honey! My eyes are not that good," Thida replied under her breath.

However, Cha-Cha thought he looked familiar. She tried to recall where she might have seen him before. He looked like one of her father's acquaintances from Krabey Riel. "Do you think that is Keo?" she asked her mother. "From Krabey Riel?"

"It could be. That part of the state was long controlled by the Regime. I think since the day that the war broke out in our state," Thida answered.

Upon her answer, Cha-Cha felt even more desperate. If he knew them, then they would be unable to hide their identities. Yet, he was so friendly to them. He must have recognized them. Thida looked so sweet, like an angel. Everyone always wanted to help her.

After half an hour on the highway, the crowd turned off to the right. Everyone was worried. *What was next?* No one dared to ask. They continued walking all morning and all night through the fields and the jungles. Nobody knew where their destination would be. Would this be their last walk on earth?

Despite the frightening walk, the jungle was so beautiful, like a giant wonderland of greenery filled with abundant wildlife. The moss covered grounds offered softness and mystery underfoot, which was at least more comfortable for walking than the dirt and pebbles. The soles of their shoes were nearly worn down to their threads, having journeyed so far and for so many months. Occasionally, the walkers spotted a deer or a wild animal running across their paths, as they screamed in awe. It was no wonder Ponleau loved his trips through the mountains, with the splendor that surrounded them.

Most of the group were from the city and had never seen wild animals before. But by midday, they had walked their way out of the forest to the other side. It was merely a shortcut to a Buddhist temple that the gunmen were taking them to. By then, everyone was hungry and exhausted.

This temple was somewhat like the first one Cha-Cha had seen along her travels. This time, she wondered if the outcome would be less favorable. By then they understood the Regime's quest to kill. Nevertheless, the soldiers fed everyone lunch. It seemed like a good sign, until one of the leaders took the microphone and ordered everyone to turn in any weapons or knives, both big and small. Any sharp metal objects within their possession were to be confiscated on the spot. Valuables were to be released. That is, if anybody had anything left.

Upon orders, Narin had to turn in the motorcycle and the bicycle. Without the bikes, the Longs were unable to carry all of their stuff. This posed a huge predicament. Cha-Cha was worried, because over the past few days, baby Sophea had developed diarrhea and was running a fever. That was a dangerous combination for an infant, and one that as a mother, she simply couldn't accept.

She looked around and spotted something that caught her eye. Under the monk's house, Cha-Cha saw a few carts that people used to carry merchandise. She darted fast to get one and load the baby into it, along with their belongings. This was after all of the valuables had been turned in. For a fleeting moment, Cha-Cha didn't care about consequences, or what her mother or husband would say about stealing. Upon instinct, she just loaded everything as swiftly as possible into the cart and then pushed it away. If the soldiers caught her stealing, she was certain to be killed. However, whenever Cha-Cha didn't see any other solution, she acted on impulse.

The people who were dismissed were free to go anywhere and did not get sorted into groups. Again, it was dependent upon the results of their interrogations. The people who saw Cha-Cha with her cart asked her why she was allowed to keep it. She ignored them. She pretended to be mute.

Silently, she was thankful for her moment of courage and bravery. Because of her quick thinking, Cha-Cha's family was able to move easier and a little faster. Thida was finally able to walk freely by placing the heavy baby in the cart, instead of carrying her. The cart was a lifesaver and a godsend to their family.

As they traveled with weary feet, the smell of death surrounded them like an ominous vulture. The flies swarmed over the shallow holes of mass graves, which held thousands of people. Cha-Cha came across one man who had dug himself out one night. He was one of many people who had been buried alive. Cha-Cha recalled meeting up with the man again one day later on in life. He had gone to the U.S. and became a widely respected engineer. How fortunate he was to have dug himself out of a grave and then continued with his journey to become successful in life. But he was only one exception. Millions were not so lucky.

The Longs continued on, still hoping to make it back to Siem Reap at some point. Cha-Cha came across another student of hers, Colla, who she was very happy to see. But the girl was dazed, bewildered, and frightened. Her hair stuck out in every direction as her eyes filled up with tears. She looked like she had just stepped out of a nightmare.

"What happened?" Cha-Cha asked Colla with a troubled tone.

The young girl showed her the deep, fresh gouges that wrapped around both of her wrists. They were still red from recent bleeding. Her clothes were soiled and stained with smudges of blood. Then, Colla described her escape:

"The soldiers brought all of the teenagers to the temple. Everyone was stuffed in there, like cotton balls stuck together. It was overcrowded. They locked most of us in there. Some suffocated to death. Guards stood outside . . . so the people couldn't get out," she took a breath. "Those who didn't fit inside were tied to the outside of the temple by their wrists and ankles," she said, pointing to her ankles and extending her wrists for them to see. Colla hyperventilated as Cha-Cha reached in to hug the young girl.

She went on. "Then, the soldiers sprayed the temple with gasoline and set it on fire. There were thousands of people still inside, screaming to their deaths. The guards shot whoever tried to escape. The gunmen hid in the trees nearby, just watching as the people screamed to death in the burning temple." The girl puffed, flapping her hands animatedly. She was breathless just from telling the story.

Horrified, Cha-Cha and her family gasped. Thida clapped a hand over her mouth. "You poor honey!" she exclaimed.

Colla was only one of about ten people who escaped. She ran deep into the forest, despite the tigers and dangerous wild animals that lurked in there. Given the two options, tigers were less fierce than the soldiers who tried to kill them. Behind her flee of terror, the temple burned flat with the charred souls of those inside who had met their living hell.

Guards continued chasing her through the woods, as Colla ran for her life. Finally, they caught her because she had nowhere to run. They bound her bleeding wrists together and then had the nerve to ask why she ran away. "Please! Let me go," she begged the ruthless gunmen.

Cha-Cha asked Colla, "Where did they take you next?"

"With you, and this crowd," Colla answered. "Wherever you are going. Do you know where that is?"

Now even more fearful, Cha-Cha said, "No. We were ordered to follow so we're just going with the flow. I hope they are not taking us to our death, but it doesn't sound good."

The teacher hugged her student, whispering to her not to let on that she was ever a teacher. Colla nodded in acknowledgement. She understood why.

The next day, the journey started out again. It was early, as usual. The herd of people got up and moved on, wherever they were made to go. Like cattle that were rounded up and shuttled to the slaughterhouse, no one asked why. They just followed the crowd.

This time, the group came into a different jungle, where the leaders searched for a certain village. The village was infinitesimal compared to the vast foliage of the Cambodian jungle. It was close to Prey Chkar in the middle of nowhere. Finding the tiny community was like looking for a single coconut amid a giant stack of bamboo, especially because of the heavy rain. The monsoons had made their way for their summer rampage, which increased the humidity and bleak undertone of the peoples' moods. The smell of the dreadful rains added to the thickness in the air and the hopelessness of spirit among those who walked to their unknown fate. The darkness of the skies came early.

Many people just sat in the rain in despair, as pellets welted their skin. Hardly anyone had a plastic tarp to cover themselves. The water dripped down their foreheads and soaked their clothing. By now, no one needed to put themselves in someone else's shoes. Everyone was wearing the same shoes. No one felt the pain and terror that each of these people felt individually, although they shared in the same experience.

As they trudged into the village, the rows of houses made a path through the center of dwellings. Huts had been built on each side of the path. They were lined in two rows, one on the left, and the other on the right. Most were no more than little shacks on bamboo stilts. The stilts were in place to keep the tigers from breaking in, as well as being necessary to avoid flooding during the monsoon season. The Comrades finally told the new people they were going to stay. They were ordered to settle in by the end of the night. The residents of the village were told to share their living space with the new people. Each family came forward to offer a space within their dwelling.

"You will stay here!" One of the leaders addressed the tired walkers. "You will work. Many of you will be sent to the rice fields when it is time."

For a moment, the people were relieved that they were going to live. On the other hand, it sounded much like slavery. Which was worse, death or slavery?

Only twenty families lived in the tiny community. These villagers were born and raised in the forests. Even though they had an abundance of high quality wood surrounding them, they didn't know how to build a nice house. Just a small shack was sufficient for them to live in. Without an education, it was a carefree, yet primitive way of life. They didn't know any better and were content with what they had. Up until now, it had been a peaceful and quiet existence.

Each of the villager's houses added one or two new families to join them. The bigger houses held as many as three or four additional families, although it was hardly comfortable for anyone. Some stayed upstairs. Some stayed under the house. Cha-Cha didn't care where they ended up—whether it was upstairs or under the house—just as long as they stayed dry and out of the rain. She was concerned for her baby and her elderly mother.

The Comrades introduced the mountaineers and peasants who lived there to the new bunch who had arrived. "This is your new home until we tell you otherwise! And these are now the first class citizens!" The leader pointed to the village people, who had always been thought of as third class by society. The people who were evacuated from the cities were now third class citizens. This was a complete reversal of how it had been before.

The educated folks fell to the bottom of the totem pole and the laborers were appointed with high-ranking positions and control. It was one of Pol Pot's strategies to build up power by shifting control to the poor and taking it away from the middle and upper classes. Therefore, even barbaric mountain people had the authority and permission of the new Regime to kill. They became Comrades. They were allowed to be as ruthless as they wanted to be. They were taught to hate, not to love. It was the dictator's plan to put the former city dwellers to work, digging ditches, and planting rice and vegetables. They had much work in store for them. Some of them had never held manual labor positions and were physically unable. Those people died. If someone was of no use to Pol Pot's new government, they were as good as dead, not even worth the bullet that killed them.

The Longs were chosen to stay with Chuck and his family. Their home was humble and sparse, hardly protection from the elements. At night, the jungle was especially scary. The pitch-blackness was filled with wild creatures like tigers, elephants, monkeys, and poisonous snakes. Nobody was allowed to travel on the road alone.

After two nights in the jungle without sleep, baby Sophea was now very ill. Cha-Cha was too. They both had a fever and Cha-Cha also had a bad migraine that would not go away. Most likely, it was caused by dehydration and lack of sustenance. She had already been thin even before their ordeal began, but the last couple of months had taken its toll on her frail physique.

Thida gently asked one of the Comrades if they could move into the community kitchen, at least while her daughter and granddaughter were sick. The amazing spell she had on people was miraculous. Even the killers wanted to help her. They couldn't resist her sweet face and soft-spoken voice. It was like trying to look into the eyes of a sweet kitten and say no.

Through a stunning effort, the Comrades agreed. Although the kitchen didn't have any walls, it did have a roof. The Comrades let them stay there. It felt like a luxury hotel just to have a roof over their heads. Sophea and Cha-Cha were both critically ill by then. One of the gunmen, Comrade Pat, passed by to make sure everyone was where they were supposed to be in the village. Upon seeing the elderly woman crying, he stopped and asked, "What is wrong with them?" He pointed at Cha-Cha and Sophea.

Weeping, Thida answered. "My granddaughter has diarrhea and a high fever. My daughter also has a high fever and a fierce headache. Comrade, please have pity on me. These are all the family I have. Please . . . help me Comrade!" she implored.

Pausing for a minute to decide whether he should help, Comrade Pat told her, "I'll be back with medication."

When he returned half an hour later, Comrade Pat brought an assistant with him. He delivered an injection to both Cha-Cha and her baby girl. After an hour or so, Cha-Cha's headache calmed down and she was able to sleep peacefully through the night. She was amazed for his help, knowing that their plan was to kill, not to heal.

For Sophea, the recovery was slower. But the baby persisted. The medication helped and Sophea's condition improved.

The heavy rains put a damper on the Regime's plans to start work immediately. However, they found work for everyone in the group, including things that could be done in preparation. For now, the fields were too saturated from the heavy outbursts of rain that had been dumped upon them.

When she felt better, Cha-Cha got the most honorable job of carrying buckets of human feces to be used as fertilizer. Although it was gross, the job was better than what some people had been assigned to.

However, Cha-Cha had not completely recovered from the illness and was still weak. She could only take baby steps as she carried the burdensome buckets. Her aging mom now had two patients to take care of, her daughter, and granddaughter. Their family had run out of food by then. Thida was growing desperate to do something.

Early one morning, Thida got up and chose a few sets of clothes that she intended to barter in exchange for rice. Her plan was to walk to the next village. Thida was stubborn enough at her age. "I'll be back in a little while!" Thida yelled to her daughter.

"Be careful." Cha-Cha warned her mom. Thida was unfamiliar with the territory. The forest swallowed her from the very minute she set foot in it. There were tigers in the woods and strange, wild animals to contend with. It was no place for a seventy-four-year-old woman.

By evening, Cha-Cha grew very worried when her mother had not returned. She was devastated and heartbroken. She pulled Sophea tightly to her chest and rocked her back and forth. She cried herself to sleep and let the baby cry too.

At night, the people of the village never came out of their houses. They were dreadfully afraid of the tigers, and rightly so. The tigers were vicious and liked to prowl for food. They scrounged for meat or any morsel. There had been attacks on the village people over the last couple of decades, so the locals knew better than to come out when these creatures were prowling through the jungle. The tigers were stealthy, with their quiet padded feet and glistening white teeth, eagerly drooling for a piece of flesh.

One of the newcomers had not listened to the warnings. In an attempt to escape, the recent arrival found himself as dinner for one of the hungry beasts. The village people discovered his hands and what was left of his legs only three or four hundred yards away from the main path in their community.

Cha-Cha was afraid.

Where is Mom? Her thoughts ran rampantly. The next day, Cha-Cha got up very early. With her baby by her side, she sat on the side of the road to wait for her mother. She sat there all day, becoming more and more distraught as her mind raced with many thoughts about her mother. *Had she been caught by the Khmer Rouge?* One of the guards could have reported her to the main powers, the ones who had authority to kill. No one was pleased with the new leadership. Their freedom was lost. They had been exiled from their home. They lost their normal way of living.

Was she eaten up for dinner by a hungry tiger in the forest? Cha-Cha's thoughts made her crazy with speculation. She spent the whole day worrying. She had grown accustomed to her dependence on Thida for everything. *What would she do now?* Cha-Cha wondered if she could even live without her. Her mother was her whole world, her rock.

As the blue sky filled with stars and a crescent moon rose high into the sky, Cha-Cha finally picked herself up from the path and wrapped Sophea gently in her arms. As a mother, it was her job to protect her baby with her own life, even if she would have rather waited for her mother on that path forever until she returned.

Alas, it was another night without Thida. The third morning came and Cha-Cha no longer had the energy to sit by the road waiting for her mom's arrival. So, she sat under the house with baby Sophea. She was a good baby and didn't cry. Instead, they just sat there looking at each other. It was as if the baby knew her mommy was upset, so despite feeling sick, Sophea sat still.

Meanwhile, Cha-Cha was heartbroken.

Chapter Fifteen

"Tiger's Eyes"

The small hint of sunlight peeked in through the cracks of the tattered palm leaf roof. Morning had come. Suddenly, Thida came walking miraculously out of the forest! Cha-Cha and Sophea's faces both lit up in utter shock. Sophea began jumping up and down, cooing and smiling with her three teeth showing as she saw her grandmother's face. She wrapped her little arms tightly around Grandma and giggled, as Thida picked her up. Sophea's face was filled with the joy of a child who had suffered great hardship, yet who still had love in her heart.

Thida turned to Cha-Cha and squeezed her hand tightly. She said, "Honey, everything's alright. I am safe . . . I am here." Then she massaged Cha-Cha's chest to help her breathe better, since the girl was hyperventilating.

Thida then told her the whole story. "I am very sorry to make you worry. When I left here, I went from house to house and everyone told me that they were running short of rice. They were very kind to me; they did not lie to me about their supply and even showed me how much they had left in their house. Everyone around this area is hungry, just like the rest of us. They told me the nearest village I might have luck finding food in was Phum Tnot. Then they gave me directions to get there. My thinking was that if I left right away, I might arrive before dark. I had no time to come back to let you know. I just left. I thought I would return by the next morning." She paused, as Cha-Cha listened intently.

She continued. ". . . but I was lost in the forest. I was so scared. I walked briskly. I ran and prayed to God that he may preserve my life to come back to you. Never before have I ever been so afraid of losing my life; but I knew that you and Sophea both need me more than anything in the world."

By now, both mother and daughter were weeping. Amazing powers protected the elderly woman from the tigers and showed her the way to go. Even more astonishing were the things that Thida was capable of doing at her age. Running, jogging, and walking many miles with no lunch or dinner in her body would have been enough to kill many healthy young people, much less a seventy-four-year-old grandmother.

Yet, Thida's strength came from the love she had to save her child and granddaughter. Cha-Cha was amazed and overwhelmed by Thida's courage and dedication. She only hoped to be as good at raising her daughter as Thida had done in bringing up such a difficult child as her. Thida would have laid down her life to protect her own children.

After they both dried their tears, she continued with her story. It was almost dark when eventually Thida had come upon a building in the middle of the forest. It was a dangerous hour to be in the woods. The building was also risky, as it turned out to be one of the headquarters for the Khmer Rouge. A gruff voice yelled to her from the darkness. "Is anyone there?"

"Yes." Thida walked closer to the building because she had nowhere else to go. She knew she had to appear before them. They let her in and asked her a lot of questions.

"Where are you from?" asked one of the soldiers.

"From the village, Prey Chkar," she replied.

"What's a woman your age out walking in the dark this time of night for? Surely you must know the tigers are hungry," said one of the Comrades.

"Yes, Comrade," Thida agreed. "But my daughter and granddaughter are very sick and no one in the village has much food to spare. I was on my way to Phum Tnot to find something to bring back. But I got lost."

"Here, eat something," the officer said as he pushed a plate of porridge and fried fish to her. She wolfed it down hungrily.

The officers let Thida spend the night in their headquarters and were very kind to her. In the morning, they asked her to stay and wait there. "Some Comrades are coming here and will be on their way back to Prey Chkar," instructed one of the officers. "You will go with them."

Not wanting to cause a disturbance, Thida complied. She didn't want to wait there but was afraid to say anything that would make them angry. All day long, Thida waited with the soldiers, but none of the new Comrades came by as expected. She had lost a whole day and knew her daughter was probably stricken with worry. She had no other choice than to obey them and spend another night. The jungle was too risky. While Rachana worried, so did Thida. They had a strong connection even when they were apart from one another. It was a parent and child's bond that few could ever experience.

In the morning, the soldiers handed Thida a basket of fresh corn. "You can go. Sorry to keep you from your granddaughter. If we come across a Comrade coming your way, we'll ask them to pick you up." They were very kind to her, although they could have easily killed her. It was in their nature to kill, but Thida's warm persona could melt even the heart of monsters.

Carrying the basket of corn, Thida hurried back to the village as fast as she could. Three days of worry was enough to make anyone crazy. As she jogged back, the cover of the forest was a leafy umbrella of protection from the hot sun. She passed by several mounds of graves where the spirits of the deceased were interspersed between the trees. The village people believed that the dead should be buried far away from the community because their spirits were happier within the forest.

Cha-Cha was thankful for the corn, and so was their host family. She started a fire to cook it, smiling in gratitude for her mother's safe return. They were both thankful and vowed to take care of each other, no matter what. Cha-Cha begged her mother never to leave the village without her again.

After a while, Cha-Cha regained a little strength back, at least enough to go work in the fields. The Khmer Rouge ordered everyone to work. Narin had already been working from sunup to sundown. His family rarely saw him.

Sometimes the soldiers let the workers leave at about one o'clock in the afternoon to go to the forest and eat table roots or pick them to feed their families. They tasted disgusting and bland. Cha-Cha was still so weak and frail that she could barely go with the others. They walked too fast and she was afraid to be left alone as bait for the hungry tigers. Being so thin and weak, she was also at a huge disadvantage. Many of the other people had already died from starvation, at least those who had not been killed by the Regime. Still others had killed themselves. They couldn't endure the hardships and had lost loved ones. Some had no desire to live anymore. But Cha-Cha still had her family. She knew she must do whatever it took to stay alive for them, for her baby daughter and elderly mother.

Since most of the workers left without her, Cha-Cha had to find another means to feed her family. She discovered a small creek on the other side of the village. In the summer, it was dried up, so there was a lot of wild bamboo growing along the banks. While everybody else went for the roots, Cha-Cha went for the bamboo shoots. She knew they were a very useful vegetable for cooking.

Cha-Cha brought the bamboo shoots home to her mother, who sorted them out. Thida chose the good stalks–the biggest ones–and took them to exchange for salt. She got just barely enough for each day's need. This became their ritual. It was Cha-Cha's daily job to earn their living. They ate bamboo shoots for lunch and dinner, mixed with a little rice.

There was a bucket in one place that all of the villagers had to use for the bathroom. Specifically, for number two. It was quite an archival means of relief. The Regime had appointed Cha-Cha as the poop patrol. They made her remove the bucket of poop every day and carry it to the communal garden, where it helped the vegetables grow better. It was her daily chore. However, Cha-Cha figured it to be an easier job compared to others who had to dig, dig, dig, and carry heavy rocks and perform hard labor.

One day, as Cha-Cha approached the empty creek on her daily routine, she heard a noise that she had never heard before. It sounded like a few baby animals. It was not exactly like puppies or baby cats. She crept slowly, trying to listen intently. *What kind of baby animals were these?* Cha-Cha couldn't distinguish the whimpers. With cautious steps, she peered through the bamboo. *Could it be a baby deer?*

As she got closer, Cha-Cha made the distinction. A voice inside of her told her to run, run fast. It sounded like kittens. Aha, it was a tiger's babies! Her instinct wouldn't let her wait to find out where they were or where their mother was. She knew if they were close enough to hear, that it was too close for comfort!

Cha-Cha's hair stood on end as she whirled around. Her heart beat faster and faster as the adrenaline kicked in. *A tiger and her babies?* Her feet kicked in with heart-pumping adrenaline as she immediately ran as fast as possible. She ran until she made it underneath the house that they were staying in, within the village.

The lady of the house, Peach, poked her head underneath, full of surprise. Chuck and Peach never had much of a relationship with their intrusive guests, so Cha-Cha and her family just stayed in their own corner of the house, went to work, and came back. It was rare they even spoke to one another.

"Cha-Cha, what happened to you?" Peach asked.

Breathlessly, she said, "I was so scared . . . I just ran for my life."

"From what?" asked Peach.

Cha-Cha took a deep breath. "When I approached the creek, I heard a sound like a lot of baby cats near the creek. I couldn't see them because they were behind the bamboo."

Peach nodded. "Oh! It was probably a mother tiger and her babies. This is the time of year they are born. Good thing they did not see you. You can never outrun them. Nobody in this village has ever outrun a tiger. Many have died. In fact, the women of the village do not go to that creek with any less than ten people and when we do get close to the forest or close to the creek, we all yell and scream to alarm those ferocious animals. We take turns to make noise and keep yelling to each other."

Dumbfounded, Cha-Cha thought about the many days she had gone down to the creek all alone. Peach added, "Every day I was worried about you. I wasn't sure what makes you so courageous to go to the creek alone and come back in one piece so many times. Are you not afraid of those wild animals?"

"Yes, but I didn't know . . ." Cha-Cha said, naively. "What should I do now?"

"Why don't you go with your people in the fields, instead of going off on your own?" suggested Peach. "They all go for the roots or yams. Don't you like those?"

Cha-Cha replied, "Well, I did go with them once, but I couldn't keep up with them. I was lost but I thank God that I found my way back. You remember that day; I came back with nothing?"

Peach warned her, "Do not go anywhere alone. It is not safe. You learned a lesson today. It was a warning for you."

It was nice of Peach to tell her this, but that left Cha-Cha now with only two choices. One was to stay safe at home and starve everyone in the whole family to death. She could bow down to fear and become obedient to death. Alternatively, she could face the danger and fight for more than one life, including those of her family members.

After she calmed down from the fear of the moment, Rachana chose the latter. She decided to get up and give it another try. Most of the new people–the people who had become third class citizens–had died of hunger. Every day, more of the dead were buried in mass graves on the hills and plains of Cambodia. Many died in the rice fields too. They dropped from exhaustion, dehydration, or starvation. Pol Pot did not care. The Comrades didn't care either.

It was a blessing that Thida was not put to work by the Regime because of her age. Because of this, she was able to go to other villages to barter. Their family had already run out of the silks and valuable clothes and materials they had brought with them, but thankfully, they still had some jewelry to offer in exchange for rice. They didn't get very much rice for every good piece of jewelry. Bamboo shoots had to be added to the rice when cooking to make it thick enough to eat, since the supplies were sparsely stretched. Nevertheless, it was enough to keep them fed and still alive.

Bravely, Cha-Cha came out from under the house and began to walk slowly back to the creek. She was reluctant. Her feet told her no. She mumbled to God along the way and asked him to chase the dangerous animals away. *Please, keep me safe,* she prayed silently. She knew she had to do this for the sake of her family. She would not lie down and die without a fight.

Hurriedly, she rushed back to the edge of the stream. Cha-Cha had never cut bamboo as fast in her entire life. She grabbed and pulled the stalks as if the tiger were already chasing her. Cha-Cha did make it home safely, although she didn't pick quite as many bamboo shoots as usual. Thida wondered why there were fewer than usual, but didn't question her daughter about it. She knew there must have been a reason. It was best not to complain.

One day, Thida addressed her daughter. "I am going to visit Tevy."

"Oh, who is that?" asked Cha-Cha. She was a new friend that Thida had met in the village.

"A woman who is nice," replied Thida. "She told me to stop by today and made sure that I would not forget to swing by her home."

"Enjoy, Mom," Cha-Cha smiled. After a couple of hours, Thida came back with her hands full, lugging a big satchel full of wraps with banana leaves. She was so happy as she opened the satchel.

Cha-Cha's eyebrows rose with delight. Thida said, "They asked me to eat all I could, but I asked them if I could bring them home to you instead, so that I could share them with you." Her daughter was touched by the gesture.

During the first year of the Regime's power, nearly two-thirds of the prisoners of war in their area died of starvation. People hid food from each other, but not in Cha-Cha's family. If anyone had so much as one bite, even one morsel of food, they took it home to share with the whole family.

Their family faced many intense challenges, but they quietly bared them within their own hearts. Once the rice-planting season came upon them, the Regime sent all of the healthy adults far away from home to work in the rice fields. Therefore, Cha-Cha had to leave her young two-year old daughter with her elderly mother to care for while she went to work. Narin was with another group of men who were sent to a separate location. The women and children were required to work in a different place. The men went south and the women went north with the children.

The Regime called the group of men "The Great Army." They were all men and young teenagers who were mobilized far away from home. They started their days before daybreak, even before the sun rose. They stopped only after the sun went over the horizon and the darkening sky was too dim to see what they were doing any longer. They slept under the stars in the open fields.

Those who got sick were killed. The Regime's rule was "*If there is no benefit to keep them, there is no loss to take them out.*" People were afraid of becoming ill. The healthy ones were made to work seven days a week, often twelve to sixteen hours a day amidst unfit conditions. There was nothing left to live for.

Chapter Sixteen

"Survival"

I t was difficult for Cha-Cha to be away from her baby girl and mother. She missed them terribly, and thought about them all day. Every day she monotonously planted the rice seedlings in the muddy fields, alongside the other women and children who were sent to work there. Her new job was not what she had wanted to do with her life. Cha-Cha's education had not paid off after all. The fact that she held a diploma was now of insignificant inconvenience. If the Regime found out she held a degree, she would be killed. It was a secret to withhold instead of something to be proud of. Her accomplishment was her shame.

Thankfully, her mother was taking good care of Sophea. The only solace to her new life in the rice field was a friendship she had struck with another woman named Minnie. Minnie was a second class citizen. Cha-Cha was now considered third class. They were the lowest on the chain of power and the first to be killed, even for something as miniscule as looking at an officer the wrong way. The second class citizens were in between slaves and leaders. The first class citizens were the mountain people and all of those who had joined forces with Pol Pot's new order.

One day after work, Minnie taught Cha-Cha how to catch rice crabs with her bare hands. They were not allowed to have any weapons, nor any means of getting food. A net, knife, or spear would have been confiscated. Cha-Cha still had some powdered milk cans that she brought from home for Sophea, when they had fled their home in April of 1975. After the milk was gone, she was able to use the empty can to put crabs in. The slaves (third class citizens) didn't go home at night most evenings, so the only way to get the crabs to her mother and daughter was through a messenger. And the messenger who helped Cha-Cha was a most unlikely assistant.

He was a first class citizen, Comrade Keo. Every night, he walked from the rice fields back to the Prey Chkar village, where he slept. It was highly frowned upon for any first class citizens to be caught helping those who were second or third class. However, Comrade Keo had a soft spot for Thida and Cha-Cha. He delivered the can of crabs to Thida every evening and then in the morning returned with the empty can for Cha-Cha to refill with crabs again throughout the day.

In this way, she was able to accomplish two things. For one, it was a subtle message to her mother that she was alright, plus she was able to supply her with meat for the day. Cha-Cha felt like she was still taking care of her family.

There were not many crabs in the can, usually only three or four. Cha-Cha always kept the smallest one for her own dinner. It was barely the size of her big toe, which was smaller than an average woman's foot.

Both mother and daughter were thankful to God for Comrade Keo, who had never before helped anyone to carry things from one person to other. Miraculously, he was willing to bring the can of crabs to Thida and return the can every morning to Cha-Cha. This was unknown to happen to anyone who was a prisoner of war. Perhaps there was a supernatural thing working in his heart. The Comrades were assigned to kill, not to save. It seemed to the mother and daughter that this was just a small glimpse of hope. It also represented a very important message to both of them that they were both alive and well. A lot of times, Comrade Keo engaged in conversation with Cha-Cha to report on her mother's wellbeing. The two women became very fond of him, which proved to be an important asset in times ahead.

As the harvest season drew to an end, there were many hundreds, maybe thousands of people who worked in the rice fields. Those who had not fallen to their death from starvation, exhaustion, or dehydration were to be sent back to their villages. They had come from many different directions to converge and work in these fields, per the order of the Khmer Rouge.

One day, an ominous mood overtook the sky with a charred pink and muted gray exterior. The clouds rolled in as the workers looked at each other, not knowing what was about to transpire.

Across the hillside, they strolled in.

Men with machetes, they were from the military. The Khmer Rouge was done with the prisoners of war. Their time had expired. For no reason, they were to be slaughtered. Soldiers baring clubs, tools, hammers, and machetes crept in as unexpectedly as a pack of lions coming for the elk, attacking the weaklings first. The workers had no weapons and barely enough energy to run for their lives.

Hundreds of people ran, screaming, panicking, and scrambling. Many were stabbed, decapitated, or beaten to death as the fields became littered with human bodies–innocent human lives. They were no guiltier of a crime than a slave at the hands of his master. The Regime chose people to kill with no rhyme or reason. No harmony. No recourse. They were of the devil.

Many more that were captured were taken to Phnom Penh, where the Chao Ponhea Yat High School became the site of a grim prison camp. People there were divided into schoolrooms that had been turned into crude cells. Prisoners of war were then processed for execution by interrogators, who were ruthless criminals of the Regime. As many as 20,000 people were massacred. No one could escape the grounds after they arrived at S-21, due to the razor-blade barbed wire that wrapped around the perimeter.

S-21 and other prisons were turned into concentration camps. The prisoners were forced to make up confessions of acts of treason against the new order. Some folks just made up stories in an attempt to save themselves, but were then tortured regardless of their cooperation. First, they were starved and tortured. They were sleep deprived or neglected. After the Comrades ran out of places to bury them, the innocent people were taken to an extermination site with their entire families. Men, women, and children were not exempt from being killed by a pickaxe, machete, iron bar, or a club. No matter their ages, from toddlers to elderly. Ammunition was scarce, so the Regime used other weapons.

Then, whether they were dead or alive, the people were thrown into the mass graves. These were the rules that the Khmer Rouge required of all POWs:

You must answer accordingly to my question. Don't turn them away.
1. *Don't try to hide the facts by making pretexts this and that, you are strictly prohibited to contest me.*
2. *Don't be a fool for you are a chap who dares to thwart the revolution.*
3. *You must immediately answer my questions without wasting time to reflect.*

4. *Don't tell me either about your immoralities or the essence of the revolution.*
5. *While getting lashes or electrification you must not cry at all.*
6. *Do nothing, sit still and wait for my orders. If there is no order, keep quiet. When I ask you to do something, you must do it right away without protesting.*
7. *Don't make pretext about Kampuchea Krom in order to hide your secret or traitor.*
8. *If you don't follow all the above rules, you shall get many lashes of electric wire.*
9. *If you disobey any point of my regulations you shall get either ten lashes or five shocks of electric discharge.*

Meanwhile, the majority of the remaining Cambodian citizens became prisoners of war who were sent to work. They too were used unfairly, although at least they were able to move about. Many were killed randomly. After the rice season was finished, the remaining workers were sent back to their own communities, whereupon they were made to work in the villages.

After returning from the fields, Cha-Cha saw the condition of her beloved mother. She had become very frail and weak from lack of nutrition. As she took her mother's pale hands between her own, the daughter worried with eyes of tears.

Thida spoke, "Honey, I can hardly walk. I think a bowl of chicken soup would give me my energy back."

"Huh? Chicken soup, Mommy?" Cha-Cha looked at her inquisitively. A few chickens strolled near the front stoop of their dwelling. They had bartered for the birds so they could have eggs to eat. Since they were alive and walking about, Cha-Cha wondered who was going to kill one of the chickens to feed her ailing mother. She considered herself much too frail and peevish ever to kill a living creature.

Her heart was troubled. As she looked into her mother's eyes, they were glassy and wet from feeling sick. It was a struggle for her mom to even lift her arms and legs. Never before had Thida asked for anything, no matter how tired, sick, or terrible she felt. This day was the first time the superwoman had asked for any particular food. It was the first time Cha-Cha could remember such words ever coming from her mouth. She knew she had to do something, but what?

Cha-Cha looked up the road to see if there were any signs of her husband coming home. Surely, he could kill a chicken for them. But there was no hope, even after she waited and prayed for Narin to arrive.

After a day went by and darkness covered the earth, Cha-Cha lay beside her mother, awake. She could not sleep and spent most of the night thinking, *what should I do?* Just thinking of killing a chicken scared her to death, especially with her bare hands.

The next morning, Cha-Cha got up early to do her daily duties as the poop patrol. At lunchtime, she came back with a bowl of rice as her reward for the day. Using a few pieces of salt they had, Cha-Cha was able to make their lunch and dinner. The rice was better than the banana trees the Regime had given them to eat when they first arrived. Some of the victims had died of indigestion from the toxicity of the banana trees. Or from starvation, just from choosing not to eat it. However, Cha-Cha's family had overcome that. Now, Thida's old body was calling for a little protein, which they had lacked for quite some time. She could barely swallow her food and was growing weaker every day.

Once again, Thida said, "It would be very good to have a bowl of chicken soup."

Cha-Cha was sad to hear these words again from the mouth of a woman who never asked for anything. She knew she must choose between two things—being a coward and not coming through for her aging mother, the same woman who had given up her entire life in selflessness for her daughter—or get up and do something that would be a small form or repayment.

As she sat by the door dangling her feet over the chicken coop, Cha-Cha suddenly stood up and threw down her leftover porridge. She watched the chickens and tried to muster enough courage to do what she needed to do. The chickens gathered by the porridge, as they were hungry and took advantage of the free meal.

Suddenly, she grabbed one of the chickens with two hands and held it. The others scurried away in fear, and Thida jumped up and down, afraid of what her daughter was about to do. Funny, she had no strength to walk but when she saw her daughter catch the chicken, the old woman ran around the corner as fast as she could. She ran even further away than the chickens.

With her heart beating faster than if two tigers were chasing her, Cha-Cha trembled. Her heart was pounding so hard that she thought it would knock her breath away. She picked up a knife from Peach's kitchen and cut off the chicken's head in one brave swoop! With that, she thought her duty was done until low and behold, as she took her grip off the chicken's body it got up, flapped its wings all over the place, and ran away!

Now petrified, Cha-Cha thought she was seeing a ghost with the headless chicken running every which way. Her face was bright red and she thought she might have a heart attack at any moment. The chicken hopped like a rabbit as Cha-Cha ran all over the yard after it. Not only was she afraid of the headless chicken, she was also afraid that if anyone saw her kill it, they would kill her for doing it.

The animals belonged to the Regime; even if it was yours and you were raising them. If anyone was caught killing a chicken, they would kill you for failing to contribute and for going against their rules.

At last, Cha-Cha caught the decapitated animal and this time she stepped on it until she heard its bones break. It was a hack job and ruthless death for the chicken. However, if anyone had witnessed her chasing the beast around the yard, it might have been good for at least a chuckle.

She bundled up the meat and took one good-sized breast to prepare it for a meal. One piece of chicken made enough soup for all of them. In fact, it made many meals for the next few days. Thida was appreciative of the effort and made an amazing recovery. She just needed some nutrition, some protein to circulate through her body and to replenish her energy.

Meanwhile, Cha-Cha was happy to have done a good deed for her mother. She had surprised herself with having enough strength and courage to do the unthinkable to save someone she cherished. When faced with life or death, sometimes women were able to do things they would never normally do, especially if it meant saving her loved ones.

Not long thereafter, Narin finally made it back to their family after being gone many months with his crew. He too had worked in the fields. The men were treated much worse than the women. He had witnessed many deaths at the hand of the Regime. Nevertheless, Cha-Cha was happy that he had made it back safe and sound to their family.

Chapter Seventeen

"Trip to Talien"

In 1977, there was another small change in the Regime. They burned all of the books and all of the history of Cambodia. Their goal was to start again from year zero in accordance with the new order, a model that was based on communism and Marxism. For that reason, the citizens of Cambodia lost their identities. Many of the towns and maps were also destroyed. They wanted to renew the country with their wave of policies and strict control.

Within the village of Prey Chkar, there was a shift in power and the Khmer Rouge began sending some families to Talien, which was about twenty miles closer to the highway. For Cha-Cha, this was welcome news as she viewed the closer proximity to the highway as a better life that was more populated. The people there had more knowledge and some were educated, although she could not have known the condition of the town from her small, sheltered life in the forest. Instead, she saw an opportunity. She bravely went to the leader of the village.

"Comrade Keo, I wish to ask a request," she said, with much respect.

"What is it, Cha-Cha?" asked the stern Comrade.

"I have heard that many families have been transferred to Talien. I would like to ask if we could be sent there?" she asked nicely.

"Cha-Cha, you are safe with me. I like you and your family a lot. I will send other people," he replied.

"How many families are you going to send down to Talien?" she responded.

Comrade Keo told her, "They instructed me to send twelve families."

She thought for a second. "Please let us go."

Now wondering what she was up to, he asked, "Why, don't you like us?"

Without skipping a beat, Cha-Cha answered, "Yes, I do like you a lot. But, Comrade, I miss my family. My mother has five daughters, who she cries for every day, and my father. With this move, who knows? We might be able to find someone who knows the whereabouts or some news about my family. Please, have mercy on my mother. She does not expect to see them but if we just heard any news about them it would give her peace."

Comrade Keo pondered this. "Okay! I understand her. They say men don't cry, but they are very wrong," he confided. "I have all my family except one I long to hear from—my only daughter. I have cried about this sometimes. It is difficult not knowing. But I warn you ahead of time. You should prepare for the worst."

Cha-Cha had no way to know that Talien was where the Regime had executed thousands of people. By now, well over a million people had perished from executions, concentration camps, beheadings, mass killings, and death by gas chambers. There was mass starvation and some just ending their own lives to avoid dying at the hands of the Khmer Rouge.

However, in Cha-Cha's heart, she felt a strong need to go there. She had a compelling urge for them to move. Her internal instincts were guiding her. It was time to go. God had a plan for them that they knew nothing about.

It was the best decision to make. Before they left, Cha-Cha and her family thanked Chuck and Peach for their hospitality, although they hadn't really done any more than what they had been asked to do. The village family did have a soft spot for them, regardless of whether or not they were supposed to. The Longs set out on their new adventure with their toddler and elderly mother. It was an arduous journey, but not one that was any worse than they had already become accustomed to.

After walking to Talien with eleven families and three Comrades, Cha-Cha and Narin scoped out the layout of the land. She knew that she'd be able to find better food there for her mother. She did. The salt was aplenty, more than enough for Thida to enhance her main menu.

Their family had bartered for a small kitchen knife that was barely big enough to cut meat. This was the only tool they had to build a shelter with. Narin used it to start cutting down small tree branches, as the two women gathered sticks to build with. They settled upon a place near the edge of the forest so they could live off the land. Their plan was to use the abundance of the fields and the roots, herbs, and other treasures that grew wild amongst the leafy vegetation.

This was to be their next home. They became gardeners and planted tobacco, eggplants, sweet potatoes, taro, green onions, and other fruits and vegetables. They smoothed the dry ground with sticks, rocks, and some debris such as boards that they had come across.

The garden would provide more than enough food for them, as well as giving them something to barter with. Now they could trade for rice, salt, or fish and have much better meals. On her lunch break from working for the Regime, Cha-Cha went fishing. All of this food was more palatable with the salt they had available to them.

They were hard workers and the garden kept them occupied. Narin also dug a well so they would be able to draw water. Life was still hard, but much better than it had been in the rainforest. At least now, they felt optimistic, even proud of their little handmade shack just on the outskirts of the jungle.

The better meals and nutrition gave them all more energy. Thida and Sophea were healthier and happier, as well as being more energetic. Sophea was now a toddler and wanted to play more. Things were fine for a few months. However, even though they were no longer living in the forest, their family was not out of danger. A few months later, there was another change in power to clean up the Regime.

One morning, Thida got up with Cha-Cha to talk to her. Normally, her daughter left just before dawn to commit to her day's duties working for the Khmer Rouge. On this day, her mother had just experienced a terrible dream. Thida said, "Honey, listen to my dream! It must mean something, but I do not understand it. It was so real."

She told it as follows, *"Sophea and I were walking from the little pond. Suddenly, I heard a loud voice screaming with a most frightening shriek. Tiger! Tiger! Tiger! Tiger! It was a voice from the village. As I turned my head to see where the scream was coming from, I saw a big, huge, ferocious tiger running straight toward me. I was so scared! I looked for any branch or just a piece of wood within reach so that I could scare the fierce animal away. Its teeth were long and sharp with a snide growl and snarl. But I could find nothing within arm's length except a meager piece of straw. Then, I was astounded as this vicious beast lowered itself on the ground and let me and Sophea get on its back to ride it. Just after we mounted the great tiger, I woke up."*

"What does this mean?" Thida asked Cha-Cha, as if she were an interpreter of dreams.

The pond Thida spoke of was a small man-made pond that had been dug by some of the workers for the Regime. At the time, one of the Khmer

Rouge headquarters had been built within close proximity to the place that Cha-Cha's family had built their dwelling. The soldiers had since moved on, leaving the place to be abandoned for some of the migrant families who still worked nearby. The Longs were one of those families, but unbeknownst to them, there were many hundreds of bodies buried close by, right near the pond. The spirits of the victims lingered nearby.

"Wow. I don't know, Mommy, but whatever it means, it will be good for all of us. Do not worry," Cha-Cha reassured her. With that, she left for work because it was against the Regime's policies to be late. If you were late, you were lazy. Lazy people were killed. The armed men made them work hard doing laborious things like digging, building, planting, harvesting, and other busy work that would benefit their new order. Being one second late was a sure inducement for insults by the guards, or even worse. The insults were done by placing the person in the center of a group of people to set an example for the rest.

Cha-Cha had witnessed the ramifications with her own eyes, as one fellow was ordered to dig his own grave. He was spit on, kicked, and made fun of by the soldiers. Then, after they hit him senselessly with shovels, they rolled him into the shallow hole that the man had dug for himself. No one was sure whether he was still alive or not when they put him in there and covered the hole with dirt. No one was allowed to cry or show any sign of emotion; or they were warned that they would join him. The witnesses cried silent tears within the privacy of their own thoughts.

That evening after Thida's dream, Cha-Cha came home and took a bath with a bucket of water and a rag. She rested for a few minutes before putting herself back to work in the garden. She was thankful that Narin had built a well for them so their family would have water and the privacy of bathing, as well as using the water for tending to their garden. Thida had also planted things around the well to hide it while they were drawing water, so as not to attract too much attention to their small slice of luxury, albeit rustic.

After relaxing for a few minutes and re-gathering her strength, Cha-Cha went out to tend to the garden. It was a beautiful night with a full moon, making the pulling of weeds and sorting much easier by the light of God's natural splendor. In fact, Cha-Cha was actually enjoying herself. The stars were brighter in the country, with no pollution, no fog, no factories, and virtually no civilization. It reminded her of home, where the river behind her parents' home had been surrounded with nature. At night, the moon danced across the water like a lullaby.

While everyone else went to bed to get as much rest as they could, Cha-Cha was working yet another shift of duty. But this was more enjoyable, since it was for her own family. Just as she was about to draw water from the well to water the vegetables, a loud voice called out from the dark, coming from the front walkway of their humble house.

"Cha-Cha, are you sleeping yet?"

She recognized his voice. She hid the bucket behind some tall plants within the triangular-shaped parcel of the garden and started walking toward the voice. "*Drat*," she mumbled under her breath. She smelled danger.

Sure enough, around the corner at her front stoop stood two leaders of the town. First class Comrade Chan and Comrade Odom were killers and Odom in particular was the meanest of all. He was especially violent. Word was he hated Cha-Cha and her family right through to their very bones. He tried hard to persecute them, however the whole village did not agree. Their lives had been spared, until now.

A lady who was once the richest of their community before the communist party took over had warned Cha-Cha one day. Although their roles were now reversed and the rich fell under the power of the poorest ones, everyone still respected the woman and valued her opinion. People listened to what she said. She was a person of influence. The Regime had shown mercy on her. She often spoke up on behalf of Thida and her family and had also point blankly warned Cha-Cha to keep her mouth shut to save her life.

The Regime was purposeful, in a way. By handing power down to the peasants and village people that never had any control, or power, or even any say in the goings-on of the country's government, it gave them new-found importance.

Comrade Chan and his wife were actually quite fond of the Long family and Thida. Chan had more compassion than the other leaders of the Regime. His wife was with him on their visit to the Long's home this evening. However, Cha-Cha knew that no one who was in a position of leadership could be completely trusted.

A third leader, the top guy of Talien, was not present with them. Comrade Sambo was the quietest one. He was the thinker. First and foremost, he was the one in charge even above Comrade Chan and Odom. Within each village, the leaders were appointed by the Khmer Rouge based on the new order of Pol Pot. The third class citizens would have died if they disagreed.

Therefore, the new first class citizens were allowed to kill because they became part of the Regime. Some were nicer than others. The Long family had met a few who had developed compassion for certain individuals, although they too had taken part in many killings. As she stared at the three unexpected guests on her doorstep, Cha-Cha's guard went up, knowing there must be a reason for their late night visit. She had to be very careful with her words. She had no choice but to invite them inside.

Comrade Chan began the conversation. "Comrade Cha-Cha, were you a rice farmer or a gardener?"

It was a clue. She knew right away that this was a very important interview and that Comrade Chan was trying to give something away. Cha-Cha had never been this smart before, but this evening she was totally on point. She understood that Comrade Chan had something in mind and saw the danger right before her very eyes. It was a life or death situation.

She paused for a minute. Cha-Cha knew that if she told the truth and said teacher, student, professor or anything of that nature, then by morning she would be dead. So would her entire family. They would all be killed.

There was a big difference in being a farmer or a gardener. One was a peasant tilling the fields, while the other was a city dweller with a middle-class position. Being one saved your life, while the other was doomed for death.

"I was a rice farmer, Comrades," she said without delay.

Comrade Chan continued without giving Comrade Odom a chance to speak. "Why did you choose Narin to be your wedded husband? Why not a good-looking, handsome man?" he asked.

Without skipping a beat, Cha-Cha said, "Oh, you must not have heard the old saying; 'Love can make you blind and deaf.' I tell you, at the time we married, no one could surpass my husband's beauty. He was the one and still is the most handsome man on earth." They all started laughing hard, even Odom. So Rachana continued, "You know what we did to each other?"

"No! Comrade Cha-Cha, please go on and tell us your entire story," said Comrade Chan. At this point, Thida had overheard their voices and gotten up out of bed. She brought them each a package of tobacco and they all rolled a cigarette, in anticipation of Cha-Cha's joke.

Cha-Cha went on after they were all happy smoking. "My husband and I lived in adjoining villages. Whenever he wanted to see me, he climbed up the coconut tree. From there, he could see me in the next village. He knew what I was doing or where I was going. When I missed him, I climbed up the mango tree to look for him."

This made them all laugh like crazy. Even though the interview was a very serious and a dangerous one, Cha-Cha had turned a life or death situation into a brilliantly good time. She was a natural comedian and storyteller.

Comrade Chan asked all of the questions, leaving Comrade Odom no time to engage in anything except the laughter. After they were finished with their interrogation, the three visitors got up and bid Cha-Cha and Thida goodbye. They had their share of tobacco and then left for the night.

Her gift of tobacco and laughter had spared their lives, at least for now. The visitors went from house to house interrogating people, especially new families who had just moved to Talien. They were looking for all the rest of the educated people who must be killed. So it was vital not to tip them off in any way that you had ever gone to school or had any higher learning.

The next morning just before dawn, there was a loud knock at the door. Cha-Cha opened it to find her frantic neighbor standing there. She was trembling with fright, as if she had just seen a ghost.

"Cha-Cha, where is your husband?" asked the neighbor.

"Why do you ask for him?" she replied, now worried about Narin's whereabouts. "I think he is at the community garden. He doesn't come home very often."

The neighbor broke down, weeping. "They took my husband a few minutes ago. Did they not take your husband too?"

Without warning, the woman's husband had been taken by the leaders to be killed. As the lady sobbed, Cha-Cha began shaking like a 9.9 earthquake. She held the neighbor's hand and murmured in her ear, "Hush. Lower your voice, honey. If they hear you crying, they will come for us too. You do know that, don't you?"

After she comforted her distraught neighbor, Rachana went back into the house and told her mother everything. Thida sat up and said, "You know what, honey? That was what my dream was all about."

Her daughter agreed. "Yes, Mother I believe that God turned the tiger into an angel to save our lives. But mother, we must be on our guard, okay? Remember, we are farmers, and say nothing more than this. We are going to be alright."

"What about Narin?" asked Thida.

"I don't know Mother, keep praying. I have to go to work now." With that, Cha-Cha left for another long day in the fields.

Along the way to work, a lot of the other workers who traveled the same path were crying. Some asked her, "How come you look okay? Didn't they take your husband too?" Cha-Cha learned that they had taken all the other men that night except Narin and three others. They took all the lazy ones, as well as any of those who didn't have the right answers during their interrogation.

Her response was, "Crying doesn't help to save me or the rest of my family. Hold back your tears and think of your sons and daughters, they need you. Be strong." Cha-Cha saw the need to offer a gentle reminder that all of their lives and that of their children were in grave danger. They held back their tongues and their tears, as if turning off the running water of a faucet.

Everyone was quiet that day at work. They barely said a word as they performed their grueling duties in the field, working for the Regime. They toiled in silent resentment for the killers who had just taken their beloved husbands away forever. The soldiers were merciless. These were good people who did nothing to deserve to die.

Some with good hearts looked upon Cha-Cha with silence and sympathy, but those filled with evil mocked her all day long. No one could feel the heavy burden that was suffered by the prisoners of war. Only those who had their feet in the same boots could relate to the cross they all had to bear.

Some gave up hoping for miracles. Yet, a handful of people were still optimistic. They held on to the hope that change would come. They fooled themselves with the fairytale of a happy ending for themselves and for their loved ones. Everyone lost someone. It was those who never gave up hope that the ways of the supernatural would work in favor to their highest good. It was more difficult for those who endured suffering because they had no one to back up their need for hope. They felt alone, helpless, and lost.

However, Cha-Cha knew she had someone. She could not see, hear, or touch that someone, but she felt his presence with her at all times. Whenever she asked for his help, she was confident that he could do the job. Although she didn't know God well at the time, she knew someone was there. Was it an angel? A higher power? She didn't know, but she believed that she would make it. Whenever doubt set in, she had to ask for the courage to get through whatever brave thing she needed to do. Cha-Cha did so without complaining or discussing her problems or insecurities with others. She was quiet in her beliefs. It was for the best.

They were under the watch of the Regime. If the leaders saw anyone together that whispered or engaged in conversations, they listened. Their ears were as quiet as cats listening for the rustle of a mouse, stalking low in the cattails and ready to pounce. When they had their chance, they leapt upon them with claws of steel knives. If the third class citizens made them mad or talked back, it cost them their lives. Indeed, human life was fragile. Anyone could be killed at any time.

That night, the Comrades had gone interviewing from house to house. Their house had been the last one, just on the edge of the forest. Hence, Cha-Cha's family was the last to be interviewed. Perhaps the laughter or the tobacco had spared them, or perhaps their answers. However, the very next morning the leaders rounded people up from their homes and took them off to be slaughtered. Cha-Cha's family was one of the few who survived.

Chapter Eighteen

"Dangerous Days"

T he Khmer Rouge became even more ruthless after a couple of years in power. Only two years after they took over the country, by 1977, they had eliminated all of the old provinces and split Cambodia up into seven zones, plus a couple of sub-regions. The conditions were dire throughout the communist reign, but the terror escalated as time went on. The people of influential and metropolitan backgrounds, who were the ones that had been driven out of the big cities after Pol Pot's victory, endured the majority of the suffering. The "old people" were the poverty-stricken peasants and people who remained in the villages or rural countryside, just on the outskirts of cities. The peasants dubbed the third class citizens the "new people," mainly because they didn't belong there and were unwanted by the villagers. Some of the villagers had been born into these rural areas for generations after generations, so they didn't want to share their space with the snobbier folks from the city.

Although they professed having a commitment to the radical party, there was a distinctive separation between the former overthrown government and the new elite members of the corrupt armed forces under Pol Pot's leadership.

One of the goals of the Regime was to build a dam near Chork Thom Village. It was a crappy design, built by the slave labor of the third class citizens, who were often not skilled to do manual labor and thereby lacked the techniques of true builders. Any citizens who had not yet died of starvation, killings, and weakness or through self-inflicted suicides were recruited to help with the construction of the dam. The crowd of villagers that lived in Talien was ordered to attend a meeting given by the leader, Comrade Sambo. He sternly reported, "The Regime has instructed me to send all of the last remaining forces within Talien to join the strongest forces, who are our sons and daughters. He or she who does not have elderly family members to care for will leave by tomorrow to help build the dam. No exceptions. The Regime must finish the dam before the next rainy season comes upon us."

Comrade Odom then spoke. "I suggest sending Cha-Cha and her family, for her little girl can be cared for by her mother."

Forgetting about the danger in disagreeing with anything they ordered, Cha-Cha piped up with a protest. "But, my mother is now seventy-seven years old and my daughter is under three years old. They both need care. My mother is older than all the senior citizens in the village. If those seniors can keep one person to stay home for care, can I stay in the village too?"

This inflamed Comrade Odom. Like a raging machine gun, he instantly yelled and screamed an order to discipline Cha-Cha for her backtalk.

Although she didn't understand at the time what he had been saying, later on it came to her attention that several times Comrade Odom had been calling out for one of Cha-Cha's homegrown sweet potatoes. "Oh! I am craving for sweet potato; whoever has it should bring me some!"

Cha-Cha had heard him, but didn't get it. He was referring to a time that he wanted the vegetable and had been ignored, which further added to his fury in this instance. He didn't get what he wanted, therefore why should Cha-Cha get anything that she wanted? Comrade Odom saw her as defiant. Defiance equaled death.

And Cha-Cha misunderstood. She didn't think that Comrade Odom would yell about something so unrelated to what they were discussing now, which was the future of her family. *What did sweet potatoes have to do with leaving the village?*

Not having paid close attention to what he was saying, Cha-Cha could have saved her situation. Ironically, there had been a lot of sweet potatoes in their garden that had rotted due to her being too darn tired to dig them up and cook them.

Until that evening, Cha-Cha had always wondered why Comrade Odom was so mad at her. Now it was clear. He made it known that she had ignored his need–not because she had deliberately tried to be unkind by withholding the vegetables–but because she didn't know what Comrade Odom wanted. Because she wasn't a mind-reader, now Cha-Cha was in a lot of hot water. Comrade Odom used the potatoes as an excuse to turn a criminal case against her. She was persecuted.

The very next day, all of the women in the village who were third class citizens or prisoners of war were taken to the headquarters, where they also gathered women from other villages. From early morning, they had transported most of the women by carriages. However, Cha-Cha was made to sit alone, apart from the rest of the women. She anxiously waited in front of the community building. She knew she had done something wrong and that she was probably going to be punished, or even killed. So, she just sat there, silently wondering what the next step would be. Until late afternoon, she waited in the sweltering heat. Her thoughts raced as she questioned God what was to become of her, of her daughter, or of her mother.

Finally, the leader of the village came with a special carriage to pick Cha-Cha up. She knew that she was standing on very dangerous ground, like quicksand. She recognized the carriage as the one that the Regime used to transport criminals. They took many of them to the concentration camp they had set up in the capital city. Great horrors took place there.

Even though she had no reason to fear death and had faced it since the beginning of their forcible destiny, Cha-Cha knew that her mother would be the worst to suffer when they killed her. Thida would be faced with the burden of care for Sophea in her daughter's absence, which was difficult to imagine for a woman of her age.

While the carriage traveled on the unknown road, Comrade Sambo began grilling his prisoner with many questions.

"Cha-Cha, where is your birthplace?" he asked, sternly.

Without hesitation, she replied, "Puok, Siem Reap."

"And what did your parents do for a living?" he asked.

"They are farmers," Cha-Cha said. "But my husband and I did not want to do rice farming, so we became vegetable farmers. We planted all kinds of vegetables. Every morning I took vegetables to the market and tended the farm in late afternoon until dark. In the morning, my husband tended to the farm by himself."

Still not satisfied, Comrade Sambo asked, "How many sisters and brothers do you have, Cha-Cha?"

"I have four sisters. My brother died when I was a little girl," she replied.

"Do you know their whereabouts?" he continued.

She said, "No. But I am not so worried about my sisters and my father because they are probably north of Puok. All my relatives and best friends are up north and they all joined the Regime back in 1970. I'm sure they are taking care of my family."

With a furrowed brow, he asked, "Why are you not with them?"

"We were sent this way by mistake. We were separated. My cousin is a big leader of the Regime. He's in the region of Varinn and came himself with his motorcycle to search for my mother and me, but we had already left for Prey Skar," she lied. Cha-Cha made up the entire story to save her neck.

At the end of her carriage ride, she was placed with another group of workers. They got up very early the following morning, even before sunrise. There were thousands of people in the group, from very young to very old. They were put to work immediately to build the dam, where they stood side by side without speaking and under watchful eyes of the guards. The group was allowed one lunch break for a very short time and that was the only break they took. After a few days of hard work, Cha-Cha's back was searing with pain. It had already been hurting since the very beginning, but now the pain was crippling with intensity. She couldn't lie down, nor sleep. Instead, she sat up all night in severe pain.

Now, she had double trouble. Cha-Cha would either receive the miracles to survive or be killed. Her divine creator knew what she needed.

Meanwhile, Cha-Cha's husband had also been sent with a separate group of workers who were required to do heavier labor. They lifted boulders for the dam, stacking them one by one, as if building an empire. It was becoming increasingly difficult for Narin and Cha-Cha to maintain their cover as farmers. The Regime was cleverly vigilant in their record-keeping and tracking of the movements of individuals and families. The Longs were lucky to still be alive, although the Khmer Rouge did need some of the third class citizens to use as slaves to build their dam and work in the fields. Other families were separated into the work brigades according to gender and age and were then divided into one of the new seven zones the Regime had created.

From sunrise to sunset, Cha-Cha and her husband worked separately amongst the armies of marching ants, under the careful watch of many guards. One wrong move or sneeze or inappropriate whisper meant death. They could be slaughtered at any moment. Many of the killers were kids. They too were Comrades and participants of the communist army. Some were assigned to manage the workers in the rice fields and at the dam.

They were just as ruthless as the adult Comrades. Thankfully, Sophea was still too young to be taken away by the hands of the communists, at least for now. Instead, she continued living with her grandmother.

But Thida had struggles of her own. She was an elderly seventy-seven-year-old woman and it was difficult to care for children at her age. She did the best she could. When Cha-Cha was sent to Chork Thom Village to work on the dam, her baby girl was only three.

Due to the hard labor and having an already frail physique, Cha-Cha's back pain worsened. After only a few days of hard work, the pain increased to the point where it made her sit up straight in the middle of the night. Whenever she lay down to try and sleep, it felt like someone was slapping a hard board across her back. The pain was excruciating.

However, medical care given to third class citizens was either nonexistent or quite primitive. Instead, the Regime's law was, "Those who can't work, die"–simple as that. Cha-Cha knew this. But she couldn't help the fact that her back pain was plainly unbearable. She simply couldn't work without her back feeling like it would snap in half.

Bravely, she mustered the courage to walk into the Khmer Rouge headquarters. A few of the intimidating leaders were sitting at a heavy, bench-style wooden table. They were in the midst of a burdensome discussion. When they saw her walk in, one of the Comrades winked at another. She sensed they had been talking about her.

One of the leaders spoke first. "Cha-Cha, what do you come for?"

"Please, I would ask you for mercy. I need just a few days off to heal my back or perhaps to ask for the opportunity to go to the care center?" she asked with unbridled hesitation.

They all laughed in ridicule. "Sure, sure. We'll send you home in two days," one of the men stated in jest. It was at that moment; Cha-Cha realized it was the end of her life. Those who couldn't work were axed down, like broken toys discarded after a child's interest changed.

"You are dismissed. Go back to the dam until we tell you otherwise," instructed another one of the Comrades. She finished out the day, nearly keeled over in pain. But Cha-Cha never complained, for she knew what became of those who spoke of pain or illness.

That evening, she returned to the shacks they used for the laborers. Facing death, Cha-Cha wondered what would become of her mother and daughter. She had seen death all around her. Yes, she wanted to live. However, death was not something she was scared to face any longer.

Truthfully, she wanted to live mostly because of her family. If it weren't for them, she wouldn't have had anything left to live for. Living in day-to-day terror was no way to spend your life. At least it was not the plan of anyone who had lived in Cambodia peacefully. It was not what she had in mind when she had enrolled in school so many years ago. Had she known what the consequences would entail, she may have reconsidered her quest for achievement.

Somehow, Cha-Cha made it through another night. By the next morning, the village courier stopped by to bring the workers food. Comrade Yin was a guard who was part of the Regime, however his demeanor was more compassionate than most of the other leaders. He stopped by Cha-Cha's housing to question her about her back pain. She was nervous of his intent, since she had never met him before. She wondered if he had been sent to kill her.

Instead, Comrade Yin gave Cha-Cha a warning. "It is very, very dangerous to have the illness you have because nobody can see what is wrong with you. It is internal pain," he explained, pointing to her lower back. "If you had a fever or an open wound, then it would be obvious that you are sick and they might send you to the care center."

"I am not lying. Trust me, I would rather work than to suffer this pain," she replied. After their talk, Comrade Yin left. Meanwhile, God worked behind the scenes to save her.

Later that same afternoon, Comrade Yin returned. He asked her, "If I send you to a care center at headquarters, will you stay there?"

She replied, "Yes I will."

"You promise?" He needed reassurance.

Once again, Cha-Cha said, "Yes."

Comrade Yin added, "Because if you don't remain in the care center as promised, it will be my own life on the line. No matter what, do not go home. Even to see your daughter or mother." The Regime knew all family members and kept close tabs on everyone. If Cha-Cha were to disobey, she would jeopardize the wellbeing of her entire family.

Cha-Cha could tell that Comrade Yin was afraid the Khmer Rouge would kill him for helping her. She was a complete stranger to him; therefore, he had no vested interest in her life except through the kindness of his heart. If he sent her to the care center, he wanted validation of her motives or they would both die. It was that obvious. "I promise," she pledged to him a third time.

Comrade Yin proceeded with specific orders. "Tomorrow at dawn before anybody gets up; you must go out to the road. Don't take anything with you. Walk fast like you have to go to the bathroom. Do not let anybody see you. There will be a man with an ox and cart waiting for you. Don't say anything to him. Just get in the cart and go wherever he takes you."

She nodded to let him know she understood the instructions. With that, Comrade Yin left. He put his own life at risk.

The next morning, before anybody else got up, Cha-Cha got up and walked to the road as fast as she could, pretending that she had to go to the bathroom. Sure enough–a little farther down the road–there was a man with a tan ox hooked to his cart. He was ready to take off. She didn't ask any questions, nor make one single peep. She simply climbed into the back as she had been told to do. The middle-aged man beat the ox with a bamboo stick to make it go as fast as it could.

At the same time, the Khmer Rouge killed people left and right. By now, nobody tried to save anybody anymore. The weak were dead and the strong that were leftover were rapidly becoming weak also. It was certain death to even attempt helping someone.

As she sat with her eyes tightly shut under the hay-filled quilt in the back of the oxen cart, Cha-Cha couldn't figure out why one of the Comrades had saved her life for no reason. They were the killers. Indeed, Cha-Cha felt that the oxen cart was a first class escape for a prisoner like her.

The man slowed down as he neared the care center. He pulled the reins to halt the cart. Upon arriving, he pointed a finger at the building to indicate that she must go inside. She nodded and smiled in silent gratitude as she slowly bent down to get out of the cart, trying not to cause more damage to her back.

There was only one other patient in the care center with her. She was a lady from the village who was considered a first class citizen. The woman barely spoke to her, even though they were staying in the same room. Cha-Cha sensed the woman's disdain for her. She was a woman of higher authority and one to be feared. Maybe she was one of the wives of the Comrades.

After a few nights there, Cha-Cha's back pain got the better of her. She had gone many nights without sleeping or with very little rest. Although she didn't do it intentionally, one night she sleepwalked right into the headquarters that were located adjacently to the care center. She unknowingly strolled right into the lion's den. It was forbidden to go into head-quarters without permission.

At the same time, Cha-Cha's quiet roommate walked in through the door on the other side. After heavy interrogation, the woman staunchly defended Cha-Cha's actions, much to her surprise. The lady told the soldiers, "At first I thought she was healthy and not sick at all. I thought she was just a lazy woman who didn't want to work. But then, I noticed that she's in a lot of pain every night and can't sleep."

The Comrades studied Cha-Cha. She looked healthy enough. The woman had been one of the Comrades wives, just as she had suspected. Yet, her sour attitude towards her roommate had turned to sympathy. "I have observed her every move. She is not faking. She is truly in pain," the woman added.

That night, an elderly man brought his folding bed to the care center and placed it in between Cha-Cha and the Comrade's wife's beds. He was ordered to observe her. He had a long silver beard. The man was a medicine man in his village.

She tried to sleep, but Cha-Cha was in more pain than ever. Her back was agonizingly sore. In a way, it was a blessing for this to be so. She could barely lay still and squirmed and whined from the throbbing. The elderly man got up and worked his magical hands on her back. His healing touch massaged the aches, as he turned to Cha-Cha's roommate and said, "It is a good thing that you told us about her condition! She would have been killed. Headquarters already decided her case."

Then he turned to Cha-Cha. "You are a very lucky lady. If your roommate had not spoken up, you would have been killed by the very next day. Tomorrow I will get the medicine for you." She was still afraid, not wanting to be in pain because it was a red marker for death. If she was no longer needed, the leaders would not waste any time ending her life. Her daughter would be without a mother. Her mother would be without a daughter. Her husband would be without a wife.

In the morning, the medicine man made his report to headquarters. He brought Cha-Cha a bitter, murky solution of roots that he had brewed for her to drink. That was the extent of the medical care she got. It was more than most. They let her rest in the care center for another three weeks. When she was finally sent back to Talien, Cha-Cha learned that the Regime had recently been there. She had just missed a mass killing of nearly all the villagers.

Was it a coincidence, or God's miracle?

However, a new challenge was there waiting for her. Every morning, Cha-Cha got up to draw water from the well for her mother and toddler. It was enough to last them for the entire day. Then she was called upon to go to work, now that her back was in acceptable condition to resume her duties as a laborer.

On one particular morning, after she lugged the water to the house, Cha-Cha went to wake up Sophea and give her a goodbye kiss. The little girl got up and fell back down. She laughed. Her mother laughed with her.

"Hurry up, honey!" she told her daughter. Again, Sophea got up and fell back down.

"I can't stand up, Mommy," said the child.

"Honey, we don't have time to play right now," warned the tired mother. For the third time, Sophea tried to stand up and once again, toppled over. This time, she crawled to her mom. But when Cha-Cha tried to pull her daughter up, Sophea's knees gave way a fourth time. Now she was truly afraid of what was happening to her little girl.

Without wasting any time, Cha-Cha rushed in to wake up Thida. She told her what was happening with Sophea. Neither of them knew what to do, however Cha-Cha couldn't risk being late for work. She rushed off to the rice fields and left Sophea home with Thida, even though she was desperate to stay behind and was seriously concerned with her condition. Cha-Cha had already pushed her luck as far as it would go. She would never ask the leaders for anything again. Besides, there were no sick days to be taken from this job. It was "do or die."

The next morning, Comrade Odom appeared at her door for some tobacco. Cha-Cha and Thida were the only people who grew tobacco in the village. They always complied because they had no other choice. Besides, it kept them in his favor. However, on this day as she handed him his share of tobacco, Cha-Cha bravely discussed her daughter's situation. "My daughter is having a health problem, Comrade Odom. She can't stand up."

"Take her to Mr. Slav in the next village." With that, he got up and put a pinch of tobacco under his lower gum. The rest that she had given him, he lightly wrapped into a handkerchief, and with a nod he was off to work.

Who is Mr. Slav? Cha-Cha wondered. Just the sound of his name scared her. It was Thida who took her granddaughter to Mr. Slav, right after Comrade Odom left their house.

Mr. Slav was another medicine man. The Regime needed people like him. Quite often, their lives were spared because of their healing knowledge. Despite his scary last name, Mr. Slav was a gentle man who spoke very little. He assessed the young girl's weakness and put his hand on her legs, much the same as a doctor would check his patient. Without saying anything, Mr. Slav mixed together two different kinds of roots from the jungle and instructed Thida to add the stem of a special squash with a particular fruit and to grind together finely, as if stirring them for a recipe. She was told to wipe the mixture over Sophea's knees every day.

Thida followed his instructions precisely, making a ritual out of it every morning as the girl awoke. Low and behold, young Sophea's knees got stronger and stronger every day, until eventually, she was able to walk normally again.

Narin had not been home for a long time. They often wondered if he was still alive. One day he came bursting through the door, sweating profusely and scared for his life. He ran straight for the back of the house and hid in a corner, trembling. Cha-Cha and Thida looked at each other, shocked not only to see him after so long but by his spectacle of an entrance.

His wife made him some tea, in hopes to calm his nerves. She wrapped her arms around his neck. "We missed you," she said, not wanting to ask what had happened or if she should be worried that someone may be coming after them. All night long, he crouched in one spot in the corner of their house. He didn't sleep. He trembled.

Finally, in the earliest hours of morning, he dozed off for what seemed like a few hours. When Narin awoke, he reached for his wife's hand. "They are killing everyone," he said quietly.

"Are they coming for you?" she asked.

"I don't know. One minute we were working in the field and the next minute they came along with machine guns and opened fire. They sprayed bullets everywhere. There was mass panic. I just ran, as fast as I could. People were dying next to me. They dropped like rain."

Cha-Cha started crying as he told his story. It was no wonder Narin had been shaking when he arrived. There was no reason for their killing. They just did. Innocent people scattered and most were left to die. The Regime had guns and machetes. They decapitated some and shot others, as many as they could. The rice fields were open grounds with nowhere to go. Those who could make it to the woods were lucky.

One man who ran away next to Narin had just seen his wife for the first time in months, by happenstance. He had been happy to see her, only moments before the gruesome attack. It was completely by coincidence. She was carrying their two-month old baby and walking towards him. The man had never met his child yet, because they had become separated while she was still pregnant.

When the Regime opened fire, the man's wife was one of the first to get shot. She looked at her husband and yelled, "RUN!" The man tried to go back and grab his infant, a baby boy. Just as he crouched down by her side, the baby was hit with a bullet. The bullets sprayed everywhere, with no warning of the attack. "Run . . . run . . .," she pleaded, as she laid choking on blood and dying in the grass. Their son was already dead. He died instantly; just an innocent baby who had been born into the wrong part of the world at the wrong time.

The man ducked and looked into his wife's dying eyes one last time, as tears smudged the dirt on his face, turning it into mud. He saw the soldiers pass by with their guns as they chased more of the people deep into the woods. When he saw a flash of opportunity, he finally ran the other way—but without his family. His wife's helpless stare and the blood splashed on the back of their newborn baby haunted him every night for the rest of his life. He escaped the killing, but never the memory.

Chapter Nineteen

"The Sick Shall Perish"

To celebrate his safe return, Narin and Cha-Cha rekindled their relationship. She got pregnant with her second child during one of the most difficult times of the war; a time when it seemed unfair for any new life to be born amidst such turmoil. The Regime did not care whether the third class citizens were men, women, children, or babies. Most of the leaders did not have empathy for life. Women who were pregnant were usually killed, because they were no longer able to work. Therefore, they were of no use to them anymore and had to die.

The Khmer Rouge did look most favorably upon children who were of the age to be taken away from their parents, so that they could brainwash and train them to adhere to the new order. It was usually by six or seven years of age, up to adolescents. The communist policies were disturbingly harsh and ascetic. Child soldiers were easier to train than adult soldiers and they became just as ruthless.

Most of all, it was undeserved for any newborn infant to be born under such circumstances. It was not the baby's fault to have been given life at a time when millions died. It was also unfair to the mothers whose job it was to give life and to nurture, to support their offspring. Their starving bodies yielded very little resources of breast milk. Some babies were born with defects from lack of nutrition.

One blessing for Cha-Cha was that while she was pregnant, many of the other women in the village were also pregnant. Hence, the Comrades couldn't kill every pregnant woman in Talien because there were too many. So, Cha-Cha's life was spared, for the time being. She was able to work in their garden while pregnant and do other light chores, at least until she was far enough in her pregnancy to need bed rest. Cha-Cha's tiny frame could not withstand the extra pressure on her back.

While she was with child, she had a craving for watermelon. It was about two o'clock in the afternoon one day and without thinking, Cha-Cha announced, "On a hot day like this, watermelon would taste just heavenly!"

With that, Thida stood up and stepped down from the house. "Where are you going, Mom?" asked Cha-Cha.

"You said you wanted watermelon. Didn't you?" replied Thida.

Cha-Cha answered, "Yes, but no one has it. Don't go anywhere Mom, please! Last time I was worried sick for three nights. Remember?"

Thida said, "Yes. Very well then. I'm just going to visit my friend." Cha-Cha could do nothing to stop her mother once she made up her mind. It was apparent that both mother and daughter shared in the same headstrong nature. If she could have, Thida would have given Cha-Cha and Sophea the whole world. They were blessed to have her. She was nice, kind, gentle, sweet, and an entirely loving mother. Also, she was a wonderful wife, hardworking, never complaining, and good to all neighbors. She was a God-fearing woman, patient, honest, and faithful. She meant the whole world to Cha-Cha and everything revolved around her. Cha-Cha thanked God every day for her mother. She had been a savior in helping with Sophea too.

One hour passed by. Two hours. Three hours. The sun was already setting over the pink and purple horizon, as the last cloud faded into the night. Yet, still no Thida. It was like déjà vu. Once again, Cha-Cha began to worry. At that time, people could be killed just for visiting the next village. People were absolutely forbidden to move around, because it made it easier for the Regime to track them if they stayed put. If they caught you, they would kill you.

Cha-Cha sat in the dark and waited for her mother's return. It reminded her of those three nights she had been afraid for her in Prey Chkar, when she feared she would never return. Again, Cha-Cha was losing hope that her mother would come back that night, because it was very dark. *Perhaps she stayed at her friend's house?* She hoped that her mother was safe. *How could a seventy-seven-year-old lady find her way home at night with no light?* Cha-Cha prayed and hoped that somebody was kind enough to keep her for the night. Meanwhile, she couldn't sleep, so she just sat in the dark and waited for her, even though she doubted that her mother would be able to come home.

At midnight, Thida was at the door, calling for her daughter. With tears of joy, Cha-Cha stepped out and welcomed her with outstretched arms.

"Why are you so worried?" asked Thida. "No danger will come close to me. People are always helping me." Then she dropped the tattered satchel from her shoulder. Out rolled three small watermelons.

Proudly, she told Cha-Cha, "Get the knife. What are you waiting for?"

"No, Mom. I'll eat tomorrow. Let's go to bed." Cha-Cha was just relieved to have her home safely. Thida had once again risked her life walking at night through the jungle to bring watermelons home for her pregnant daughter. She wasn't afraid of the tigers, nor the killers. Somehow she knew she was safe from harm.

As Cha-Cha laid her head on the pillow made of straw and leftover cloth, she was overwhelmed by her mother's love. Because of this, the craving for watermelon left her body and she had to force herself to eat the watermelons the next day. Of course, Cha-Cha didn't tell her mother this, after so much effort had gone into getting them.

Despite the killings that raged on every day around them, new life made its way into the cruel world as Cha-Cha's baby was born in 1978. As soon as Cha-Cha's contractions started, a midwife was sent to their small abode. The midwife was a peasant woman who lived in the village. After a day's worth of labor pains and no medications, nor tools to deliver the baby, the woman finally pulled out a baby girl. And how could Cha-Cha possibly be disappointed when she looked into her newborn daughter's eyes for the first time? She could not. She felt only happiness and gratitude for her baby's good health.

Her name was Neary, a gentle girl. Baby Neary's disposition was much like her grandmother's. There were no accidents in God's plan—only miracles.

As it turned out, the midwife who was hired to help deliver Cha-Cha's baby had never performed childbirth before. In fact, she had only witnessed one birth as a spectator. She didn't have any experience in nursing or health care. The villager was just a kindhearted woman who came to help, posing as a midwife so as not to upset a mother in the midst of labor pains.

Not long after giving birth, one morning Cha-Cha woke up with diarrhea. There was no healthcare. No doctors. No nurses.

After the third time of going to the bathroom within an hour, Cha-Cha was exhausted and laid down. At that time, cholera was rampant.

Cholera often occurred during wars, famine, or in poor sanitation regions due to overcrowding and by ingesting contaminated food or water. The infection affected the small intestine with watery diarrhea, which released toxins throughout the body, causing severe illness, or even death.

As Thida watched her daughter suffer, she was in distress. Her body had taken its toll of agony amidst the famine of the war. Now with a sick daughter, a one-month-old baby, and a four-year-old to look after, the seventy-seven-year-old woman was scared and overwhelmed. "I'm too old to take care of these two children of yours," Thida said, as tears dripped down her wrinkled countenance. "I wish I could trade places with you, honey!"

Her words made Cha-Cha teary-eyed too. The last thing she wanted was to see her dear mother in great anguish. She knew very well that without modern medicine, cholera did not give humans much of a chance of surviving. In fact, both mother and daughter remembered that only twenty years prior, they had lost a dear sister-in-law to the very same sickness. Cha-Cha saw the fear in her mother's eyes.

"Mother, you have nothing to worry about. I am not that sick. I am going to be better in a couple of hours," she reassured her. "I am young and full of energy. I am fine."

Suddenly, two faces appeared in the doorway with a quiet tap. "Is anybody sick in this house?"

Everyone in the house turned their eyes to see two young women at the door. They had never been seen before by anyone in the village. They were mysterious strangers who showed up quite unexpectedly. They climbed the stairs and entered the door as everyone stared, dumbfounded.

Both women had the exact same hairstyle, with the same brand new clothes that were well made with designer fabric. Yet, there were no dressmakers in the war. Most people made their own clothes, at least those of whom knew how. The availability of material was scarce, almost non-existent. The women were vibrant and colorful amid a society of rags, dirt, and unkempt faces that had not bathed in weeks, or longer. They were nice and friendly with generous smiles, unlike the Comrades. Who were they?

At the same time, Thida exclaimed, "Yes! My daughter is sick!"

Whilst Cha-Cha said, "Yes! I am sick!"

"We know that," said the two ladies. "That is why we are here for you." They opened a box and pulled out two pills from an ornate pillbox that was decorated in brass and leafy scrollwork. The pills were made in France and were very rare.

Still awestruck and skeptical, Cha-Cha asked, "Where are you from?" One of them smiled.

Then, she asked, "How did you know that I'm sick?"

One of them replied, "Oh, we do the routine daily checkup searching for people in the neighborhood who are sick or need help."

Still in disbelief, Cha-Cha said, "I wasn't aware they had a program like this!"

The other woman replied, "Oh, they do. We go from house to house. If there is anyone who needs help, we do it. We make the route every day."

"Every day?" Cha-Cha questioned, once again.

"Yes, every day," they replied, still smiling. Cha-Cha took the pill and gulped it down with some water while the ladies watched.

"You'll be fine now," said one, as she winked.

"Where are you going next?" asked Thida.

"Well, we will go and check on the other houses down the road," the women stated. "Then we will move on to the next village, Phoum Tnot."

After Thida and Cha-Cha gave them a warm thank you and said good-bye, the two ladies went back down the stairs. Quickly, Cha-Cha said, "Mother, please take a look to see which direction they went."

Thida scurried to the window just in time to see the two women walk off in the opposite direction as they had said they were going. They walked into the forest, instead of down to the rest of the village. They were talking loudly to one another and even laughing, perhaps stricken with delight by the astounded faces they had caused.

Even four-year-old Sophea knew something was different about them. "Mommy, who were those ladies?"

"I don't know, honey. Maybe they were angels," she told her inquisitive daughter.

"Angels, Mommy? What are angels?" asked Sophea.

She didn't answer. She looked at Thida in awe. Both were suspicious, yet grateful.

The next morning, Cha-Cha returned to work feeling much better. She asked everyone she knew about the program the ladies had spoken of. Nobody had ever heard of such a program. The Regime were killing people, not trying to save their lives. Those who Cha-Cha asked were considered first class citizens. They were the first and only people of that time to receive any kind of medical benefit. The people she asked became upset after learning that Cha-Cha had been the beneficiary of such a program. She was a third class citizen and not supposed to get any help. Their answers were all much the same. "No! I have not heard of anything like this. And if there is one, why should you be the one who receives it, and not us?"

By the end of the day, Cha-Cha had stirred up the whole village. The two ladies' mysterious visit during a time of need was something she never learned the answer to. They gave her medicine that saved her life. People simply didn't go knocking on doors to ask if you needed medicine. The only knocks on the door came when the soldiers were sent to kill you.

During the war, death called upon each member of their family day and night. Yet, God preserved their lives in order to fulfill the purpose he had in mind for each of them.

Even Narin was not exempt from physical difficulties. Fortunately, his were not at the hands of the ruthless soldiers. While walking home one night from working in the fields, he tripped over a large tree trunk and twisted his ankle, as well as puncturing the skin around it. He was off from work for a while but because there weren't any medicine, the wound became badly infected. The local Comrade sent him to the care center, where Narin could stay out of sight so that his defective presence wouldn't aggravate the other workers.

Once a week, Cha-Cha was permitted to bring rice and salt to him. Upon returning one day from visiting Narin, Cha-Cha entered her house to see her mother crying hard. Her eyes were swollen as if she had been crying for hours. It looked as though bees had stung her face many times, and yet the tears continued streaming down her face uncontrollably.

Worried, she asked, "What's wrong, Mom?"

Thida could barely get it out. "They came for you."

Cha-Cha nodded in quiet understanding. She knew this meant she was to be killed. Quite honestly, Cha-Cha was tired of living the nightmare. Wearing rags, working to death, being hungry all of the time, not knowing when the Regime was going to kill you from day to day; all of these factors had taken their toll on people's spirits. She wasn't afraid anymore. But she did wonder, *Why now, after making it this far?*

Thida explained, "They told me to tell you to go see the leader when you get home. But come in and see your children. I will go meet them instead. I wish to request they take me in your place."

"No, Mother," Cha-Cha said. "It doesn't work like that. You know it."

"Ple-e-e-ase! I implore you. Your children need you. If they kill me instead, you will be able to take care of your kids. I'm too old to take care of them!" she cried. And she was. Age seventy-seven was considered to be living near the cusp of death.

"Mom, listen. They want me. I must go. They don't want you. Besides, I am no longer afraid of dying. What are we living for anyway? It is better to die than to live in this condition." Cha-Cha was not afraid. At that very moment, something strange happened within her heart and mind. She felt tranquil, secure, and peaceful.

Somehow, within the very core of her being, Cha-Cha knew that she would not be killed. She had the strength of a woman who had outrun tigers, defied killers, and who had survived. She had just given birth to a beautiful baby girl and had another gorgeous little girl too. Angels had just saved her life by showing up on her doorstep with a rare pill. Life was precious. Life meant everything.

Cha-Cha changed the course of the conversation with her mother right away. With a smile of newfound confidence and conviction, she said, "Mommy, wait for me here at home. It won't be long before I return."

Thida begged, tearfully. "No, oh no! Honey, no! Please, take us all with you to be killed. I would rather be killed and buried in the same hole with you than to be left behind and grieving for you every day."

Cha-Cha was touched by her mother's love. "Have faith, Mommy."

As she hung her head in despair, Thida muttered, ". . . but when you leave and go to them, you won't come back. I will never see you again."

"I will," Cha-Cha promised. "You'll see. I will be right back." She hugged her mother and eldest daughter. She gave the baby a kiss. Then she turned and looked back over her shoulder as she closed the door behind her, leaving Thida to cry in mourning over the loss she already felt.

Chapter Twenty

"Fragile Words"

As her feet crackled upon the leaves on the path to the killer's headquarters, Cha-Cha felt a newfound confidence within herself that she had never experienced. After living in sheer terror for the last three years, it was perhaps her last walk ever. She took in the surroundings and the beauty of nature. She felt God's presence with her, holding her hand in peace. She knew not what her fate would determine, but she felt his presence guiding her. Cha-Cha sensed she was not alone.

The building was only two houses away from the interrogator. Comrade Sambo had already singlehandedly killed hundreds of people. He was the quiet killer, the one who questioned, waited, bode his time, and searched for the right moment to pounce, like a panther stalking a rabbit. He enjoyed his new position with the Regime. He relished the control and having power over the people who had been placed beneath his leadership. In the past, he had been a third class worker and had spent most of his days toiling hard in the hot sun. When he was promoted to first class as the country fell to the Khmer Rouge, his lowly stature had been moved into a position of authority. Comrade Sambo hated all the educated ones.

Cha-Cha knocked, meekly, not waiting for an answer to let her in. As she entered the dimly lit building, Comrade Sambo sat in silence. Nearby, his weapons lay still, next to his wrist, as if waiting to be used.

She initiated the conversation. "My mother told me to come see you as soon as I got home," she offered. "So, here I am."

"Yes! Yes! Come in, Cha-Cha." Comrade Sambo replied. "The leaders want you to be honest. If you are honest, I can help you."

He pointed to a chair. With respectful obedience, Cha-Cha sat down in the sturdy bamboo chair.

She knew it was a lie. Being honest with the devil? Hardly. His intent was not to help her, but to seek the truth. She knew of their manipulative strategies and had been warned by those before her. She knew better than to trust him.

He went on. "We were told that you were a teacher and that your husband was a colonel in the army. Is that the truth? An honest answer can save your life."

Faced with a serious decision, Cha-Cha wondered how they knew she was a teacher and who had told them. She knew that either way—truth or lie—would provoke them in some way. Yet she had to respond, quickly.

She knew all along that they killed every single educated individual or high-ranking official from the former government, of which she and Narin were both. Yet without any fear or hesitation, Cha-Cha spoke boldly.

She thought of a bedtime story that her father had told her as a little girl, in one of a few tender moments they once shared. "Let me tell you of a story of the millionaire's dogs and the thieves . . ." Cha-Cha began telling the Comrade:

"Once upon a time, there was a very rich merchant. Many thieves had tried to break into his house to rob him, but none ever succeeded. The merchant had two watchdogs that were very mean and very good at protecting their master's property. The thieves tried and failed. One day, one of the thieves got a brilliant idea. He took several scraps of meat, attached them to a string, and dragged it in front of the dogs, leading them off the property. After going quite a distance, the burglar started shouting, "Mad dogs! Mad dogs!" Upon which, all the neighbors armed themselves and chased after and killed the dogs. After that, the thieves broke into the house and stole all of the merchant's belongings."

Then, Cha-Cha paused. The room was sticky with anticipation for the rest of the story. She looked into the eyes of the Comrade and said, "My story is the same, Comrade. The person who lied to you about me and my husband does not have the power to kill me. But they are very smart. They are using you to kill me. The thieves yelled '*Mad Dogs!*' These people say that my husband is a colonel and that I am a teacher. Therefore, if you kill me you will be used by them. But I believe you are smarter than they are. I hope you find out the truth about my husband and me. We are just hardworking farmers. My husband is no colonel; he is much too short to even carry a rifle. And I am no teacher; I can't even spell my own name."

"Then your real name is Cha-Cha?" he asked.

"Yes, it is a name given to me by my father," she replied. For that was true.

After another thoughtful pause, Comrade Sambo said, "Well, if you are what you say, then you can go home now." It was that quick and easy.

As she left the building breathing a sigh of relief, Cha-Cha looked up into the heavens without saying a word. God had intervened with his miracle once again. For during this period of the war, the Killing Fields were filled with death. People were slaughtered without a trial or without any fairness, nor validation. All it took for some to die was to have been accused by another. The Regime rarely questioned, they just took the individual and their whole family to be murdered instantly. Cha-Cha's case had been handled differently, and for no apparent reason.

Even though she had slid by death yet again, Cha-Cha and her family were on high alert. Not long thereafter, she was assigned to work with a group of people who prepared rice for the entire community of villagers. Everyone who was able to work was separated into their appointed groups. They ate together and were obligated to share their portions of food with the whole neighborhood, including the Comrades. Those who didn't share often suffered severe consequences, or even death.

The leader of the community kitchen was a robust man named Borin. Even though most people were terribly thin and emaciated from starvation, Borin was a heavyset guy with a sour expression. He was loud and boisterous, the kind of fellow you could hear yelling from a few hundred yards away, even if he was just talking in a normal tone of voice. Borin was in charge of dishing out the portions. The people got whatever he said they could have, and that was that. If there was only enough for one spoonful apiece, that's what he would dole out. If you were lucky, on a good day, there might be two or three spoonfuls of rice mixed with the catch or kill of the day, be it a crab, bird, fish, or chicken. And even if you were the person who caught it, you weren't entitled to have any more than those who had contributed nothing.

Borin was also in charge of the food storage and knew exactly how much rice, sugar, salt, or fruit there was, right down to every last grain and seed. Because of his job as the kitchen leader, Borin also held an authoritative position with the Regime. This also gave him the power to kill or be the tattletale on those who he thought should be punished.

One afternoon, one of the supervisors said to the workers, "Let's get the work done fast, so we can go fishing." So they all scurried to get their work done and went fishing for the afternoon. People caught a few fish. But they had stirred up the small pond to the point that the water was now murky, making it too difficult to fish. They just left and went home.

However, Cha-Cha lacked the right fishing equipment. She didn't have nets or poles and couldn't catch anything, so after everyone went home, she was left alone in the pond with nothing but a fishing basket, a bucket and her bare hands. Frustrated but not ready to give up, she started to pray. *God, my mother is old and weak and she is craving for fish. Please have mercy on my dear mom.* She mumbled it over and over again. To eat only rice and salt every day was taking its toll on Thida's health. She was fatigued and grew frail from lack of nourishment.

It was a very small pond, barely bigger than a giant puddle. After half an hour or so after the other villagers had left, the murkiness dissipated and the water began to clear up. At least now, Cha-Cha could see the fish, although she still lacked adequate tools to catch them properly.

Finally, the fish began to resurface up to the top for breath. All the tramping people had done made the fish confused. Cha-Cha dipped her basket in just as a school of fish brushed by her feet. She held still at the right moment and scooped up an entire basket of fish. She emptied the basket of fish into the bucket on the ground. She went back into the water and scooped up another basket of fish. She put the basket of fish on her head, while carrying the full bucket of fish in her right hand. There were so many fish that she could hardly carry them all home. It took all of her physical strength to carry the bucket and she had to set it down every few feet to give her arms a rest.

Upon walking by the community house and dining area, Borin was standing atop the upper deck like a watchman, studying Cha-Cha as she carried her heavy bucket of fish. His eyes followed her. She looked up at him as Borin kept his eyes on her, but he looked puzzled. He wanted to say something, but did not. Instead, Cha-Cha returned his glare with a smile. Borin opened his mouth as if to speak, but still said nothing. She felt his eyes on her as she passed by and just kept walking briskly along the road back to her house.

Thida was thrilled to see all the fish. It was enough to last them for months, which it did. They dried it, salted it, and made fish sauce out of it.

It was policy to share everything you grew, caught, or acquired by way of food with the rest of the villagers. The following day, as lunch time came, Cha-Cha brought exactly one fish with her in her pocket. The small crowd gathered and ate the rice and salt that had been slapped down on their plates by Borin. Cha-Cha asked aloud, "What, nobody brought fish for lunch?"

Someone said, "What fish? Didn't they take away your fish? They took all of ours and took our equipment too."

A second person said, "Yes, this is true. They were even going to take us to jail for going fishing this afternoon. The leaders were furious at us. They said next time they catch us fishing, they will discipline us thoroughly."

Another person said, "Borin didn't see you? With a fish?"

Cha-Cha clamped her mouth shut. She didn't take the fish out of her pocket. Instead, she ate the rice and salt in silence with everyone else. But she couldn't help wondering, what made Borin deaf, dumb, and blind? He could have confiscated her fish, taken her to jail, or at the very least, insulted her. Cha-Cha realized that she could have been disciplined or even killed for having fish that she did not share with the rest of the hungry people, especially the superiors. That was in part why she had brought a fish with her to contribute, figuring the others would have also done the same.

Throughout the next few months, everyone walked on eggshells. Killing became such a commonplace event. People stopped wondering if they would die and just wondered when, and how it would happen. The thought of heaven was a better option than the hell they had succumbed to under the power of the Khmer Rouge. This, they knew, was not how life should be. They knew because they had seen the way it had been before, when people lived in better times and had good jobs and the ability to make decisions for themselves and for their future. It was something many had taken for granted. Now they tiptoed through life, having to lie about who they truly were just to stay alive. They were not teachers, doctors, lawyers, or police officers any more. They were no longer first class citizens. They were just a hairsbreadth away from death every day, trying their best to escape the evil that had encompassed their land. They went from being something to being nothing, which took away their hope. Without hope, there was nothing.

Somehow, Cha-Cha and her mother still had hope, although they didn't know if the conditions would change anytime soon. Nevertheless, they remained hopeful of living. They maintained hope on behalf of the two precious little girls, baby Neary and young Sophea. *Would they ever have the chance to experience a normal childhood, or go to school, or meet friends and go to college, or find a husband, or any of the things that parents and grandparents wish for?* Thida and Cha-Cha fought to stay alive for them, and for each other. The two little girls were precious little human beings that were now theirs to care for and cherish. Both women wanted something better for the girls and although they couldn't foresee how it would be possible, it was enough of a reason to live.

Suddenly, one morning they heard voices outside their little house. It was February of 1979. There had been another turn of politics. They saw some people they knew passing by with their belongings. Confused, Cha-Cha appeared at the frame of her doorway. Someone yelled to her from the path. "We can go now!"

"Go where?" she yelled back.

"Wherever you want. Go home!"

Nobody knew what was going on. *Were they being sent somewhere else again? Was the war over?* They were confused. But Cha-Cha told her mother to get ready. Narin gathered a few of their vegetables for the journey while she stuffed their raggedy clothing into the tattered suitcase they had carried with them now for the past four years. Within half an hour, they were ready to go. They placed the children in the small cart that they still kept stored underneath their dwelling.

Their family joined others who walked by; some who had come from other villages and who were just now passing Talien. Still confused, they asked another person. "What's going on? Where are we going?"

"Home." It was a simple reply.

People were afraid and many started moving or traveling back to their birthplace, as a change in the Regime came to pass. Although the Killing Fields had ended, people still felt unsafe. Plus, they really didn't have anything to return "home" to since most of their properties were in shambles, including the eco-structure of their communities. Without rice fields, trees, supplies, and marketplaces, there was nothing for the Cambodian citizens to live on.

So, many of the survivors ran away to other countries such as Thailand, Laos, and Vietnam. Since they were finally free to move around, Sophea traveled with her parents, her baby sister and seventy-seven-year-old grandmother, Thida.

They all walked back to Siem Reap, wondering what was to become of them and what it would be like to return home. Everyone walked in pensive silence, lost in their own thoughts. Thida wondered if her husband would be there. She missed him. Cha-Cha wondered what their home looked like now. Most of the land had been ruined, bombed, and destroyed. The country was in shambles. The dam that they had worked so hard to build only stood for two years because it was so poorly made. It was a fitting symbol of the failure of the communist Regime by the end of their reign of horror.

Most of the overthrown communist military fled into the wilderness of Cambodia's jungles and rainforest and to neighboring countries. Pol Pot escaped by helicopter when the city of Phnom Penh fell under his power.

As a new prime minister took the seat of leadership, the citizens of Cambodia were told they could return to their homes, wherever that may be. They were no longer under the severe dictatorship that had been inflicted by Pol Pot. In actuality, there were probably close to four million deaths in this human genocide, one of the worst within the twenty-first century. Most history books only listed a third of those numbers, perhaps not accounting for the suicides and those who died of starvation and other causes. Close to 2.5 million died directly at the hands of the Khmer Rouge, while even more died from famine, suicides, and politicizes.

In any case, all of the citizens that had survived hell on earth were finally free to begin their long march home in much the same way as they had left in 1975. Some hoped to find relatives they had lost contact with. Along the walk back, the countryside was blemished with sunken hollows of dirt, as if hell had engulfed the land above it. The pockmarked landscape of mass graves was the reminder of a human catastrophe of the worst kind.

The Long family finally found their way back to the Sim property, which was Cha-Cha's birthplace and Thida's lifelong residence. When they arrived, they were stunned to discover nothing left. It was both unbelievable and believable at the same time. The only distinguishable building left standing on their parcel of land was a restroom made of concrete. It was a mark of where they used to live. All of the beauty that had been there before was now just a memory. The trees, the riverbank, the lovely yard and barn—and most importantly, the house itself—were all casualties of the war. Nobody was there.

Thida walked to the spot where her lovely home had once stood. The rubble revealed a few tidbits of her old life, the one she had shared with Lee and their five children. *Had they all died?* She picked up a small piece of paper with singed edges. It was a picture that had been sitting near the hutch in the entryway. All of that money Lee had once stashed away, unwilling to share with his family, was long gone, along with all of their possessions.

Silently, Cha-Cha marveled at how stingy her father had been with his money and how insignificant it now was. It was gone, perhaps burned in one of the bombs as the frame of what was once their home burned up high into the fiery skies of war. Money hadn't mattered after all; it was her family who mattered. She wished her father had realized that. It would have benefitted them well during some of those financially trying times.

It was difficult to recognize the property as theirs. The fruit trees, the murky river that was now nearly dried up, and the rotten wood scattered around their yard made their land indistinguishable. The acreage had been destroyed, along with most of their community. Nevertheless, it was still home. It still had great significance.

The Long family stayed there for a few days and nights. They slept on the ground under the cold stars, with no shelter. There was no roof to separate them from the heavens. They knew not what their fate would be or what would become of them. All they knew was that they were still alive, when so many of their own countrymen and fellow citizens had not been so fortunate. They still had each other and had circled back to the beginning, from the very place their torment had begun.

Once the Killing Fields came to an end and the people were free to go wherever they wanted, many of them had no place to go. Every town had been destroyed. There were virtually no homes left. Some had burned to the ground or been bombed. The squatters took over land from the previous owners of property; so many had died that whoever came and claimed a piece of land were the new owners. But with everything destroyed, it was not a treasure to own land. In fact, it was hard to even distinguish where your plot of land was. It was a time of uncertainty.

Chapter Twenty-One

"The Merchant"

Even though it was discouraging to rebuild their property again from scratch, Narin and Cha-Cha began gathering remnants of wood, aluminum, and whatever they could find to build a shelter. They found pieces from their own lot and from places in town that had leftover shingles and scraps. They used rocks or old nails that had to be pulled out from demolished construction and began the arduous task of rebuilding.

She still went by Cha-Cha, whenever addressed. It was safer not to reveal her true name until they all knew if the coast was clear.

As she had always done, Thida managed the children while her daughter and son-in-law started the process of reconstruction. Narin and Cha-Cha were not builders and they lacked the tools to remake what was once there before. Just as she was carrying an armload of broken materials, Rachana noticed a family walking towards them. It was Phary and Pitch, along with their children. They ran towards each other with outstretched arms of glee.

"I can't believe you survived!" shouted Phary to her beloved younger sister. "How did you do it? They killed all of the educated ones. We thought you would be dead, and Narin too."

Their warm embrace was long and heartfelt, as if they never wanted to let go of each other. Thida saw them too and trotted over happily as Phary's smile revealed the tears of joy. "Mommy, I can't believe this day! I never thought we would see you again," she gasped. Everyone was thrilled to be back together.

Hoping to see her husband with them, Thida asked what had happened to Lee. Sadly, he had died only twenty days before the crowds of leftover survivors had been freed. He was eight-six-years-old and had nothing to eat. He died of starvation. It had never been easy to feed him, as Lee was a picky eater. The fact that there was no food for the third class citizens made things even more difficult. He literally wasted away to nothing, as a thin and frail man who died with too much pride to endure any more cruelty from the Regime.

Lee had stayed with Phary and her family throughout the duration of the Khmer Rouge's brutal infliction upon Cambodia. They had hidden away, far within the thickest jungle mountain regions of a place where few ever traveled. Their friends were the very same people that had befriended Ponleau so many years ago and who Lee and Thida had always welcomed into their home. They returned the favor, and even through the twisted transition of power to the poor becoming first class citizens, the mountain people had protected them and spared their lives. They snuck Phary's family rice to eat and hid them whenever the Regime came by, which was infrequently in those parts.

Lee had once been an influential part of society and his being cast down to third class was something he had difficulty dealing with. It was astounding that he had endured the entire four years. And like most everyone in Cambodia, Lee had suffered from severe malnutrition and depression that contributed to his lack of will to eat.

Nevertheless, the rest of them were finally reunited. They felt happy and blessed to see each other and to know that their family was still alive. A few days later, Tina, Rachel, and Kalianne also joined them, along with their families. Only one brother-in-law died; it was Tina's husband.

They were all joined again with one another, by the grace of God. The next few days were spent with many tears of joy, hugging, and telling tales of survival as each of them had experienced close calls with death on their own personal journeys. All of them were in disbelief that Cha-Cha in particular–the weakest and frailest of the Sim siblings–had made it. Not just because of her feeble body frame, but also for the fact that she had achieved a diploma and had married a government employee. They had all surmised that their baby sister would be long dead and were astounded by her determination and success in sneaking by the Regime's strict guidelines to kill all of the professional and educated citizens. They didn't think that Cha-Cha had the strength, energy, or tenacity to make it. But she did. Seeing their youngest sister was like seeing a ghost.

After everyone rekindled their bond, they set out to work again on reconstructing the once beautiful home they had all shared. It was their birthplace, one of pride, nostalgia, and sentiment. Although they were never able to fully rebuild the structure, they did construct a cabin that offered sufficient shelter and comfort. Extravagance and material things were no longer important to them. Just having a roof over their head and having each other to cherish was the greatest gift of living.

Most of Cha-Cha and Thida's jewelry had been used for bartering throughout their trek. It came in handy for food to survive. So when the country became free, they were very, very poor. The family had nothing to their name except the shirts on their backs. Cha-Cha's sisters returned to their own parcels of land after they had all spent some time together, so Narin and Cha-Cha were left to manage the Sim property.

Some of Narin's family had also survived. They had become very bitter over the past five years and were spiteful of his marriage to Cha-Cha. They began influencing him negatively. They blamed her for strange and ridiculous things, like everyone getting separated during the Killing Fields. After visiting with them, Narin returned as a different person. He was Dr. Jekyll and Mr. Hyde.

As soon as he saw his wife nursing baby Neary, he initiated an argument with her. The fight escalated whereupon Narin smacked her across the face, shockingly out of character. Narin then beat her up while she was most vulnerable. Even though they had gone through horrific and unimaginable adversity together, he didn't appreciate Cha-Cha.

After that incident, Narin went to live with his family. She demanded that he should never return. In a sense, they became separated, although it was never official.

Sadly, Cha-Cha was left alone once again to care for her mother and two daughters. She had no way to earn a living and had not a single riel to her name. They were in destitute poverty.

Like Ruth from the bible who went to Boaz's field to harvest wheat, one day Cha-Cha took young Sophea with her to work in the rice fields. They picked the spare rice remnants, which were tiny pieces leftover from where the harvesters had cleaned the fields to near bare. On their way back from the rice fields and with nothing much to show for their efforts, a man loading up a rice wagon took pity on this feeble mother with her young girl and handed them a few handful of rice.

Quite thankful for his generosity, Cha-Cha and Sophea brought the rice home and pounded it down. For all of that days' worth of work, they only had one can of rice. She dared not cook the whole can, so instead they made porridge with a portion of it. One can of rice was all the food they had in the entire world. It was barely enough to last a day for two grown women and two children.

Not to be discouraged, Cha-Cha took Sophea back to the rice fields the next day. This time, she brought the fishing basket with her back to the rice fields. There was some shallow water there, so she was resourceful and used the basket to scoop up some shrimp, minnows, and small crabs. On their way home, mom and daughter stopped by several houses to see if she could barter her catch of the day in exchange for rice. She was successful and managed to get four cans of rice as a trade for her fish.

However, she knew she had to do something more or they would barely make it. Because she could no longer teach and had nothing of value, out of desperation Cha-Cha went to visit Phary. She told her sister about the split-up with Narin and his sudden outburst of abusiveness towards her. Phary had little to offer in advice, but she gave her baby sister the reassurance that God would bless her in some way if she remained faithful.

On the way back from visiting her favorite sister, Cha-Cha took a different route than she had traveled on the way there. It was a longer road that was less traveled. She had made that walk so many times before the war, but now her inner instinct told her to go that way. It was not a shortcut.

While holding the hand of her precious Sophea, they came upon four people who were sitting at an old school building. The structure was crusty now, with many of the bricks befallen and the asphalt broken off. Only five years of war had aged the building by half a century.

The four strangers were there, trying to start up a market. There was one Chinese lady who was selling barbecue chicken. Cha-Cha had seen her somewhere before, many years before the Killing Fields. Her name was Ping. Ping also sold medicine and bamboo shoots. She was an eccentric, yet sweet, middle-aged woman with long braids to hold back her wispy black and graying hair away from her face; which was hidden underneath a colorful hat. Her clashing patterned blouse enhanced her character as a semi-toothless grin beckoned Cha-Cha to come see her. Between the alluring smell of chicken and the friendly face of Ping, she couldn't resist.

"Come! Come!" said Ping, as she crooked her finger to lure them in.

Cha-Cha walked over to Ping and sat down to chat. Little Sophea busied herself by drawing in the dirt with a stick. After getting reacquainted, a man on a bicycle showed up.

It was not by accident, as he had already prearranged to visit Ping on that day. His long gray beard and straw hat was mysterious, with its extra-large brim that overshadowed his eyebrows. He called himself "Toto" and was a trader with the black market in Thailand. On this day, Toto had sarongs and children's clothing for sale. He was very hungry and wanted to trade his items for the barbecued chicken. But Ping did not want clothing. "No deal!" she exclaimed. Ping only wanted gold or rice.

Cha-Cha stepped in. She happened to have a small piece of gold, which was quite scarce in her diminished collection of jewelry. But the timing was right. So, she offered Toto the small piece of gold for a toddler pair of shorts, tank top, and two bags of peppermint candy. Toto then gave Ping the piece of gold to buy the barbecue chicken to eat. Hence, everyone was happy with the exchange.

The clothes fit baby Neary perfectly, and the candy was thoroughly enjoyed and appreciated by Grandma Thida. In fact, all of the girls made themselves sick from eating too much peppermint candy, although they didn't regret it for one second.

This was the beginning of a new friendship between Cha-Cha and Ping. As an old acquaintance from the past, Ping was never kind to Cha-Cha during her teenage years. Her scrappy and fragile appearance made her the target of ridicule. However, God touched Ping's heart that day and granted her a newfound desire to help Cha-Cha. The funny Chinese lady decided that they had more in common than she previously thought and that perhaps she had misjudged this entrepreneurial single mother. Hence, she had a change of heart.

"I have a proposition for you," said Ping. With that, she held out her calloused palm to reveal a handful of pills. "For every pill you sell, you will give me four cans of rice. I will give the pills to you now."

At that time, it was a rare arrangement for anyone to trade without any possessions in return for barter. Ping trusted her and basically gave Cha-Cha the chance to feed her family based on the honesty system. Cha-Cha very easily could have taken the pills and never returned again with anything. But she was a woman of integrity, if nothing else.

"Very well. But I can't sell these in the same place as you and compete with you. If you trust me, give me some pills and I will go from house to house selling them for you," replied Cha-Cha.

Ping thought for a moment and nodded. "Okay, I believe you will do it."

Being the shrewd businesswoman that she was, Cha-Cha turned around and sold each pill for eight to ten cans of rice instead of the four cans that were offered by Ping. Therefore, she profited by four to six cans of rice per pill. After doing this for several months, Cha-Cha stocked up on a lot of rice to feed her family. She and Ping established a great arrangement and trust between them. Plus, they were not infringing upon each other's territory because Cha-Cha took her allotment of pills door to door, instead of staying exclusively in the marketplace, where Ping sold hers.

After she had a pantry full of rice, Cha-Cha began trading some of her rice for gold. Having gold to barter with was always a good tool, even when cash seemed worthless. Eventually she built up a sizable stash of gold to replace all of the pieces that had been bartered or lost during the Killing Fields.

Ping also made out well and added sarongs to her collection of items to sell wholesale. The sarongs were very pretty and well made. Some had floral patterns or woven designs on them. Ping told Cha-Cha that she wanted 20 km of palm sugar for five sarongs.

Again, Cha-Cha went house to house selling them. Most of the women in the area had very little clothing to wear except the rags they had been wearing for years, so the sarongs were a big hit. However, instead of selling five sarongs for 20 km of palm sugar, Rachana sold one for 20 km. She sold two sarongs, gave Ping 20 km of sugar as agreed, kept 20 km of sugar for herself as profit, and also had three extra sarongs. One she gave to her niece, and two she kept for herself to wear. The sarong exchange was a double benefit in that they were lovely to wear and gave Cha-Cha a boost in confidence. She was a great saleswoman—a natural.

By now, the recent "divorcee" was looking good in her new clothes and business was going well for the single mom. Essentially, Ping, Cha-Cha, Toto, and a few others had created a new little marketplace in the community. Nearly all of it was done through bartering since there was no exchange of riels or money. The use of money had not yet returned to their ecosystem after the war ended.

Nevertheless, Cha-Cha saved up on some pure silverware, gold, new clothing, and enough food to feed her family. She became a merchant. Both women were pleased with the business, as it was going very well for them. They became great friends and Cha-Cha continued taking things from Ping to hock for huge profits. Saving money turned out to be a huge asset to Cha-Cha throughout her lifetime. Her entrepreneurial pursuit with Ping enabled her to accumulate a fair amount of gold, which she cleverly stowed away for the future.

However, this merchant lifestyle was rather hectic. In the morning, Cha-Cha went to the market to buy and sell material. Their distributor, Toto, imported the clothes from Thailand. Cambodia was still in shambles and there was much chaos. It was still a very dangerous place to be. On a scale of zero to ten, the beauty of Cambodia was subzero. So, every week Toto risked his life to get the goods to the new marketplace. It was worth his while in financial gains, since everybody in the country started over again from scratch.

During the day, Cha-Cha also volunteered as a teacher in their village. Teaching was what she most enjoyed. It was her passion. Retailing kept her family afloat and gave them a good income. She still believed in the value of education, despite the fact that it had nearly cost her family their lives.

Aside from a few who had found and fixed a bicycle or who had acquired a cart, there was no transportation. People walked everywhere. The market was about seven miles from Cha-Cha's cabin on the Sim property. Every day, she ran and jogged to and from school and the market. She got up at four o'clock in the morning to breastfeed baby Neary and left both daughters with her now seventy-nine-year-old mother. She left the marketplace earlier than the other merchants to do the volunteer teaching job and to feed her baby in between.

Times were frantic because the school and the market were of great walking distance and the time to travel was very little. She ran every day. Running built up her strength. On the return trip home, every day Cha-Cha stopped at the river to take a quick bath to freshen up. Thida prepared her lunch and had it ready for her. She grabbed the lunch and ate it on the run, right after her quick bath. Very often, Cha-Cha only had time to take a few bites of her lunch before she arrived at the school. But she was healthy from the exercise and felt stronger than ever. She achieved the endurance of a marathon runner.

On the weekends, there was only a little more time to relax, although there was still much work to do. Thida kept their cabin pretty clean and did a wonderful job helping to raise Sophea and Neary. Cha-Cha helped her catch up with chores on the weekends because there was no school.

Quite unexpectedly, one day Kim Sivorn showed up at their small home. She was Cha-Cha's cousin who had betrayed them in the Killing Fields. Cha-Cha had never forgotten that deed, or the kindness of Kim's husband, Thom. He gave them the tarp and helped them to cross the dangerous river just before the monsoon rains of that depressing summer in 1975. Unfortunately, Thom had died later at the hands of the Khmer Rouge.

Her cousin's uninvited visit was barely cordial. Cha-Cha's snide expression towards Kim was one of unwelcome intrusion. She hardly spoke and simply opened the door to let Kim in.

By now, Cha-Cha was doing very well in the marketplace and sold nice clothing. She suspected Kim was there for handouts, rather than just a *"How do you do?"* visit. Before the betrayal, she had given Kim and her husband everything. Cha-Cha had cared for her with the same love as a sister.

Just then, Kim had the nerve to ask for a skirt for her daughter. Cha-Cha didn't say a word. Her cross expression was one of perfidy and disgust. Then, Thida spoke to Kim for a few minutes, but Cha-Cha still didn't say one word. After a brief ten minutes of discomfort, Kim's visit was cut short when she realized that her cousin refused to talk. So Kim got up and left, without ever apologizing. She had come to the area to visit her sister and mother, who lived nearby. It was the last time Cha-Cha ever saw her again, although Kim did send a letter to her once again, well after they had moved to the U.S. Her correspondence or attempts to connect were always done in greed or desperation, asking for help. However, Cha-Cha never responded to Kim's requests then or at any point thereafter.

Another time, Thom's brother's family contacted Cha-Cha with a letter. It read:

Dear Cha-Cha:

We would love for you and your family to come stay here with us for a visit if you want to stay. We don't know what the future holds for us or for your family. But what will be, will be. We are reaching out to you as friends and family and want you to know that Thom loved you and that we all love you too. We know how kind you were to my brother and his family.

Although Cha-Cha held no resentment towards Thom's family, the timing was not right. Only a few weeks later, in May of 1980, a stranger came to visit her. He had been hired by Narin as a messenger. The guy was young, in his early twenties. He found Cha-Cha working at her volunteer teaching job and handed her a scribbled piece of paper. The short note from her wayward husband read:

Please honey, come join me. Bring our two daughters and go with Sok. There is an opportunity to go to France or America, or others. – Love Narin

Confusion manifested in Cha-Cha's throat as she swallowed a lump of astonishment. Narin had escaped to a refugee camp on the border of Thailand and Cambodia, which was a place that many people ran to because of the haziness of what was to become of their country. It was still dangerous and people didn't know if history would repeat itself again. Some worried that it could, as there were still many political pushes and pulls for power at the head of the country. Everyone still lived in fear, always looking over their shoulder to see if soldiers might return to chase them through the streets and fields with machetes or machine guns.

The messenger said, "You must make your decision quickly. I will only be here for three days."

"You are Sok?" Cha-Cha asked the stranger.

He nodded yes. "I will take you and your daughters to him if you choose to go," he said.

With her heart beating rapidly, Cha-Cha wondered what to do. It was such a big decision to make and without much time to think it through. So, she sought the advice of all her sisters and her beloved mother.

Thida was sad upon hearing the news. "Honey, it isn't easy living in another country that is not ours. How would you make a living? We don't speak their language or know anything about their culture. We don't know anybody. There is no family to rely on."

"Well, it hasn't been exactly easy living here either," she replied.

"Right now I have all my daughters close to me and you have all of your sisters and the same neighbors, for the most part. We all know each other so well and can count on each other. Why would you want to leave this place? For the unknown?" asked Thida. She didn't want to lose her daughter, especially her favorite one.

"For my daughters," explained Cha-Cha. "If we lived overseas, maybe they could become something in life instead of living like this. Maybe they could have a better future. All they have seen is destruction, misery, despair, and death . . ."

A tear sprouted from the corner of Thida's eye. They had been through so much together. Cha-Cha had devoted her life to her mother's wellbeing, and vice versa. It was a tough decision to make and not one to be taken lightly.

Phary came to visit. She heard the case was very serious and made a painfully slow walk to her baby sis's house, which was seven miles away. Phary's love for her sister was more important than the pain in her hips and joints that caused her daily distress.

Phary also dealt with a tough time handling things and putting food on their plates. "Is this what you think is best for your family?" she asked her baby sister seriously.

"I don't know," said Cha-Cha. She was so torn by the love of her family and the prospect of a better opportunity for her two daughters that she still did not have the answer.

Then, Phary turned to her elderly mother. "If Cha-Cha leaves, I want you to come and stay with us. We will take care of you, Mother."

Cha-Cha tossed and turned for two nights. By the third day, she still felt unclear. Questions wrapped around her mind like, *What kind of life will these two girls have if I stay here? Will there be more killing? Are there more wars looming ahead? More destruction?* Yet Cha-Cha found no answers to her own questions; because nobody had the answers of what was to become of Cambodia and its people. They were at the mercy of the leaders, whether good or bad.

Quite honestly, there was nothing left to stay for, except for their families. No bicycles, no cars, no jobs, no buildings, nothing. The future there was as uncertain as the next monsoon rain that could come and wash away the landscape in a moment's notice. The citizens who remained didn't know if the Regime would come back. All the houses were destroyed, including the farms for which most of them relied upon for food and to support their families. It was all gone. Cha-Cha came to the conclusion that she was in search of a better life; one that was safer.

Deep down, Cha-Cha loved her mother more than any other human being on earth. But she also knew that Thida had four other daughters who would not neglect her. Sophea and Neary represented the future and her decision as a mother was to do what was best for them, even if it hurt her in the process. She realized that either decision would leave her with a big regret. On one hand, she might regret not giving her daughters a fair chance at having a future, but on the other hand, she would regret leaving her mother, who had chosen to live with Cha-Cha instead of her own husband. Thida never even had the chance to bid farewell to him, because Lee died only a few short weeks before the country was freed in 1979.

After much deliberation and self-reflection, the urge to go to the refugee camp was greater than the urge to stay. Thida was now seventy-nine years old and needed care, but not a future. Therefore, Cha-Cha chose to seek the best opportunity for her two little girls, who needed her most and who would rely on her just as much as Cha-Cha had relied on her own mother throughout her upbringing. She could only hope to be as wonderful and loyal of a mother as Thida had been. Cha-Cha also hoped that after she got to the refugee camp and saw what kind of condition it was in—or if there was in fact a promising life elsewhere—she could retrieve her mother and persuade her to join them.

Thida had given up her whole life for her daughter and it was the most difficult decision Cha-Cha had ever made to leave her behind. The feeling of a broken heart was looming and both mother and daughter were so sad when Cha-Cha announced that she would be leaving for the refugee camp in hopes of getting a chance to bring Sophea and Neary to a country such as the U.S., France, or Canada.

When Sok showed up at their cabin to pick up Cha-Cha and lead her to the refugee camp, she gently asked him to wait outside for a few minutes.

Thida wept as never before and her heart was crushed like that of a giant boulder rolling over her small physique. She sobbed and sobbed and sobbed, as Cha-Cha tearfully wept along with her and promised that they would see one another again. She gripped her mother's hands and embraced Thida for what seemed like hours. She repeated over and over again how much she loved her more than the whole world multiplied by a million.

Then, Cha-Cha lifted one-year-old Neary and took the hand of her five-year-old Sophea. The three of them turned back to look at her mother one last time, still crying. Both little girls knew that something was changing. They sensed it, especially Sophea. She reached up to her grandmother's face, touched her cheeks, and kissed her. "I love you," said the sweet little girl.

Sok knocked on the door behind her. "I don't want to interrupt, but we have to go now if you're coming," he said. The sun was setting over the horizon as Cha-Cha departed, feeling emotionally spent and still unsure if she had made the right decision.

Chapter Twenty-Two

"Refugees"

They had to travel through the jungle at night, which was enough of a danger in itself. Cha-Cha had the courage to do it after having survived in the jungle for the past four years. Even with her two young children, it was treacherous to move. A widow also journeyed with them, along with her four young children. She had lost her husband in the Killing Fields. Keeping six children quiet was a challenge for the two women, but they followed Sok and did as he instructed. They stayed as quiet as possible and walked with light feet and whispers, although they rarely spoke unless necessary.

Sok had warned them of the dangers of getting to the refugee camp at Khao-i-Dang. Although it had been put in place by the new prime minister of Cambodia, the refugee camp had already reached its limit with an average of 1,600 people going there every day between its opening in November of 1979 to January of 1980. The base was made to hold 300,000 refugees. However, because of the vast numbers of Cambodian citizens who were fleeing in hopes of getting out of the country permanently, the new government promptly shut off the entry to Khao-i-Dang by January of 1980. Most of the people there were professionals, such as teachers, engineers, doctors, nurses, and lawyers. They were those who had survived the terror of the Khmer Rouge, like Cha-Cha's family.

However, the closed entry to Khao-i-Dang did not deter people from trying to get there. They knew that if they eventually made it behind the walls of the refugee camp, there was a chance they might be able to obtain Visas to go live elsewhere. Plus, some of them had relatives whom they hoped to reunite with. Many refugees had died trying to get there, because they first had to go to the holding camp on the Cambodian side and be shipped to Khao-i-Dang on the Thai side. The two camps were about 20 km apart from one another. The base was administered by the World

Food Program and UNICEF, the Red Cross and the UNBRO (United Nations Border Relief Operation).

Narin had apparently been in the refugee camp for a few months, ensuring his place there and an opportunity to move elsewhere once the Visas were issued. However, Cha-Cha's trip wasn't until in May of 1980, which was well after the open door policy had been cut off. Her decision was dangerous, since guards patrolled day and night to make sure that no more Cambodian citizens would be allowed to escape the country. Entry to Khao-i-Dang was no longer permitted and the ruthless border patrollers were very trigger happy.

The children were frightened and clung to their mothers with tight grips. The scary noises from the jungle came from every direction and the half-lit moon made it difficult to see anything, especially through the thick foliage and vegetation. The ominous vines hung over their heads like giant monsters, waiting to swallow them. There were eyes on them that could not be seen. Owls, tigers, snakes, and other strange critters crept stealthily through their natural habitat, lurking upon the new strangers who dared to invade their territory.

Sok was a good guide, considering the group had no trail to follow.

Suddenly, a flashlight shone into the sky from somewhere up ahead and the small group heard voices. The border guards were patrolling. The footsteps were only a few feet away. Sok silently signaled to the two women to crouch down and keep the children very still. They nearly smacked right into them. Danger was barely a few feet away as the crunching leaves echoed in the thickness of the night. One cough, sneeze, or noise of the baby would have alerted the guards. All of them would have been robbed and killed for trying to cross.

Cha-Cha's heartbeat was as loud as a set of drums. She feared they would hear it as her adrenaline made the sweat drip down her forehead in the muggy night. The troopers passed by as the women managed to keep the babies from crying or stirring. Cha-Cha held baby Neary very close to her bosom in order to muffle her and keep her still.

Although the first camp was not their ultimate destination, they did make it there. However, the camp on the Cambodian side did not allow people to leave the country without permission. After staying there for a few days, Cha-Cha followed protocol to obtain a permit to reach Khao-i-Dang on the Thai side. The immigration office denied her request, stating the refugee camp had already reached its limit.

Sok was unable to continue with Cha-Cha and the widow, so he found a second guide to lead them to the other camp. This was going to be even more dangerous he warned. They decided to take their chances. Cha-Cha had to reach her husband somehow. She had gone this far. It was too late to turn back. So, with blind faith, she decided to take her children all the way through and attempt to cross the border.

The second guide was less compassionate than Sok had been. There was something about him that caused Cha-Cha a feeling of distrust. However, Sok had assured her that if they reached Khao-i-Dang, they would be safe and accepted. It was just getting through that proposed a challenge.

The second guide told them to follow closely. Again, they were taken through the dense forest, which was laced with mines. Their guide navigated them around potential hazards. The last thing either of the ladies wanted was to step on a mine or to have one of their children step on one. They would be killed instantly or maimed permanently.

After walking for a couple of hours, the guide spotted flashlights up ahead. By then the nine of them had already crossed the Thai border, although there were no markers to indicate the point of passage. They were not out of the woods yet, figuratively speaking. The voices came closer and closer, so the guide pointed quickly to the women to turn away, so as not to walk into the guards. Cha-Cha clutched Sophea and Neary very close. The other woman did the same with her children, putting a finger to her lips in a gesture of hush.

Just as they were trying to walk quietly through the night to get away from the voices, the other mother and one of her children fell into a well. It was dark, damp, and extremely scary. However, it was fortunate that the well had been stopped up or that it had instead been a mine. Thankfully, the guide pulled the woman and child out safely. Her little boy was a bit muddy, and trembling with fright. Their small band once again managed to get around the patrolling enforcement that was looking for fugitives, such as they were.

Cha-Cha's tribe kept moving and walked throughout the night until about 4:00 a.m. They finally reached the second refugee camp. However, instead of taking advantage of the fact that most of the Thai guards were sleeping, he told Cha-Cha and the other woman to sleep nearby until close to morning. It was a mistake on his part, since after the sun rose over the red gravel of camp Khao-i-Dang, so too had most of the guards awakened from their few hours of rest.

"C'mon, I'm going to get you through the barbed wire fence and push you in," the guide told the two ladies. They seemed uncertain, yet they did as they were told in order to stay alive and not get caught.

"Who goes there?" yelled a guard.

They found themselves facing two armed men with machine guns pointed at them only a few yards away, just as the first child was about to sneak underneath the prickly barbed wire on the outskirts of the base.

"Put your hands up!" ordered the second patrolman.

They had been caught. All of them raised their arms as fear gripped the two women and their kids. One of the children started crying.

The guide swiftly spoke something in Thai. The women didn't understand what he was saying, although they could make out the gist of it. Then the guide cautiously removed something from his pocket. It appeared to be a fistful of silver trinkets. Their guide was trying to bribe the guards.

It worked. Although they were still trembling with fright, the two guards finally dropped their weapons and turned their back on the women and kids. They yanked the silver out of the guide's hand and sputtered something to him as they turned to leave.

Then, instead of helping them to get inside the fence, the guide pointed to the direction that Cha-Cha and the woman were supposed to go—but not before a surprising turn of events.

"Before you go, empty your pockets," he instructed. He was robbing them just before they left. The two women complied. Both of them turned their pockets inside out and dumped out their small satchel, which mostly contained food and items for the kids.

Thankfully, Cha-Cha's hunch of mistrust towards the second guide had given her the instinct to hide her valuables. She had pinned her bag of jewelry in a small cloth wrap that she had made special just for the trek. It was carefully positioned on the hem of her skirt, where it remained virtually invisible to the untrained eye. The guide patted both of them down. Cha-Cha had purposefully left out a couple of less important items that she gave him.

"That's all I have," Cha-Cha remarked as she handed the shady character a couple of gold bracelets. Perhaps he felt entitled to steal from them.

"Take off your clothes," he said to both women. They stripped off their blouses and dropped their skirts to the ground. He reached down Cha-Cha's skirt and did not find her hidden jewelry because she had done such a clever job in hiding it. After copping a feel from both women's breasts with a disdainful expression, he turned away. Behind his back, Cha-Cha gave him a stare of disdain. He would get what he deserved someday, she surmised.

"Good luck," he whispered. They both stood there in their undergarments, a bra, and panties. Both were exposed to the outdoors and vulnerable to the creep who had just saved them and then betrayed them all at once.

As they all watched him retreat into the forest, the women redressed and went in the direction he had told them to go. They finally made it into the second refugee camp, which was their ultimate destination. By the end of their terrifying journey, Cha-Cha felt a compassionate bond with the woman she had traveled with. She also felt bad for her that the lady had four small children to raise all alone and that she had lost her husband at the hands of the Regime.

Narin, on the other hand, had been safely staying at Khao-i-Dang. The camp was situated on a partially wooded field very close to Cambodia's southeast border. At least 160,000 people stayed there.

Once inside, Cha-Cha quickly searched for her husband. The World Relief organization fed them and brought all of the refugees' food at least once every week. Although Cha-Cha was somewhat happy to see Narin, the happiness faded quickly. Instead, her focus was on her baby, Neary, who had developed diarrhea and a high fever. The baby's condition was very risky as her temperature soared. At only thirteen months old, Neary was unable to cope with the difficult conditions that she had endured.

After spending only a few hours with her husband, whom she had not seen for close to a year, Cha-Cha knew the baby needed emergency care. Narin took them to the hospital, where he worked during the day. The hospital was in one big open room with a few partitions to separate the operating stations from those who needed bed rest. It was a field hospital with limited tools, medications, and resources to care for the patients.

Indeed, baby Neary's condition was quite severe and the hospital staff explained to the worried mother that she would need around the clock surveillance until she recovered. Cha-Cha stayed close by her infant for the duration of her care, which took eleven days. Little Sophea also stayed next to her mother the whole time, although she could have gone back to the shelter with her father. Sophea never really knew him that well and didn't feel comfortable with him. She was mommy's little girl. Narin had not been around much during the Killing Fields when he was sent to the rice fields to work. Ever since her parents had been separated, Sophea felt even more distant from him. He never spent any time with her even when he was around. Narin was never "kid friendly" in a sense that most fathers try to bond with their children.

Even more disturbing was the news Cha-Cha learned about Narin while at the hospital. While sitting next to her baby Neary, a nurse approached her. "You are Narin's wife?" she asked.

"Yes," answered Cha-Cha.

"That's strange. He had told some of the girls at the cafeteria that he was a widower," replied the nurse. "How long have you two been married?"

"Eight years," she said.

The nurse looked at Cha-Cha sympathetically. "Is there something else I should know?" she asked.

Thinking for a moment, the nurse said, "No . . . not really."

Looking puzzled and inquisitive, Cha-Cha gave the nurse an odd expression. So, the girl added, "I just think he seemed to be hitting on a couple of the women. But I don't want to start any trouble for you," she added.

"No problem. I appreciate your honesty," said Cha-Cha. Her heart filled with disappointment and regret. She had left her wonderful mother behind for this terrible experience. Most of the trip was spent sneaking through a monstrous jungle and dodging robbers and now sitting by the bedside of her dying infant. Suddenly, Cha-Cha felt responsible for putting her children in jeopardy. She doubted her decision to come.

After the infant girl was finally better and discharged from the field clinic, Cha-Cha finally got to stay with her husband. They had not shared a bed together in a long time. It took a bit of adjustment. He acted happy to see her. But after the news that the nurse had disclosed to her, Cha-Cha felt a new coldness towards him. He was her husband, and had been her choice to marry. She felt anger and fury, much the same anger and resentment she had felt towards her father when she learned of Lee's infidelities. Cha-Cha suddenly looked at Narin differently. Sometimes she even wondered if she had made a mistake and what her life would have been like if she had chosen to marry Phon instead. *Would she have been happier? Would they have survived the Killing Fields together, as she had with Narin?* These were questions that could never be answered. Time was something that could never be replaced; therefore, dwelling on past hurts and wrongs was futile.

On the third night in her new home at Khao-i-Dang, an RPG explosive hit the refugee camp. It was 1:00 a.m. on May 31, 1980; exactly fifteen days after Cha-Cha had arrived on the grounds. Even though the bases were set up to provide exceptional care to the refugees, there was also a dark side for them all to endure. There was still much hostility between bordering countries of Cambodia. Rumors of abuse in the camp, including conscription, extortion, and even physical punishing of refugees were not uncommon. The Thai soldiers set off the bombs. They didn't want the Cambodian citizens in their country.

At first, the loud explosion from a first bomb awoke the Long family. They were frightened. Cha-Cha reached for her children. Everyone in their building was screaming and confused. Unexpectedly and unluckily, a second bomb landed right next to her bed. Their peaceful slumber was violently interrupted.

That was not the worst of it. The entire Long family was badly injured, along with eight other people within their building. Strangers ran in to help all who had been wounded. Chaos ensued.

One lady lost the side of her breast. The shrapnel pierced the lungs of another man, putting him in serious condition. The bits and pieces of the bomb were lodged deep into his lungs, making it difficult for him to breathe. Narin's injury was to his knee. Baby Neary was bleeding from the side of her head, yet astoundingly she didn't lose her ear or hearing. Little Sophea's arm was also wounded. Everyone was crying, screaming, and panicking. They didn't know if more bombs were coming and the hysteria ensued.

All of the victims were taken to the care center that was set up by the world relief efforts. It was staffed by volunteers and missionaries from different countries.

The most serious of all the victims was Cha-Cha. The bomb had landed right next to her bed, causing critical wounds from head to toe. She was covered in shrapnel internally and externally, to the point that her body was barely recognizable. Cha-Cha was bleeding so badly that nobody thought she was even alive, so they placed her on a gurney in a corner of the back of the field hospital and placed a white sheet over her body. They doubted she would make it, so they attended to the others first.

Meanwhile, the German surgeon and nurses cared for the children first and then the adults, including the man whose lungs were severely damaged. Since there were limited tools and medication to help the victims, the process was excruciatingly painful and meticulous.

From 1:00 a.m. until noon, they worked on the victims, removing bits and pieces of the explosives with tweezers and small tools. Cha-Cha still lay bleeding in the corner, fading in and out of consciousness. Her memories were scattered. She thought of her mother and her daughters. Her condition was critical. Whenever a nurse or someone came close to her, she barely had the strength to speak. She worried about the wellbeing of her children as she lay on the gurney dying.

A nurse came over to check on her. Cha-Cha whispered, "Please, take care of my children." She knew that if she died, Narin would not likely stick around to take care of their daughters. His behaviors were not indicative of a caring father. Instead, he was a womanizer. Cha-Cha worried that he would abandon their children to pursue his own life with a new wife. She wondered what would become of them. All she ever wanted was for them to have a future.

Finally, she passed out, gasping and choking on her own blood. The pain subsided as her body adjusted to the loss of blood. She was near death and knew it. After surviving the Killing Fields, she had mistakenly left Siem Reap in exchange for this disastrous journey.

Finally, the German surgeon finished bandaging all of the victims. He pulled back the sheet on his last patient, expecting the woman to be dead. He put his stethoscope on her and could barely make out a heartbeat. "I'll experiment to see if anything comes up," he said to the nurses. He put his ear down next to Cha-Cha's bloody face and asked everyone to be still.

Spectacularly, there was just a faint breath coming from her lips. Cha-Cha had been unconscious for some time. They carefully placed her lifeless body on the operating table. She opened her eyes for just a second and everything was blurry. She sensed their presence. "My babies . . ." she whispered.

"They are going to be okay," said the kind doctor. His face was long and lean. He had a balding head and crystal blue eyes. The doctor shook his head in disbelief of the woman's will to survive. He pulled up her blouse, which was soaked in blood and tattered. "Just rest," he instructed. Cha-Cha blinked.

Moments thereafter, she fell into a coma. The German doctor had to cut her intestines open to remove the pieces of explosives and shrapnel. It took many hours to carefully pick out the pieces, but they were unable to get them all. She would live with some in her head and throughout her body for the rest of her life. But they were able to save her by the grace of God.

For the next two months, Cha-Cha stayed in the care unit. Her recovery was slow and painful. While there, she met another friend at the Refugee Camp who knew Lynn, Em, and Lana from before the Killing Fields. They had all been such great friends when Cha-Cha was a single teacher. Unfortunately, Em and Cha-Cha were the only ones who survived out of their great group of girlfriends. But Em's husband had been killed also.

One day while resting in the hospital, a seventh day Adventist missionary came by the ward and gave a slide show to the patients. He was a young, lean fellow with an American face and different accent. His name was Kyle. He was dressed in denim slacks and a collared shirt, indicative of a foreigner. For the first time, Cha-Cha saw the face of Jesus portrayed high from a projector screen. His name registered in her heart and mind. She had never heard about Jesus before, since most of the Asian countries celebrated Hinduism or Buddhism.

Although Cha-Cha didn't become a member of the seventh day Adventist community, the seed of God was planted within her soul. She saw the good in Jesus and the kindness in his face.

Later that day, a group of teenagers came to her ward to sing. It was strange, since she couldn't really understand what they were singing. Their chorus was beautiful and timely. A translator spoke to the patients about the word of God. Cha-Cha and some of the other patients listened with intent. The guy said:

24 "Therefore everyone who hears these words of mine and puts
   them into practice are like a wise man who built his house on the rock.
25 The rain came down, the streams rose, and the winds blew
   and beat against that house; yet it did not fall, because it had its
   foundation on the rock.
26 But everyone who hears these words of mine and does not
   put them into practice is like a foolish man who built his house on sand.
27 The rain came down, the streams rose, and the winds blew and beat
   against that house, and it fell with a great crash."

Cha-Cha had never heard of anybody building a house on sand or rock. The students didn't introduce themselves, nor explain the meaning of the song they had sung. However, the impression it left was memorable and touching.

They all left after singing. Then two hours later, they returned. All of them knelt around Cha-Cha's bed, placed their hands across her body and started to pray. She didn't understand what they were doing, but she closed her eyes and lay very still. They began to speak in their foreign language. She couldn't understand them. They stayed still, praying and all closing their eyes in a big circle surrounding the stranger for whom they had never met, yet whom they all seemed to sincerely care about. After they were done with their words of prayer, the missionaries got up and smiled at her. One by one, they placed a hand on her forehead and smiled as they touched Cha-Cha and left. She couldn't ask them any questions and didn't know what was going on.

It wasn't until many years later that she would remember the meaning of what they had done. However, Cha-Cha couldn't help but to feel better after the teens' visit. Her body suddenly felt reinvigorated. She wondered if they knew magic.

The next day, she asked one of the caretakers for a bath and if she would help her get out of bed and learn to walk again. It was a miracle but she had newfound energy that came within her suddenly and unexpectedly. Only the day before their visit, Cha-Cha had felt so weak and tired that she could barely turn her body from its left to right side. One day later, she was feeling so good, well enough to ask for help to walk just a few steps.

The very next day, the same group of people returned again. They came to Cha-Cha's bed and the bed across from her, and knelt down in prayer. One spoke and they all ended their prayer with "Amen." They did not speak to any of the patients, nor did they disclose who they were or what they were doing.

Again, Cha-Cha slept well and felt newfound strength within twenty-four hours. "Excuse me!" she called out to the hospital staff.

One of the workers came over. "Are you okay, dear? Do you need something?"

"Yes. I would like two bamboo poles," said Rachana in a matter-of-fact tone of voice. She was a very independent lady.

"Why do you want them?" asked the worker.

Decidedly, Cha-Cha replied, "I'm going to get up and go to the bathroom."

"We can help you," the nurse tried to reason with her.

"No!" Cha-Cha exclaimed. "Just give me two poles, please. I want to see if I can do it or not."

So, the nurse went to find two bamboo poles as her patient requested. They were not very secure, but Cha-Cha slowly pushed her legs over the bed and hoisted herself up, which took all of her strength to maneuver. The bamboo poles were not made to hold the entire weight of a grown body, but somehow she managed to take a few steps without falling down.

There was another woman in the ward next to Cha-Cha who had been seriously injured with an axe. Apparently, she had been cutting firewood to earn money to feed her family. The woman had been admitted for three days and had yet to receive any medicine, since they were short on supplies at the refugee camp. However, just being admitted into the ward gave her the comfort of people to console her and food to eat.

The day before the healing group came to pray for her, the woman lay seriously suffering in her bed. She couldn't move and the pain was intolerable. Her body was as lifeless as a log that had been struck down in the forest. All she could do was move her hand and speak, but that was about all. The doctors hadn't visited her yet, nor given her any medication to ease the pain. The head doctor from Germany had taken time off to go back and visit his family.

However, God did not forget her. The prayer group came to visit her too. Miraculously, the woman walked out of the hospital even before Cha-Cha. The greatest physician of the universe came to visit her and she recovered. So too, did Cha-Cha recover. Fully two months after her savage attack, she was able to walk out of the Khao-i-Dang refugee camp hospital on her own.

Chapter Twenty-Three

"Reflections"

"Mom, are you alright?" Sophea asked, as she reached across the seat to squeeze her mother's hand on the drive back home. The funeral had been emotionally draining for everyone. Rachana had not spoken much, which was unlike her.

"Yes, I was just doing a lot of thinking," she replied.

"I know this is very tough for you, but it is for the best," said Sophea. She had different feelings about her father's death. He was not someone she had been proud of. *Like mother, like daughter.* Sophea knew little bits and pieces about her mother's relationship with her grandfather, Lee. Although she had never known him since she had been just a baby when the Killing Fields started, she had sometimes overheard a few stories that her mother had told to others.

Quietly, Rachana said, "Yes, I know. It's just overwhelming."

Sophea understood. "I think you can be happy now. Your whole marriage to Dad was difficult."

Rachana spoke. "I remember when we left Bataan refugee camp in the Philippines. We had been transferred there after the bomb in Khao-i-Dang. The beautiful countryside passed by and I had mixed feelings. *Where is America?* I wondered what it would be like and if we would be happy here."

Sophea nodded. "Neary and I would not be where we are today if it were not for you," she said kindly. The younger sister had become the class valedictorian in both middle school and high school. Both she and Sophea had received good scholarship offers from colleges. In fact, Neary got almost all of the scholarships that their community had to offer. "Maybe our family would have been happier if you had divorced him..." Sophea went on to say. "But you did what you felt was right in your heart, as you have always done."

Sophea remembered begging her mother to divorce their dad. She had promised her that both she and Neary would be there by her side through divorce court. She felt they would be able to earn a living and search for a better life with just the three of them, as it had been before they moved to the U.S. Instead, Narin spent the latter part of their years trying to destroy his family every day. Sophea also felt the reason her mom stayed with him was because she didn't believe in divorce and that she hung in there because she had no other family in the United States.

Rachana said, "We are here because I felt it would be best for you and Neary."

"I know, Mommy," Sophea replied.

"I remember how worried, scared, and excited we were when the plane flew across the ocean after we left the past behind," she said. "But I knew you girls would be able to have a better future here than in Cambodia."

For Rachana, her biggest concern had been wondering how she would earn a living to support her two daughters. She had no money and didn't speak any English. She could hardly walk after the pain of the explosives had almost crippled her ability to walk. Even now, she still had shrapnel impaled deep within many areas of her body. Yet, she was resilient and refused to just lie down and die.

The plane had landed in California on September 9, 1981 in the big, beautiful country called AMERICA. Rachana had heard from some of the other people she met at the refugee camps just how spectacular it was and how much opportunity there was for success. Everyone was allowed to pick and choose what they wanted to do. They were free to go anywhere they wanted and could walk around without worrying about suddenly being gunned down, robbed, or bombed. They could pursue anything they chose to do in life. They could receive an education without jumping through hoops or being scrutinized.

Corvallis, Oregon had a population of only about 50,000 people. It was clean and beautiful. When they first arrived there, the family got an apartment in their small town. At first, they stayed inside because they were afraid of people. They didn't dare to look out the window because they didn't speak English and didn't know what to say to people. Narin had made the first move in unpacking, walking, and going to the grocery store. He learned to take the bus or any public transportation, but he left his family at home until he became familiar with the lay of the land and the customs of the Americans.

By the beginning of October, it was cold. Their first family outing was to the grocery store. All of them were afraid and constantly looking over their shoulders, afraid that the Killing Fields had followed them.

After a few days, they met a fellow immigrant from Cambodia, who was also a refugee. He had come two years before them and already knew what was needed. He gave the Longs a bicycle. They were thrilled, but had no idea that such things were easily stolen. So, they stored it in the laundry room of their apartment complex, thinking it would still be there the next day, which it wasn't.

Life was certainly an adjustment, especially for Rachana, who had been considered one of the "smart" citizens back in Cambodia. Because of her lack of knowledge, time, and transportation, she was unable to get an education in America. Also, Narin was adamant that she should not go to school. However, she was able to get a job, albeit low paying. Her body was still weak and she had difficulty walking. She felt incompetent because of the language barrier. But at the same time, Rachana was happy that God had given her the willpower to stand on her own two feet. And she was the best citizen she could be as a new person in the United States.

Rachana began meeting neighbors and even met people through a church she was invited to attend by another Cambodian lady, with whom she formed a friendship. Initially, she started going to church so that she could meet people. The sermons didn't make sense to her, since she could barely understand any English. She knew nothing about church. She sought like-minded people since she had no friends, relatives, or anyone to talk to. However, instead of just finding friends, Rachana found the Lord.

Another tough adjustment was the weather. September was crisp. October was chilly. November was frigid. By December, it was downright cold, especially having just moved from Asia. The Long family lived about three or four miles away from the grocery store. They didn't have any warm clothing; walking three miles through the snow while carrying grocery bags was extremely difficult.

Rachana thought about her mother all the time. She had corresponded with her while in the refugee camp and had asked her mother to come with her. At that time, Thida was too afraid to come. She wondered if they would ever see one another again. She regretted having left her in Siem Reap.

Little did Rachana know at the time, it would be another decade before she would see her dear mother again, in May of 1990. When she left her eighty-year-old mother crying that day she left for the refugee camp in Thailand, Thida's face was something Rachana never forgot. The tears of grief as Thida watched her baby daughter and two of her favorite grandchildren–whom she loved more than her own life–were tears that Rachana still shed every day. Yet they journeyed to the unknown world, where she knew not what was waiting. Rachana still couldn't live with what she had done. However, she had made the decision for the sake of Sophea and Neary. She felt she had chosen what was best for them.

Thida and Rachana never thought their closeness would end the way it did, but it happened. Her wish was that whoever still had parents alive, not to let anything come between them. It was a gift that she tried to explain to Sophea. "After your parents are gone, no tears or sorrow can do any good," Rachana told her. "People say nothing can separate faith and love, but believe me, the world can do it all. I have tasted the worst of it."

"That's why I want to spend every minute with you that I can," Sophea said.

But Rachana was still lost in thought, thinking not about Narin but about her beloved mother. Narin's funeral had stirred up many memories, regrets, and reflections for Rachana.

It was 1990 when Rachana received a phone call from a friend in California. They told her that Cambodia had finally opened the door to all Cambodians to freely come and go. This was news that shocked Rachana. She was overjoyed. She would finally be able to reunite with her mom after a decade apart. It was the best news she'd heard in ten years. Her body trembled. She hung up the phone with her friend and sat down.

Rachana called out to her husband, as if she had seen a dangerous animal. "Narin! Narin! Narin!"

He asked, "Cha-Cha, what is wrong with you?"

She exclaimed, "I'm going back to Cambodia to visit my mother!"

Narin looked puzzled "How'd you do it?" He knew they weren't letting anybody in from outside the country. But he didn't know her secret.

She replied, "They opened the door for the tourists to come visit."

He knew there was no changing Rachana's mind. "Okay," he shrugged.

After she felt better, Rachana called her supervisor. "I finally have a chance to go see my mother in Cambodia. Would it be possible to take a month off to go overseas to visit her?"

Her supervisor replied without hesitation. "Rachana, of course. I would not stop you from visiting your mother. Just tell me the dates."

After she hung up, Rachana immediately got back on the phone and started calling travel agents. However, she was discouraged to learn that none of them were selling tickets to Cambodia, only to Laos or Thailand. It took her a few days to find a new travel agency in California that was just starting up. Low and behold, the new agency had one ticket to Cambodia. After buying the ticket, it took Rachana another month to get everything planned.

By early May, Rachana boarded a giant aircraft and set sail in the sky, returning to her birthplace. None of her family knew about the trip. At that time, it was still unsafe for Cambodians to return home. But she missed her mother and longed to see her, so Rachana didn't mind taking a risk. She was not sure if she would be able to come back to America, but no one could hold her back.

She had cried for ten years over the decision to leave her mother. She had chosen a future for her children instead, which had cost her all the pain and sadness of her life. The only solace was the subsequent success of her daughters, knowing that she had made the right choice.

After the plane landed in Cambodia, Rachana quickly found a ride to her sister Phary's house, where Thida was waiting for her. Even though Rachana didn't tell anyone she was coming, Thida knew in her heart to expect her arrival. It was a sixth sense. But the surprise was bittersweet.

The two spent days crying. A lot of questions were asked, and a lot of stories told. Some were sad, some were happy. Joy and sadness took turns entertaining them. However, the reunion was not complete without Sophea and Neary. Thida longed to see her two granddaughters that she had helped to raise with her own hands.

Although Rachana was overjoyed to have spent time with her mother, the story did not end happily because Thida never got to see Sophea and Neary before she passed. By then, Thida would have been willing to come with Rachana to live in the U.S. for the rest of her days on earth. However, they were unable to bring her because they couldn't get the paperwork done that was necessary to fly her back to America. By then, Thida was ninety years old.

Because of Sophea's and Neary's schooling–they could not return to Cambodia to see their beloved grandmother. Sadly, Thida passed away in January of 1993, at the age of ninety-two. Rachana's heart forever remained rueful of what she gave up. They had experienced so many good things in the past and before the war. They had endured both bad times and good times. And even through the hard times during the Killing Fields, the good memories of her mother made her happy.

The world was cruel. Sometime, someway, and somewhere at the last minute, they were torn apart. Rachana had chosen the risky adventure to the unknown in the belief of a better future for her daughters. It nearly cost them all their lives. Whenever she thought of Sophea and Neary, Rachana was reminded of what she would have done for her mother.

Chapter Twenty-Four

"New Beginnings"

About a week or two after Narin's death, Rachana went through her savings and checking account with a fine-tooth comb to see exactly what was left. Since taking the twelve-hour job just before her husband's death, she rarely had much time for anything, not even time to look through the bank account. After spending the afternoon reviewing her accounts and looking through their bills, Rachana was happily surprised to discover that she had enough money to move to a nicer neighborhood!

At bedtime, Rachana told her daughters about the plan she had been thinking about ever since the revelation. However, Sophea was more pragmatic. "Mommy, you counted it wrong. I don't think we have that much money."

"Oh boy! Maybe you are right," Rachana agreed with her. That night, she couldn't close her eyes. She tossed and turned on her bed all night. She couldn't wait to go to the bank first thing in the morning and find out exactly how much she really had.

But in the morning, she overslept and had to get to work. All day long, the unknowing bothered her. After work, Rachana rushed to the bank. She politely asked for access to the safe deposit box and counted her money three times just to make sure the figures were accurate. Then she took a deep breath and smiled.

Rachana rushed home to break the news to her children. "Guess what, girls! The numbers were right! I went to the bank and we have enough money to buy our dream house!"

The girls were thrilled. All three of them started jumping up and down and laughing and clapping. They all felt happier than they had felt in a long time.

Every day after their classes, the trio drove around to many neighborhoods, looking for Rachana's dream house that she could share with her two daughters until they graduated and moved on with their lives. Everything seemed too high priced or unaffordable.

Finally, they found a new development that was within their budget. It was called Barley Hill. Rachana proudly picked out the lot, and chose a floor plan for the building design. However, the contractors had already plotted the flooring and carpet, cabinetry, fixings, and all the details.

So, Rachana sat down with Troy, the realtor. He was a chubby guy with a mustache and saggy cheeks. Although he dressed nice and was professional in demeanor, there was something about him that gave off a mistrusting presence. Nevertheless, Rachana handed him her wish list. She wanted a different carpet, the tile, and lighting of her choice, and no lawn in the front, just flowers and shrubs. Everything was carefully changed according to her tastes and preferences. Troy agreed to see what he could do.

However, the next day, God hardened his heart. His plans for Rachana were not Barley Hill. Troy called and said, "I'm sorry, Mrs. Long. You have to take what they give you in the design. These are predetermined things."

"But I'm willing to pay for the difference," Rachana replied.

"I'm really sorry. That's the way it is. The contractor already has arrangements with certain vendors so these are the only choices they have for you. You have to pick out something in the swatches I gave you. Nothing more," he explained.

"I don't like any of those things. If I'm going to pay this kind of money for a home, I want what I like," said Ms. Independent.

Troy said, "Mrs. Long, there's nothing I can do."

"Just forget it then!" replied Rachana. She hung up, severely disappointed. She was mostly upset about all the time she had wasted, more than anything else.

Oh well, time to look for something else, she thought aloud. *I don't like that part of town anyway.*

After searching high and low for a few months, Rachana discovered that the old houses in the nice neighborhoods cost more than what she had. She continued searching and found another empty lot on Pin Quinn, at Whispering Hill. It was a lovely lot. Rachana thought that perhaps she could buy the piece of land and find her own builder, rather than having to go through a similar ordeal than the first place she had chosen.

Upon the recommendation of a friend, Rachana found a reasonably priced contractor who could build a place the way she liked, with the specifications she liked. So she offered full price for the lot, without even trying to negotiate. This time, she chose another realtor, after having experienced such a headache with Troy.

This time, the realtor came back to Rachana two days later with a lot of anger in his voice. He said, "I have some news you're not going to like."

Already bracing herself, Rachana said, "Oh, no. What is it?"

The realtor said, "I was so excited to meet with the owner of the property that I went to his place of business to tell him that his lot was sold at full price."

Still not realizing anything was wrong, Rachana said, "Go on . . ."

"He said *NO!* He changed his mind and was taking the property off the market," explained the realtor.

"What!" exclaimed Rachana. "But I don't understand."

He went on, "The owner said the lot is a hassle to him. Now he doesn't want to sell it anymore."

"I see," she replied, disappointed. This was bad news. It was their last hope at having a new house.

After the phone call, Rachana went outside on her porch and sat in a wooden swing. A full moon crested over the August night, like a bright spotlight shining down on her. She sat there, looking up at the moon for the longest time. Then Rachana started crying, like a spoiled child who didn't get something she wanted. She couldn't sleep, wondering why her plans of having a dream home kept falling through.

Rachana went back inside to put on a sweater. It was getting chilly, as a breeze came through the early evening skies. She sat in the living room alone, opening the curtain just a bit to look out upon her front yard. Deep down, all she wanted was to get out of her present house and start a new life, one with new hopes, new dreams, and new memories. Rachana wanted to forget the past. All she could think about as she sat in her home was Narin and how his death had fueled the desire for a fresh start. *Why God? What is your plan?* She asked aloud.

Troy couldn't give her what she wanted in a house, and the owner of the lot was unwilling to sell to her, so how was she going to move out? *What is going on? Is it me? Or is it them?* Rachana had no idea that it was God who had a different plan for her. He closed the doors for a reason, because they were not his plan.

After two big disappointments, Rachana pushed the desire to move into a dream home to the back of her mind. She focused on work and helped her daughters to succeed in college. She was proud of Sophea and Neary. Both were studying hard and wanted to become doctors. Rachana couldn't ask for anything more. Even though it had been difficult to leave her elderly mother and flee to the refugee camp, the cost had been worth it so that her two girls could pursue a better life.

Growing up, Rachana had often told her daughters, "You can live without a husband but you cannot live without a job. Seek education first and then you will find a husband. That way, if your husband throws you out the window, you will still have an education and a job." She always raised them with love, just as her own mother had done for her.

As a mother, Rachana didn't always give her daughters everything they wanted, but she did her best always to give them things they needed. Even when they were quite poor, Sophea and Neary needed a computer to study with. Kids of the future did their homework on computers, rather than with a pencil and paper. Rachana worked very hard and saved up enough money to buy them one, even though they never asked for it. They accepted what she gave, but didn't ask for more. They didn't want their mother to bear any grief over trivial requests.

Quite honestly, Rachana enjoyed raising her girls. They did everything together. They cooked together, did laundry together, worked together, gardened together, vacationed together, picnicked together, and played together. She taught them to be self-sufficient and not to rely on others for their needs. They were well cared for, but without being spoiled.

Rachana also taught them the value of self-respect. When they were in high school, she drove them to a car lot. She stopped the car as the two teen girls looked at her, wondering what she was doing. She told them, "Right now, you are like a brand new car in the dealership. But if you let someone drive you out of the lot, you are no longer a new car. You are a used car. Your price immediately drops down. So, if you stay a new car, you remain valuable. Do you get what I'm saying to you?"

The two young women nodded. "Maintain your value," they repeated.

Even before they were teenagers, Rachana often drove young Sophea and Neary to the wealthy neighborhoods of their area to show them all of the fancy mansions. With decadent beams, skylights, wraparound porches, and perfectly manicured lawns, these grand homes were the ultimate sign of affluence. Sophea remembered being only ten years old or so when her mother took them by these dream homes. She'd say things like, "These are the houses that people who work hard live in. If you want to live in a house like this, you have to work hard and do well in school."

In contrast, Rachana also took her two young daughters to the soup kitchen at the homeless shelter, where they all volunteered from time to time. She wanted them to see what poverty looked like just as much as she wanted them to see what living wealthy looked like. As they slapped instant potatoes, canned vegetables, and potted meats on the trays of the homeless people, the girls got to witness appreciation in the eyes of the poorest people who lived on the streets of Oregon. Their ragged clothes were filled with holes and dirt to match their sad faces of hardship. Rachana would say, "If you don't work hard, this is the life you'll have. Look at all of these people. Is this the kind of life you want for yourself?"

She always made her point to her daughters when it came to the value of work ethic, integrity, and even self-respect.

A few weeks after the last real estate deal fell through, Rachana met a man who told her where she could find a lot that just came up on the market a few days prior. She drove through the neighborhood that he described to search for it. Low and behold, she spotted a sign that said, "For Sale by Owner." It was on top of a hill, with cute trees that reminded her of the trees that her parents had pruned in their backyard growing up. The neighborhood of Bexley Park was nice and well established. As soon as Rachana saw all of the trees, her heart jumped for joy.

When she returned home from scouting out the property, she called the number on the sign. A woman answered. Rachana explained to her that she had driven by the property and loved it. "I'm willing to pay cash!" she offered.

But the woman said, "I'm sorry, it's up to my husband. He handles all of the matters when it comes to real estate and such." Apparently, she was his wife and had no voice in their family finances. "I'll tell my husband about it. I'll have him call you," she added.

Rachana thanked her. Then she waited. And waited. And waited. Two weeks went by. So Rachana called back. The woman answered again. "I'm sorry, the property is sold," the lady cordially replied.

That was it for Rachana. Once again, her hopes had been smashed into little bits and pieces. She had not even offered less for the property and had been willing to pay cash. *What is going on?* She was confused.

The following Wednesday, Sophea called her mother from work. The owner of the lot had called her and asked if they were still interested in buying. So, Sophea arranged a meeting for the very next day. They met with the owner at the title company and signed the papers. The builder that Rachana had connected with for the second property was still available, so they commissioned him on Friday to look at the lot and confirm his price and blueprints. A week later, they finally commenced building the dream home that Rachana had so patiently waited for.

As they were making the transition to their new home and fresh start, Rachana put their old house on the market. It was June of 1996. There it stood, with no lookers. Only two families even glanced at it or did a walk-through with the realtor until February of 1997. Another house on the very same street, that was not as well kept, sold for more than Rachana's listed price. Other houses nearby were selling left and right. But not hers. Nobody was even interested in looking at it. The realtor seemed surprised too.

Rachana decided to pull the listing out from their realtor and put it up for sale by owner. She was getting really nervous because their new house was nearly ready to move into. Two weeks before they were scheduled to move into their new house, two serious buyers stopped by. There was nobody who could sell a home better than the one who lived there. Perhaps the realtor hadn't been doing his job.

The first buyer told Rachana he would return in the evening with the earnest money for a deposit. However, the second buyer came and would not leave until she agreed to sign the papers. She explained, "The gentleman who was here earlier is supposed to return this evening with the earnest money. I feel bad."

The second buyer said, "Too bad. It is sold. We will pay cash."

Amazingly enough, a third buyer was pacing in front of the house, waiting for his turn to come in and take a look. He did not get the chance. After so many months of fretting and not getting anywhere with the real estate broker, Rachana was able to sell her own house and had three buyers vying for the chance on the very same day!

It took several months to erect, but once the new house was finished, Rachana and her daughters were thrilled. It was simply beautiful. A week thereafter, the three moved into their new house. She said to her daughters, "God's timing is always just right." They celebrated with a nice dinner that evening at their beautiful new home in Bexley Park. The neighbors were sweet and friendly. A few of them came over when they saw the new people outside. "We're your new neighbors! Welcome to the neighborhood!" they said, with big smiles of welcoming anticipation.

Bexley Park was a safe place for children. Even though they were now young adults, it was reassuring for a single mother who was working in the cafeteria at a low-paying job to be able to live in an affluent neighborhood. Doctors, engineers, and professors at the university surrounded them.

Selling her old house at the same time of building a new house had given Rachana so much stress. However, she had also learned a valuable lesson. The whole time, she had wondered, *"What if I cannot sell the house on time? How can I pay for the new house?"* After the transaction finally happened and she was able to move into the new place, she realized that she needed to have more faith. She adopted a new mantra that would carry her through the rest of her life:

Less Faith = More Burdens
More Faith = Less Burdens

Within that same year, in 1997, Rachana started reading the bible. At that time, she was a member of a Lutheran Church. Whenever she read the New Testament, she learned that Jesus performed many miracles. It made her think back to all of the miracles she had lived through in Cambodia and even through their hardships with financial matters and Narin's sickness in the U.S.

Prior to her newfound interest in scripture, Rachana had been suffering from severe arthritis. It was getting increasingly worse every day, making work difficult. When she sat on the couch, Rachana had to ask her daughters for help getting up because it was so painful. However, she did not seek medical attention because she was just so busy with her life. She was always worried and focused on just trying to earn a few more pennies that she could turn into a dollar. That was all she could think about.

Rachana was insecure when it came to her finances. She often worried about ten years ahead, instead of living in the moment. The negative energy drained her, but also made her unable to ignore the arthritis pain.

After she began reading the bible, Rachana started praying for healing from the pain. She remembered the teens who had visited her at the hospital back in Thailand and it dawned on her that they had been praying for her healing, along with the other woman who had suffered injuries by the axe. Every time she took communion, Rachana prayed that Jesus would take the pain away. She repeated the prayer over and over again.

Over time, Rachana barely noticed when the pain left her. Her prayer was answered while she was busy living life. All of a sudden one day, she had an epiphany. No more pain! *How can a person who suffered from bad pain just forget that it exists?* She didn't know, but the arthritis appeared to go away completely.

Then one day in bible study, the group she often gathered with talked about miraculous healings. It woke Rachana up. She suddenly realized that she had been entirely healed of her arthritis. Before this occurrence, Rachana often sat in on the prayer group as a spectator, quietly listening. She rarely commented or even spoke. However, after this occurrence, Rachana surprised herself by jumping up and telling everyone what had happened. Not only did she shock herself, but she surprised the whole group who had thought she was such an introvert.

Someone said, "Wow! When a miracle takes place, even the mute can talk!"

Everyone laughed.

Chapter Twenty-Five

"Special Visitor"

In June of 2000, Sophea had her own struggles to contend with. She hated to face the music, but she returned to Oregon to visit her mother after flunking out of medical school. Although Rachana was disappointed, she understood. She too had struggled to pass the exams to become a teacher back when she had gone to college in Cambodia. She knew what it was like to want something so badly, yet to fail even after giving it your best. Rachana was not angry.

However, Sophea was disappointed with herself. If she had learned anything up to that point, it was not to give up on something without a fight.

Later in August, Rachana was busy scurrying around her home, preparing for work. She had just opened the door and grabbed her pocketbook and keys when the phone rang. "Honey, can you get that?" she yelled to her daughter. "I don't want to be late for work!"

Rachana slid into the driver's seat of her car when suddenly Sophea appeared. She was out of breath from running to catch her mother before she left for work. "Mom, wait!" Sophea yelled. "Mom!"

Just as she was shifting her car into reverse, she stopped to acknowledge her daughter. "Mom!" Sophea ran to the window, as her mother rolled it down.

"What is it?" Rachana's boss was very strict and mean. She had zero tolerance for lateness and Rachana had always been a punctual employee. The director of the department seemed to have a hair across her backside that most of the employees were afraid of, although her sweet exterior made it tough to discern her intent. The boss's sourness stemmed from years of working at a place with lack of appreciation. The staff did not get their way with her at all and many had been fired for trivial things.

Breathlessly, Sophea said, "Mom wait. Mom . . . I got an interview for tomorrow in San Francisco at nine o'clock in the morning. I want you to come."

"Oh, heavens. Well, you talk to them and find out everything you need to know, honey. That's great news," said Rachana.

Sophea said, "Mom, you always say that God is faithful in his promises."

"He is," she agreed. With that, she sped out of the driveway. Rachana drove as fast as she could to go talk to her supervisor. She hoped that her boss would be in a good mood when she arrived to work.

As Rachana stormed into her supervisor's office, she told her, "You can yell at me. You can fire me, but I have to go. I have an emergency. I don't know when I will be back. I will call on Saturday and let you know."

The boss smiled. She pushed her reading glasses to the top of her head. In a moment of kindness, Rachana's supervisor said, "You don't have to run Rachana. You're going to run out of breath. Just call me when you have time." She had never been as kind to anyone before.

"Thank you!" Rachana said, graciously. With that, she turned and stormed out of her boss's office before she even had a chance to change her mind. Then Rachana sped back home.

As soon as she returned, Sophea told her mother, "I've already packed the suitcase for us. I'm going to the travel agent to buy the ticket right now. Can I have the keys please?" She held out her palm with expectance and anxiety.

"I'll come with you," replied Rachana. "But you can drive."

For the rest of the day, Sophea and her mother ran around town doing errands and picking up the letters of recommendations she needed. When they finally returned home, Neary handed them the suitcase. She was coming too. The three of them were going on a grand adventure to visit San Francisco.

A cab arrived an hour later and took the three of them to the airport. They got to the gate right before it closed. On Friday, Sophea spent all day interviewing. They didn't have any time to go sightseeing or even to visit the Golden Gate Bridge. They flew back home that same night. Sophea had managed to get accepted to the school. She had said the right things and looked like a great prospect, both on paper and in person. Sophea was very good under pressure, even though she was a sensitive person at heart.

On Saturday, Rachana and her two daughters had one last family time together. They went to the lake for a picnic. They joked, laughed, and enjoyed each other's company. Their sandwiches were delicious too.

By Sunday, only Rachana and Sophea made the long drive to San Francisco. It took them fourteen tiring hours to get through heavy traffic. On Monday, Sophea started school. Everything happened so fast, but when God works, he does so at the speed of lightning.

Rachana stayed in San Francisco for two weeks, helping her daughter to adjust to her new surroundings. It reminded her of her own mother who had dropped everything and came with her whenever she had gone to Pnom Penh for college. Sophea and Rachana searched the city for an apartment. The cost of living in the city was much higher than it had been in Oregon. However, they managed to find something decent just on the outskirts of the city, near the Bay area. It was a cute place on the third floor with a gated elevator that looked like a building from the thirties style of architecture.

Upon returning home, Rachana packed more of her eldest daughter's things to send to her by train. As she thought about it, she realized she couldn't be without her daughters. Sophea and Neary were her only family in America. So, Rachana began packing everything in their house. Neary was also starting medical school in Portland the following month, so both of them would be gone.

Rachana had loved her house. She thought she would live and die in it. However, she had to give it up and go with her baby daughter. It turned out to be the best decision for her. In Portland, Rachana was able to find a much better job. The boss was also a wonderful person and extremely nice to work for. Actually, all of her supervisors had been very kind to her. Their philosophies were, "You work hard, and you get a good treat. You're lazy, we let you go."

Rachana also found her coworkers to be pleasant and she fit in easily with the company culture. Every day was fun and she enjoyed her job just as much as seeing rainbows or drinking a nice cup of tea. It was pleasant and fulfilling. Rachana was thankful that her family was so devoted to each other. She felt so blessed and happy, like a fresh breeze after a bad rainstorm.

The following year after Rachana had made the adjustment, she was given some time off for a vacation. She wanted to return to Cambodia. Phary's son had called Rachana to let her know that his mother was not doing well. Her health was failing. They didn't expect Rachana to be able to come, but the family wanted her to know. She didn't tell them it had been her plan to use the vacation time she had earned to visit them. It was by pure coincidence that they needed her at the same time she had been planning a surprise visit.

Only the following Thursday after his phone call, Rachana was on a plane to see Phary. As she flew over to Cambodia, the plane couldn't fly fast enough for her. She was so excited to see her sister, although she knew that Phary was dying. This brought many mixed feelings of anticipation. It was her favorite sister, the very same one she had thrown scissors at as a young child. If she had known then what she knew now, it was one instance that Rachana would have liked to turn back in time.

She could barely sit still on the jet as it discharged the landing gear and the wheels rolled out to land. Rachana wanted to jump out of the plane even before it came to a complete stop. After it finally did and the flight attendants allowed them to unbuckle their seatbelts, Rachana leapt out of her seat and nearly knocked people over trying to hastily run off the plane. As soon as she stepped off the plane, she inhaled the air. Breathing the Cambodian air was somehow different from the air in the U.S. It was familiar and felt good to Rachana to return to her birthplace.

After retrieving her luggage, Rachana stepped out into the street and flagged down a taxi to take her straight to her wonderful sister. Another decade had gone by since Rachana had traveled back to Cambodia to visit with her mother. Back then, the town had still been quite empty. By 2001, it was once again bustling with life.

However, upon arriving at her sister's house, she discovered that they no longer lived there. Instead, a different family had moved in. Rachana was bewildered and dumbfounded. She couldn't find Phary's house and had no idea of her whereabouts. After all of the burst of excitement in returning to Cambodia, Rachana suddenly felt lost. She cried to the cab driver, "Where is my sister? Is she dead? Do you know her?"

He did not. He was a young man. The cab driver was not familiar with their family and the population had grown since Rachana's last visit. He seemed sympathetic, but was not helpful. She got out of the taxi and let him go.

Rachana searched for the marketplace where she had worked as a merchant with Ping over twenty years prior. It was still there, now much bigger and more impressive than in its humble beginnings. She asked a few strangers, "Do you know Phary and Pitch Seng?" Everybody she asked shook their heads no.

Feeling discouraged, Rachana sat on the stoop outside an old school-house. She hung her head in despair. "Please God, help me find my sister. Please."

Not wanting to waste too much time, Rachana hailed another taxi. She got into the backseat, but didn't know what to tell the driver. "I'm searching for my sister," said Rachana. "But I don't know where she lives, so I don't know where to tell you to go."

Seeming puzzled, the cab driver said, "Okay, so what do you want me to do?"

She replied, "I guess just drive around in her old neighborhood. Maybe I can ask some of her neighbors if they know where she may have moved to."

The fellow did as he was asked. Just as he was entering the suburbs that Rachana now recognized as their old place, suddenly she pointed. "There it is!" she yelled. "I must have gotten the address wrong before. It's been a long time since I was here," she explained. The taxi driver must have thought she was crazy.

"Please, drop me off here," Rachana pleaded as she handed him some money. He got out to help her take the suitcase out of the trunk.

"Good luck," he smiled.

Rachana ran up the driveway as fast as she could, leaving her bag back down by the curb. She let herself in the front door of her sister's house and flew up the stairs like a teenager who had full strength.

Sure enough, Rachana found her dear sister sleeping in the back of the house in a hammock. She stopped in her tracks and gazed upon Phary with tearful eyes. Her eldest sister had whittled away to just skin and bones. She was thinner than she had ever been. Nobody was around her. Phary's children were off to the marketplace to earn a living. Some things just never changed. That would have been the life she could have endured, had she not made that brave escape to the refugee camp when she did. Even though she had nearly died trying to get out of Cambodia, it had turned out for the best.

In fact, many of the refugees from Khao-i-Dang who were unable to attain Visas to get in other countries like the U.S. and France were destined to stay there for many years. By December of 1982, still over 40,000 refugees remained there, awaiting repatriation to other countries or to be sent back to Cambodia. The population steadily dropped as the leftover people were forced to resettle elsewhere. However, many of the

CPSIA information can be obtained at www.ICGtesting.com
Printed in the USA
BVOW04s1257110514

353193BV00010B/277/P

"Anyway, I can never repay you for what you did. You saved my life and I am eternally grateful. But I want you to have this," Rachana said, handing the elderly man an envelope full of money. "Please, take it with my gratitude."

He nodded. Even to that day, he still didn't know why he risked his life to save a stranger like Rachana. In fact, he didn't even remember doing it. However, Rachana felt good deep down knowing that in her heart, God had chosen Mr. Yin to work on one of his miracles, of which there had been so many within her life.

With that, Rachana turned and walked back to the vehicle, where the guide still waited for her. Her visit was short and sweet, but she felt a strong warmth and ray of energy inside for having found the man who had saved her life and in having honored him with a small reward, even though he didn't remember doing the good deed. Maybe he had done other good things too. Chances are, he had.

As she put it in perspective, Rachana learned that even those who didn't know God could reap the benefits of God's love. He knew everyone. All races, all nations, regardless of rich or poor, beautiful or ugly, healthy or sick, handicapped or not, believers or non-believers, good or bad, smart or ignorant, God knew every person on earth. He knew everyone by name and knew what they had done and even what they were going to do. This was an amazing revelation.

sisters, Rachel and Kalianne lived. They were also thrilled to see their long lost sister. Rachana got a hotel close by for the duration of her stay.

For a single mother earning minimum wage with two children in the university, no other reason could have made Rachana return to Cambodia except the goodness of her sister and the amazing love they had for one another. Every night that Rachana was there, she prayed to God to ask him to keep Phary alive long enough for her to be able to tell her what she needed to. There was so much . . . where would she begin?

Aside from her sister, there was someone else Rachana longed to see. Back in the Killing Fields, there had been a man who had saved her life. Comrade Yin had gotten her the oxen cart to take her to the care center after she suffered the crippling back pain from working at the dam at the hands of the Regime.

Rachana wondered if he was even still alive. They had only met once. Since she was already in the capital, she started asking around to find out his whereabouts or if anybody knew him. After asking at least a dozen people and getting nowhere, finally there was a lady who sold tomatoes, papayas, and watermelons at the marketplace. She nodded. "Yes, I know Mr. Yin," she said. "I haven't seen him in a couple of years, but I know he lives about ten miles north of here and still works at a youth center."

Her heart filled with joy. Comrade Yin was still alive! This was indeed happy news to Rachana. The next day, she sought him out. She hired a messenger to take her to the place that the lady with vegetables had told her about.

When Rachana arrived at the youth center, she recognized him right away. He was outside, taking a lunch break and sitting with a co-worker. She approached him. "Hello, Mr. Yin?" asked Rachana.

He looked into her face, squinting. The sun was in his eyes so he couldn't quite make out her face. "Yes, can I help you?" he answered.

"You may not remember me, but I remember you. You saved my life in the Killing Fields and I have never forgotten what you did," replied Rachana.

"I did?" he asked, questioning her. He didn't remember.

"I'm the girl you took to the hospital from the dam. You snuck me there in the oxen cart. Well, I should say that you had it arranged for me," Rachana replied.

He nodded, still unsure. Life had passed by and he didn't remember everything from back during those times. It was an era he had tried to forget. "I think so," Mr. Yin said, still uncertain.

No words came out of Phary's mouth because she was so dumbfounded and still in shock. Instead, she wiped her face with the edge of her sleeve and bopped her head up and down in positive acknowledgement.

Rachana rubbed her sister's chest with one hand to help her breathe. Her unexpected presence almost killed Phary. The taxi driver didn't even move his car. He stood there in awe and wiped a tear from his cheek, watching from a short distance. Now everybody was crying.

Over and over again, Rachana reassured Phary to calm down and take a deep breath. She begged, "Don't die, please! It was not my intent to come and kill you, just lie back and relax. Relax! Relax! Take a deep breath."

With those words, Phary finally cracked a small grin. After a few minutes, she was finally able to cope with it and had toned down her hyperventilation. She was now able to breathe easier. Finally, the first words that came from her mouth were, "Oh, honey!" Phary paused for a moment after nearly choking on those words and on her tears.

Reaching up to grab Rachana's face with both of her skeleton hands, Phary said, "Cha-Cha, I have longed to see you before leaving this earth. I have stayed alive every day, hoping you would come. And here you are."

The two sisters held onto each other for dear life. The taxi driver even crept in closer to the wall so he could hold himself up against it; because he was so moved by the love of these two sisters.

"Oh, I hurt all over my body," cried Phary.

After what seemed like the longest time, they all finally calmed down. Phary was able to sit up straight. They wiped their faces and finally the laughter snuck in, little by little. Rachana helped her to get into the house, which was painstakingly difficult. Every step for Phary was like a searing knife.

A little later, the rest of the family and all those who lived close by came to join their long lost Rachana's visit. To them, she seemed worldly and cultured. They had often told stories about her and the antics she had done in her younger days. They laughed about her independence and the time she had stolen Lee's money to go to college. They were in awe about her ability to survive the Killing Fields. Rachana was someone they admired.

For about three hours of their reunion, they all enjoyed each other's company. However, Rachana had to leave because it was unsafe for her to stay overnight. There was still danger, even twenty years later. So, Rachana traveled with the same taxi driver to the capital where her other two refugees had little motivation to leave, especially considering the much better treatment they had while in Khao-i-Dang than they had received even in their home country. Many of them were rejected by several countries after countless attempts of failed paperwork.

Finally, Thailand declared Khao-i-Dang closed in 1986 and the refugees who still refused to leave stayed illegally. The camp had become their home. Many of the people were very vocal in opposing the forced repatriation. Forced demonstrations and fights made it difficult to kick them out. Nearly fourteen years after the camp was set up and hosted by world relief efforts, in 1993 the remaining 11,000 residents were sent to a second refugee camp after a closing ceremony was held to honor the tragic symbol of the Cambodian deaths.

Everyone had their own journey in life to make, according to God's plans for every individual. Some were destined to stay, while others were meant to go. Rachana's decision had not been an easy one to make and sometimes she had questioned the fate she had chosen. It was by design. She had followed her instincts and done what she thought was best.

Now as Rachana stared at her sister's gaunt frame, she couldn't help but to remember Phary's kindness for her when she was just a teen and early adult. Without Phary and Pitch, Rachana would have been unable to achieve the education or the things she had accomplished in life, including having a strong work ethic. Despite her dying figure, Rachana thought her sister to be such a beautiful person.

Quietly, Rachana knelt down beside her sister while she slept in the hammock. Carefully, she touched her hand and then reached in to hold her. She was afraid to break her ribs or touch her, but she wanted to feel Phary's presence. This was why she had traveled so far and it meant the world to see her again, especially knowing it was probably the last time.

The touch of Rachana against her made Phary open her eyes instantly. She was so shocked to see her baby sister that she wondered if she was seeing a ghost. Rachana cried out loud, "It is me, Sister!" Rachana gave her a warm embrace.

Phary trembled like never before. She was terrified, thinking that perhaps she had died and was imagining things. Her frail body shook and she was barely able to lift herself up from the hammock.

"It's okay!" Rachana exclaimed. "I am really here. Look, pinch me!"

Instead, Phary wrapped her skinny arms around Rachana's neck and wept. She wept and wept as much as a faucet running from a sink. Rachana tried to be strong. She smiled and said, "Did you miss me?"